GETTING THE OLD TESTAMENT

GETTING THE OLD TESTAMENT

WHAT IT MEANT TO THEM, WHAT IT MEANS FOR US

STEVEN L. BRIDGE

BakerAcademic
a division of Baker Publishing Group
Grand Rapids, Michigan

Published by Baker Academic
a division of Baker Publishing Group
P.O. Box 6287, Grand Rapids, MI 49516-6287
www.bakeracademic.com

Baker Academic edition published 2011
ISBN 978-0-8010-4574-5

Previously published in 2009 by Hendrickson Publishers

Printed in the United States of America

The Library of Congress has cataloged the original edition as follows:
Bridge, Steven L.
Getting the Old Testament : what it meant to them, what it means for us / Steven L. Bridge.
p. cm.
Includes bibliographical references and index.
ISBN 978-1-59856-045-9 (alk. paper)
1. Bible. O.T.—Criticism, interpretation, etc. I. Title.
BS1171.3.B745 2009
221.6—dc22 2008055377

NIHIL OBSTAT
Monsignor Charles M. Murphy, STD, *Censor Deputatus*

IMPRIMATUR
Most Reverend Richard J. Malone, ThD, *Bishop of Portland*
February 23, 2009

The *nihil obstat* and *imprimatur* are official declarations that a book or pamphlet is free of doctrinal or moral error. No implication is contained therein that those who have granted the nihil obstat and imprimatur agree with the contents, opinions, or statements expressed.

11 12 13 14 15 16 17 7 6 5 4 3 2 1

To
Sally & Ellis Gottlieb
Reginald & Tinker Hannaford
Abraham Schechter
and
Jacob Neusner

Individuals who
in a very special way
have extended to me
and to countless others
the hospitality of Abraham.

Table of Contents

Part III—The Writings (Kethuvim)

List of Tables

Preface

While writing this book, I endeavored to keep in balance a number of dynamic tensions. I have sought to produce a work that might satisfy both institutions of learning and communities of faith; one simultaneously sensitive to Jewish, Catholic, Protestant, and Muslim perspectives; one that grounds these Scriptures in their historical contexts, yet draws out their present-day implications and applications; one that might speak to younger readers as well as to their senior counterparts; one that is both informative and accurate, yet accessible and entertaining. These broad parameters are hardly the result of an ambitious marketing scheme—some ploy to capture a larger share of readership. Rather, they reflect the diversity of backgrounds of those individuals whom I encounter on a daily basis—my eighteen- to sixty-eight-year-old traditional and nontraditional undergraduate liberal arts students. They come from all walks of life and appropriate this material from a wide array of viewpoints. All of this is to say that if, in the reader's opinion, I occasionally stray too far in one direction or another, I hope my failings might graciously be forgiven and attributed to the needs of one's fellow readers, those "others" in the audience whom I am seeking to reach.[1]

Of course, no book can be all things to all people. Those who have *no* prior knowledge of the Bible may want to start elsewhere; those looking for post-graduate-level sophistication should probably likewise move on. Rather, this book is specifically intended for individuals who find themselves between the polar extremes of the learning spectrum.

[1] To the above pairings, I might also mention the male/female balance. To this end, I have endeavored to use inclusive language wherever possible. However, I have not shied away from using masculine pronouns for God. This decision is not so much a theological one as it is a historical/literary one. Rightly or wrongly, such pronouns most accurately represent our ancient authors' conception of God.

It is my sincerest desire that, for these readers, this book might deliver what its title, *Getting the Old Testament,* promises. In one sense, to "get" something means to grasp or comprehend that which was formerly misunderstood (as in, "Now I get it!"). But in another sense, it also means to receive or gain fresh possession of (as in, "What did you get for your birthday?"). Both definitions come into play here. My greatest hope is that the reader might discover, as I have, that the ancient lessons that remain to be "gotten" (comprehended) prove to be valuable gifts—godsends, even—well worth "getting" (receiving).

Acknowledgments

I want to begin by thanking those individuals whose passion for the Hebrew Scriptures has proven to be contagious. Foremost among them are Barry Bandstra at Hope College and Deirdre Dempsey, John Schmitt, and Sharon Pace at Marquette University. I hope that they might judge this work to be historically, literarily, and theologically edifying. But beyond that, I pray it pays fitting tribute to their academic and scholastic legacies.

Since much of the content that I present here has been developed and refined in the context of young-adult youth groups, small-group Bible studies, religious education programs, retreats, faith workshops, large congregational assemblies, and high school, college, and university classrooms, I remain grateful for all such opportunities afforded me over the years. In particular, I am indebted to those institutions that have extended to me teaching positions, including Hackett Catholic Central (Kalamazoo, Mich.), Mount Mary College (Milwaukee, Wis.), Marquette University (Milwaukee, Wis.), and St. Joseph's College (Standish, Maine). I have relished my time at each of these schools and have been amply blessed by the colleagues and students whom I have encountered there. In many respects, this book is my labor of love for them.

Of course, while I have labored, much of my free time has gone by the wayside. My wife, Kamal, has dutifully shouldered many of the additional responsibilities created by my absence. She and our three daughters—Heather, Erica, and Emily—have demonstrated considerable support and patience while I've attended to this project. They've also lent valuable perspective to my work and managed to keep me grounded throughout the process. For all these things I am genuinely grateful.

I owe a special debt of gratitude to St. Joseph's College for the sabbatical leave that I was given during the 2007–2008 academic year.

Without this sabbatical and the support of several faculty development grants, this book might never have been completed.

Finally, I also wish to acknowledge all those who have helped to make this book what it is. I thank my friend, Andrea Asken-Dunn, for reading the preliminary drafts of this work and for offering honest and insightful feedback. I also wish to credit Shirley Decker-Lucke. Five years ago, Shirley first approached me at a Society of Biblical Literature conference and invited me to publish with Hendrickson. Even now, two books later, I remain ever so appreciative of her initial offer. I also wish to thank my editor, Allan Emery, and all the other individuals at Hendrickson who have toiled behind the scenes to assist me with this project. Their efforts have made this book substantially better.

When I published *Getting the Gospels* in 2004, I decided to commit the majority of my royalties to humanitarian projects benefiting the poorest of the poor. Since then, thousands of dollars generated from that venture have dramatically improved the lives of residents in a small Mayan village some three hours outside of Guatemala City. The results have been truly transformational. Accordingly, I am once again committing the majority of my royalties from the sale of this book to relief efforts aimed at providing the basic necessities (food, clothing, shelter, clean water, medicine, education, and employment) to the world's most impoverished countries. For enabling me to make these commodities a little more prevalent, I thank you, the reader, from my heart.

Abbreviations

General

9/11	September 11, 2001
ABC	American Broadcasting Company
ALS	amyotrophic lateral sclerosis
BAFTA	British Academy of Film and Television Arts
B.C.E.	before the Common Era
ca.	circa
CBS	Central Broadcasting System
C.E.	Common Era
cent(s).	century (centuries)
cf.	confer, compare
ch(s).	chapter(s)
CIRP	Cooperative Institutional Research Program
CMA	Country Music Association
CSS	College Student Survey
CW	conventional wisdom
D	Deuteronomist source (of the Torah)
E	Elohist source (of the Torah)
ed(s).	editor(s), edited by
e.g.	exempli gratia, for example
ELS	Equidistant Letter Sequence
emph.	emphatic
et al.	et alii, and others
etc.	et cetera, and the rest
Gen Next	Generation Next, eighteen- to twenty-five-year-old Americans (as of 2006)
Gen X	Generation X, twenty-six- to forty-year-old Americans (as of 2006)

GSE&IS	Graduate School of Education and Information Studies (at UCLA)
HB	Hebrew Bible
HERI	Higher Education Research Institute
i.e.	id est, that is
ibid.	ibidem, in the same place
IPO	Initial public offering
J	Yahwist source (of the Torah)
lit.	literally
LXX	Septuagint (the Greek Old Testament)
NBC	National Broadcasting Company
n.d.	no date
NJPS	Tanakh: The Holy Scriptures: The New JPS Translation according to the Traditional Hebrew Text
NT	New Testament
OT	Old Testament
P	Priestly source (of the Torah)
Sci-Fi	The Science Fiction Channel
trans.	translator, translated by
UCLA	University of California at Los Angeles
UK	United Kingdom
UN	United Nations
TP de Oro	[Gold Prize for Television Programming]
v(v).	verse(s)
vol(s).	volume(s)
vs.	versus
WMD	weapons of mass destruction
WRR	Doron Witztum, Eliyahu Rips, and Yoav Rosenberg
WTC1	World Trade Center (North Tower)
WTC2	World Trade Center (South Tower)
WWI	World War I
WWII	World War II

Hebrew Bible

Gen	Genesis
Exod	Exodus
Lev	Leviticus

Num	Numbers
Deut	Deuteronomy
Josh	Joshua
Judg	Judges
Ruth	Ruth
1–2 Sam	1–2 Samuel
1–2 Kgs	1–2 Kings
1–2 Chr	1–2 Chronicles
Ezra	Ezra
Neh	Nehemiah
Esth	Esther
Job	Job
Ps(s)	Psalm(s)
Prov	Proverbs
Eccl	Ecclesiastes
Song	Song of Songs
Isa	Isaiah
Jer	Jeremiah
Lam	Lamentations
Ezek	Ezekiel
Dan	Daniel
Hos	Hosea
Joel	Joel
Amos	Amos
Obad	Obadiah
Jonah	Jonah
Mic	Micah
Nah	Nahum
Hab	Habakkuk
Zeph	Zephaniah
Hag	Haggai
Zech	Zechariah
Mal	Malachi

Apocrypha

Jdt	Judith
1–2 Macc	1–2 Maccabees
3–4 Macc	3–4 Maccabees

Sir	Sirach
Tob	Tobit
Wis	Wisdom of Solomon

New Testament

1 Cor	1 Corinthians
Gal	Galatians
Jas	James
2 Pet	2 Peter

Modern Works

AB	Anchor Bible
ANET	*Ancient Near Eastern Texts Relating to the Old Testament.* Edited by J. B. Pritchard. 3d ed. Princeton, 1969
CBQ	*Catholic Biblical Quarterly*
WBC	Word Biblical Commentary

Introduction
Overhearing the Old Testament

Why Premises Matter

High atop his tree house roof, the rambunctious ten-year-old lost his footing and plummeted to the ground. X-rays in the emergency room revealed a broken leg, requiring a cumbersome, heavy cast. For much of that hot, sweltering summer, the boy withdrew to his bedroom while his family and friends enjoyed the fun and frivolity of their new swimming pool. Feeling neglected and abandoned, the lad grew increasingly despondent—and bored. He eventually tired of television and turned his attention to the outside world, or at least to that which he could hear and observe through his open window.

Initially, the mundane scenes of the local community did little to relieve the monotony. But a piercing, high-pitched scream from an adjacent house quickly piqued his curiosity. There, he overheard his distraught neighbor exclaim, "Oh my God, what have I done? I've killed her!"

The boy was incredulous at first. He knew his neighbors well. The man, his wife, and their two sons were a harmonious, model family—the epitome of honesty, innocence, and wholesomeness. This just couldn't be what it seemed. Dismissing the incident, the boy distracted himself with TV and eventually fell asleep.

Before long, however, his slumber was interrupted by the sound of a shovel digging into the earth. Peering out the window, he spied his neighbor intently burying something in the ground. Still convinced of the man's virtue, the boy assured himself that there *had* to be another explanation. Then, as if on cue, he overheard the anguished fellow confess, "I wish there was some other explanation for this, but there isn't. I'm a murderer. I'm a murderer!"

Had the man really killed his wife? The boy's suspicions appeared to be confirmed when his neighbor's young sons arrived home later that day. "Where's Mommy?" they asked. "We miss her." "Mommy . . . had to go away," their father stammered. "She's with God now." "Can we go there too?" they naïvely pleaded in unison. "Soon enough," he sullenly replied. Our little eavesdropper gasped in horror. If tragedy was to be averted, he needed to take action immediately!

Perhaps this plot sounds familiar. It comes from an episode of one of the most popular and longest-running sitcoms in American television history: *The Simpsons*. Since its debut some two decades ago, this animated family of five has provided humorous, insightful, irreverent, and incisive commentary on a wide range of social issues and pop-cultural trends. The show has amassed numerous distinctions, including twenty-three Emmy awards, twenty-six Annie awards, and a Peabody award.[1] In fact, the critics at *Time* magazine went so far as to declare *The Simpsons* the century's best television series.[2] Even abroad, this program has been enthusiastically received. It has garnered prestigious nominations and awards through the UK (BAFTA, British Comedy, National Television), Spain (TP de Oro), and Australia (Logie). In fact, few television shows have been as widely distributed. The series airs in dozens of countries and has been dubbed into at least eighteen languages.[3]

In "Bart of Darkness," the sixth season's first episode, Bart comes to believe that his do-gooder neighbor, Ned Flanders, has dispatched his wife, Maude, and is determined to do the same to his children, Rod and Todd. Given his limited mobility, Bart enlists the aid of his sister Lisa. Once Ned and the kids leave the house, Bart convinces Lisa to break in and find evidence of the murder. But shortly after Lisa enters the

---

[1] For a fairly comprehensive and updated list of the *The Simpsons'* various awards and nominations, see "Awards for *The Simpsons*" online at http://www.imdb.com/title/tt0096697/awards (accessed July 12, 2008).

[2] The *Time* writers supplied this description: "Dazzlingly intelligent and unapologetically vulgar, the Simpsons have surpassed the humor, topicality and, yes, humanity of past TV greats" ("The Best of the Century," *Time,* December 31, 1999, 72).

[3] Those languages include English, Spanish, Albanian, French, Japanese, German, Russian, Hindi, Swahili, Italian, Swedish, Turkish, Cantonese, Mandarin, Hebrew, Arabic, Klingon [a bit of pop-culture humor], and Bengali (http://www.imdb.com/title/tt0096697/ [accessed July 12, 2008]).

Flanders's home, Ned returns . . . with axe in hand! Lisa takes refuge in the attic as Bart—cast and all—endeavors to save her. The dramatic tension culminates when Ned raises the axe above the cowering Lisa and declares, "It's time to put you away. Put you away for good!" Bart and Lisa both scream as . . . Ned casually returns the axe to its storage rack. Bewildered, Ned sputters, "What the gumdrops is going on here?" Bart confronts him with his accumulated "evidence," and the truth is finally revealed. As it turns out, Ned had accidentally "murdered" Maude's favorite ficus plant by overwatering it. (The high-pitched squeals belonged to him.) He then buried its remains in the back yard, hoping to replace the plant before Maude arrived home from Bible camp (where she was, of course, "with God").[4]

The story line of "Bart of Darkness" is not entirely original. Much of it is based on Alfred Hitchcock's 1954 film, *Rear Window,* starring James Stewart as the confined photojournalist, L. B. Jeffries.[5] Indeed, in *The Simpsons* parody, many of Bart's misunderstandings parallel those of Jeffries. However, the *means* by which they transpire are notably different. Whereas Hitchcock relied mainly on voyeurism (what L. B. Jeffries *sees*) to advance his plot, "Bart of Darkness" is driven primarily by eavesdropping. Flanders's scream and surprised exclamation, his "confession" in the back yard, his conversation with his sons, and his words with the axe are all overheard—and all misconstrued—by Bart. (*D'oh!*) Such are the inherent risks of eavesdropping.

Of course, the creators of *The Simpsons* are hardly the first to capitalize on this plot device. Eavesdropping is widely attested in literature, from classical Greek tragedies to Elizabethan dramas to Victorian romance novels.[6] The popularity of these scenes undoubtedly lies in

---

[4]"Bart of Darkness" can be viewed online at http://watchthesimpsonsonline.com/movie/413–601_Bart_of_Darkness.html (accessed July 12, 2008). A complete transcript of this episode can also be found online at http://www.snpp.com/episodes/1F22.html (accessed July 12, 2008).

[5]In a nod of recognition to the film, James Stewart's character appears twice in "Bart of Darkness," both times in scenes that were painstakingly recreated from the movie. Considered by many critics to be Hitchcock's best work, *Rear Window* received four Academy award nominations. More recently (June 2008), it was judged by the American Film Institute to be the third best mystery film of all time.

[6]William Shakespeare even paid homage to it. Shakespeare's *Much Ado about Nothing* not only employs the device but also headlines it. In Shakespeare's day, the word "nothing" was pronounced the same as "noting," a synonym for eavesdropping. Shakespeare's clever title capitalizes on this pun and suggests the true nature of his production: *Much Ado about Noting.*

their tremendous potential to alter any natural progression of events.[7] Their effectiveness as a catalyst stems from a simple principle: successful communication requires that both sender and receiver share certain presuppositions in common. Generally, this is not a problem. But when third parties—outsiders to those shared presuppositions—overhear a conversation, they glean only its content, devoid of its context. In other words, the background that originally gave rise to the words and is thus essential to their intended meaning is absent. This requires the eavesdroppers to supply the missing contexts for themselves. With no guarantees that their newly contrived contexts will match the originals, misconceptions often arise.[8]

So what does any of this have to do with the Hebrew Bible (HB—in Christian circles frequently referred to as the Old Testament [OT])? As it turns out, quite a bit. At their core, the biblical documents are forms of communication—messages between senders and receivers. Their original authors and their intended audiences would naturally have subscribed to a set of shared presuppositions, namely, to the social, political, cultural, linguistic, and religious paradigms of their day. We can think of these various elements as the *premises* on which their worlds and words were based. *Webster's Dictionary* defines a premise as "a proposition [previously] supposed as a basis of inference; something assumed or taken for granted; [a] presupposition." In this respect, a premise can be thought of as the story behind the story. It is the context out of which communication and its intended meaning arise.

In a real sense, we modern readers of the OT are eavesdropping on ancient conversations—conversations that took place in foreign

[7] For a more detailed examination of the literary use of eavesdropping, see Ann Gaylin, *Eavesdropping in the Novel from Austen to Proust* (Cambridge Studies in Nineteenth Century Literature 37; Cambridge: Cambridge University Press, 2002).

[8] Not all misconceptions are tragic. This narrative tool is equally effective at producing comedy. There are few television sitcoms, for example, that have not resorted to using it at one time or another. (Some shows utilized it so frequently [e.g., *I Love Lucy, Three's Company,* and *Frasier*] it became somewhat of their trademark.) Paradoxically, even before the sound era, Stan Laurel and Oliver Hardy employed eavesdropping in a humorous short entitled *Wrong Again* (1929). In it, Hardy plays a stable boy who overhears two men talking about a stolen Gainsborough painting, the "Blue Boy." Hardy mistakes their topic of conversation for a horse named Blue Boy. Consequently, he and Laurel decide to return it to its rightful owner. When they arrive at his mansion, horse in tow, the bumbling duo find the millionaire engrossed in his bath. Dismissively, he directs them to "put him on the piano." They deliberate briefly . . . and then endeavor to do just that!

tongues throughout distant lands more than two millennia ago. While the *contents* of such conversations lie plainly before us, the *contexts* out of which they arose—the premises on which they are based—are no longer present. To compensate, many readers resort to doing what many eavesdroppers have done: they construct their own meanings. But as we have seen, third parties are prone to err when they approach subject matter strictly from their own standpoint: "What do these words mean *to me*?" This is the same mistake Bart Simpson made. He misjudged what he heard precisely because he failed to consider—or at best, merely assumed—the premises of his source. If he instead sought to determine "What do these words mean *to the one who originally produced them*?" he could have avoided his awkward predicament. (Of course, the sixth season would then have needed a new first episode.)

The point is that just about any form of communication, verbal or nonverbal, needs to be discerned in light of the presuppositions that gave rise to it. If we seek to understand the intended meaning of a biblical text, we need to frame its content against the background of its author's premises. Otherwise, we run the risk of drawing unfortunate or amusing conclusions about it. Once we have grasped the original sense of a text, we can then go about assessing its relevance for us today.

Admittedly, this entire proposition places modern readers at somewhat of a disadvantage. After all, the OT is more than just a conversation. It is a veritable library of dozens of works of mixed genres composed over a span of a thousand years (ca. 1200 B.C.E.–200 B.C.E.). Its assortment of authors wrote in various locations at different times under diverse circumstances. Their ancient frames of reference are no longer our own, and the authors themselves are unavailable for comment. So how are *we* supposed to learn and adopt *their* points of view? Fortunately, there is a wealth of historical-critical scholarship that offers crucial insights into the ancients' social, political, cultural, linguistic, and religious paradigms. The payoffs of tapping into that scholarship, as daunting as it may seem, are well worth it. For it is only in light of their premises that the biblical authors' messages about God, humanity, the created order, and the dynamic interrelationships among them, can be fully grasped and appreciated.

So what effects do an ancient author's presuppositions have on the interpretation of a biblical text? And how does one go about reading it in light of its historical background? The chapters that follow provide a series of case studies that address these questions. For now, however, a brief, preliminary example shall suffice. Consider God's "testing" of Abraham in Gen 22:

> Some time after these events, God put Abraham to the test. He called to him, "Abraham!" "Ready!" he replied. Then God said: "Take your son Isaac, your only one, whom you love, and go to the land of Moriah. There you shall offer him up as a holocaust on a height that I will point out to you." . . . When they came to the place of which God had told him, Abraham built an altar there and arranged the wood on it. Next he tied up his son Isaac, and put him on top of the wood on the altar. Then he reached out and took the knife to slaughter his son. But the LORD's messenger called to him from heaven, "Abraham! Abraham!" "Yes, Lord," he answered. "Do not lay your hand on the boy," said the messenger. "Do not do the least thing to him. I know now how devoted you are to God, since you did not withhold from me your own beloved son." As Abraham looked about, he spied a ram caught by its horns in the thicket. So he went and took the ram and offered it up as a holocaust in place of his son. (Gen 22:1–2, 9–13)[9]

Nowadays, we are horrified by grisly headlines of parents murdering their small children. When a perpetrator claims to have acted in accordance with "the voice of God," it only heightens the bizarre monstrosity of such crimes. For this reason, modern readers might take issue with God's requirement that Abraham slaughter Isaac—and rightly so. After all, what sort of benevolent, loving Deity would ask someone to kill his or her own offspring? The fact that God stops Abraham right before the directive is carried out hardly exonerates the Almighty. (Is it really any better that God is just *pretending* to have Abraham butcher Isaac? Consider the psychological and emotional toll this would take on a father—much less his wide-eyed son.) The request is outrageous. In fact, even by the OT's ethical standards, God's behavior seems out of line. The fifth commandment clearly stipulates, "You shall not kill" (Exod 20:13; Deut 5:17), and additional ordinances expressly prohibit child sacrifice (Lev 19:21; 20:2–5; Deut 18:10).[10]

Within the immediate context of the narrative, however, God's little "test" serves a specific purpose: it showcases Abraham's unwavering faith. Here is a man whose devotion is so strong that he would withhold *nothing* from God, not even his own beloved flesh and blood. Such loyalty proves Abraham to be an excellent choice as God's origi-

---

[9] Unless otherwise noted, all biblical quotations are taken from the New American Bible translation.

[10] Granted, these laws will be promulgated long after Abraham's time, according to the Bible's narrative history.

nal covenant partner (a point to which we shall return in ch. 4). But while this episode bolsters Abraham's reputation, it appears to subvert God's. Indeed, the very necessity of such a "test" can be challenged on the grounds of the Almighty's self-proclaimed ability to judge a man by simply looking into his heart (1 Sam 16:7). Wouldn't an omniscient Deity already have known that Abraham would be faithful? Why put him (and Isaac) through this horribly twisted ordeal?

Here is where the historical context can shed invaluable light on the subject and help transform our understanding of it. As it turns out, that which offends our modern sensibilities would have been received quite differently by the original audience of Genesis. Why? Because for ancient Near Eastern people, the practice of child sacrifice was a relatively familiar occurrence. What we find abhorrent and morally repulsive was, for the most part, a common cultic ritual.

The ubiquity of this act deserves some explanation. In ancient times, people's survival as hunters, gatherers, cultivators, or herders depended in large part upon the forces of nature. The sun, wind, rain, soil, vegetation, insects, livestock, and wild game were all factors that contributed to one's survival. A community's continued existence hinged upon the harmonious interplay among them. The sudden disruption or exertion of these forces (in the form of floods, droughts, hail, frost, plagues, diseases, or predators) could easily trigger widespread starvation and death. At that time, most people believed that deities controlled the forces of nature. If they were suitably appeased, the seasons were mild and the harvest abundant. If not, then there was trouble. Sacrifices and offerings were designed to avoid the latter. In this respect, human sacrifice was essentially a utilitarian act. Better to offer a few individuals to satisfy the gods than to put the entire population in jeopardy of their wrath.

Against this background, Abraham's test acquires a radically new meaning—one that is nearly opposite that which modern readers tend to ascribe to it. Given its historical context, God's call for human sacrifice is not unusual. It's what happens *next* that's so peculiar. God prevents Abraham from following through with it. Why? Because God considers Abraham's *intention* sufficient. It is Abraham's willingness to surrender his progeny—his unflinching obedience—that God ultimately desires. Consequently, an animal (the ram caught in the thicket) becomes a pleasing and acceptable substitute for Isaac.

In light of its original premises, then, Abraham's test is not the story of a dysfunctional God playing dangerous mind games with one of his followers. Rather, it serves to illustrate an important distinction between Abraham's God and all the other deities of the ancient world. While *they* may demand human sacrifices, this One does not. Instead, it is the devoted heart (coupled, perhaps, with a token offering) that Abraham's God wants. No more, no less. Ironically, then, while this episode appears to cast God in a questionable light, at least for modern readers, the story itself ultimately serves to promote a more humane practice of religion.

The chapters that follow offer similar case studies drawn from throughout the OT.[11] For the most part, they proceed according to the chronology of the biblical narrative, with sectional divisions that reflect its early tri-part structure (i.e., the Law, the Prophets, and the Writings). Each chapter considers a popularly misconstrued passage, book, or biblical theme (i.e., that which we have tended to overhear) and then reconsiders it in light of its historical context (i.e., that which lay behind this ancient conversation). Through this process, original meanings are allowed to reemerge—meanings that not only challenge our commonly held (mis-)interpretations but also present us with a fresh set of contemporary implications and applications. It is my sincerest hope that these varied forays into the Old Testament will help bring it to life, so that the reader might discover how rich and relevant these amazing documents are and how rewarding their study can be.

---

[11] As broad as it is, this survey is by no means exhaustive, nor is it meant to be. Rather, it is intended to present a balanced and representative sampling of the sacred texts as they span the chronological and literary spectrums.

Part I תורה

The Law (Torah)

The first section of the Hebrew Bible, the Torah, consists of five books: Genesis, Exodus, Leviticus, Numbers, and Deuteronomy. Narratively speaking, they cover the earliest stages of Israel's history, beginning with the creation of the world itself.[1] From there, the story line proceeds through the fall of humanity in the garden of Eden, the great flood, the patriarchal stories of Abraham, Isaac, Jacob, and Joseph, the rise of Moses, the exodus from Egypt, the delivery of the law on Mt. Horeb/Sinai, and the wilderness wanderings. By its conclusion, a new generation of Israelites find themselves about to enter the promised land, eager to claim that which God had pledged to them.

The chapters that follow concentrate on select episodes from this narrative history. Chapters 1 and 2 examine the dual creation stories of Genesis. They explore the extent to which the biblical text can be reconciled in light of the findings of modern science, the prevailing legends of ancient Mesopotamia, and even its own, internal contradictions. Chapter 3 considers the biblical account of Noah's ark against the background of its popular representation, its ethical implications, and its historical presuppositions. Chapter 4 explores the Abraham narratives and demonstrates how the varying traditions surrounding this patriarch give rise to both conflict and hope in the Middle East. Finally, chapter 5 treats the Law itself: the 613 statutes and commandments

[1]For a narrative timeline from creation to the united monarchy, see Appendix A.

found within the Torah. This chapter aims not only to survey the contents of these regulations but also to convey their primary purpose in light of their original context.

1

The First Creation Story —Is It True?

FOCUS TEXT: GENESIS 1:1–2:4A

Throughout the history of literature, few texts have generated more controversy than Gen 1. Individuals with even a nominal exposure to the Bible are typically familiar with its story of creation. God calls into existence the heavens and the earth and all that is in them in six days. God then rests from his creative activity on the seventh day.

Defining the Controversy

From its opening verses, the OT presents a serious challenge to any modern believer who would seek to uphold its status as "inerrant," as "sacred Scripture," or as "the word of God." Taken literally, Gen 1 and the biblical chronology that follows it suggest that our planet—indeed, the entire universe—is roughly fifty-eight hundred years old. Such an assertion, of course, runs contrary to findings across a wide array of scientific disciplines. Most geologists, paleontologists, astronomers, physicists, biologists, chemists, and oceanographers judge the earth to be exponentially older—that its true age, in fact, is probably closer to 4.5 billion years.[1]

Given the tremendous disparity between these two timetables, modern believers find themselves on the horns of a dilemma. Presumably,

---

[1]This estimate comes from radiometric dating, a technique of determining age based on the fixed-rate decay of atomic nuclei. According to this method, our galaxy is 11 to 13 billion years old and the universe itself is 13 to 15 billion years old.

they must either side with Scripture and disavow a vast body of scientific research or side with science and surrender the authority of Scripture. Neither of these options is particularly attractive for those who would seek to maintain both the trustworthiness of the Bible and the general validity of contemporary scientific methods.

In an effort to resolve this dilemma, some creative solutions have emerged. One strategy is to grant Scripture the ultimate authority but then to seek out empirical data that coincide with the Genesis account. The levels of inert helium in the atmosphere, the decline of the earth's magnetic field, the accumulation of meteoritic dust on the moon, and the concentration of metals in the oceans are just some of the types of phenomena to which so-called creation scientists have appealed. But so far, these appeals have convinced neither the mainstream scientific community nor the U.S. Supreme Court. On June 19, 1987, the court ruled on *Edwards v. Aguillard* 7–2 against the Louisiana Creationism Act. A brief representing seventy-two Nobel-Prize-winning scientists and seventeen state academies of science was filed in opposition to the act, which required that creation science be taught alongside the theory of evolution in Louisiana public schools. The court ultimately struck down the Louisiana Creationism Act because it purported to advance a particular religious doctrine and thereby violated the Establishment Clause.[2]

An alternative strategy is to accept science's conclusions but then to reinterpret the biblical text in conformity with them. In this regard, 2 Pet 3:8 ("With the Lord one day is like a thousand years and a thousand years like one day") is often cited as an indication that the six days refer not to twenty-four-hour periods but to considerably longer epochs of time. It may also be noted that the order of creation in Gen 1 bears a fair resemblance to the gradual, geo-evolutionary process envisioned by scientists: light/dark, sky/sea, land, plants, fish/birds, animals, humans. But even this solution is not without its difficulties. On the as-

---

[2]Two decades later, this church/state issue continues to be debated. At present, nearly twenty states are considering bills which would require public schools to teach both evolution and intelligent design. (Intelligent design claims that certain features of the natural world are best explained by an intelligent cause rather than by unguided, random processes.) The issue presently occupies the highest of educational institutions. At the time of this writing, Harvard University has just announced that it shall allocate $1 million in seed money to begin a major research project into the origins of life, largely in response to the challenges posed by the intelligent design theory.

sumption that God was the only witness to these events and thus the source of their description, critics decry the repeated appearance of the word "day." Surely God could have foreseen the controversy caused by this term and circumvented it by providing a more accurate timeline! A more formidable obstacle lies with the arrangement of creation. According to Gen 1, the sun, the moon, and the stars are not created until day four—well after the earth and its accompanying landscape.[3] In addition, the sequence of events in Gen 1 clearly contradicts that found in Gen 2 (a point to which we shall return in ch. 2).

For these reasons, the dilemma has resisted simple resolution, and the perception of what's really at stake in this issue has only galvanized the resolve of the opposing parties. The conflict is frequently billed as creation vs. evolution, religion vs. science, or the authority of God vs. the authority of humankind. The question of origins seems to cut to the heart of who we are, why we are here, and how we should live. Is human life merely the fortunate by-product of coincidental cosmic forces, the quirky result of—as the biologists' joke goes—a sexually transmitted, terminal disease? Or has our existence and that of the universe been consciously ordained by a supernatural power? When it comes to creation, what is the *truth*? Certainly both sides can't be right, can they?

Underlying this juxtaposition of science and Scripture is the widespread assumption that both are describing the same thing. Science has endeavored to provide us with an explanation of the geophysical processes involved in the formation of our planet. But to presume that this is also the purpose of Gen 1 is like presuming the meaning of an overheard conversation. In essence, it neglects the very premise out of which this text emerged. To ignore our author's worldview and to supplant it with our own is to jeopardize the message that was originally intended to be communicated. To get at that message, one must recognize some fundamental differences between modern and ancient ways of approaching historical truth.

[3]It is on this basis that the Roman Catholic Church initially rejected the heliocentric models of Copernicus and Galileo and condemned these scientists as heretics. The church authorities reasoned that since earth was created first, the rest of the universe must therefore revolve around it. In July 1981, Pope John Paul II organized a commission to review the case. Once the commission reached its conclusion (more than a decade later), the pope officially admitted that errors had been made by the theological advisors of the church and largely exonerated the Renaissance scientists. See John Paul II, "Lessons of the Galileo Case," address to the Pontifical Academy of Sciences, October 31, 1992; in *Origins* 22 no. 22 (November 12, 1992): 371.

Historical Truth: Modern vs. Ancient Approaches

When it comes to history, we moderns tend to think of truth in sensory terms. We want to know what actually happened, as it can be apprehended by our physical senses, particularly our sight, our hearing, and our touch. We prefer to think of truth as experiential and recordable, as, for instance, in a photograph or video. To illustrate this point, consider the following photo of Earth from space.

This photograph was taken on December 7, 1972 by the crew of Apollo 17 as they rocketed toward the moon. As NASA's accompanying caption on its Web site notes, the view extends from the Mediterranean Sea area to the polar ice cap of Antarctica. While there is heavy cloud

"Earth from Space" December 7, 1972 (NASA).
Astronaut photograph AS17-148-22727 courtesy of NASA Johnson Space Center. This image can be found online at http://spaceflight.nasa.gov/gallery/images/apollo/apollo17/html/as17-148-22727.html (accessed July 25, 2008).

cover in the Southern Hemisphere, the northern Saharan region of Africa is almost entirely visible. In the center of the image is the Malagasy Republic, the large island off the coast of Africa. The Arabian Peninsula can be seen at the northeastern edge of Africa, and the Asian mainland is barely distinguishable on the horizon beyond it.

I've showed this picture to my classes and asked, "Is this true? Did planet Earth, on December 7, 1972, really look like this? Was there an island here and a peninsula over there? Were there cloud swirls here and here and here? Did clear skies prevail up here? Was all this ice accumulated down there? Assuming, of course, that it hasn't been digitally altered, does this photograph convey a true image?" Although my students usually look at me a little quizzically, they always answer affirmatively.

But there is another way of conceiving history, one more in line with the perspective of our biblical author, who wrote long before the advent of modern imaging technologies. To exemplify the difference, I call up a second image.

"Soccer-Ball Earth."
Image courtesy of *Florida Today* cartoonist Jeff Parker.

This image is a political cartoon. It portrays our planet as a ball in a soccer game. Six menacing players surround it, jockeying for position to kick and control it. Their jerseys are emblazoned with various monikers: "Overpopulation," "Global Warming," "Fossil Fuel Dependency," "Pollution," "Loss of Rain Forests," and "Species Extinction."

When I've shown this picture to my classes, I've asked them, "How about this one? Is our world really just athletic gear being kicked around by a half-dozen, cleat-clad giants on some vast, intergalactic field? Is this actually happening? Is this a true image?" This time, my students' furtive, darting glances betray their concern for my mental stability. But inevitably, they answer negatively.

The difference between the photograph and the cartoon is analogous to the difference between science's take on creation and that of Genesis. Science provides us with a geophysical snapshot of the 4.5–billion-year process by which the earth came into being. Presumably, if someone had been present throughout that period recording with a digital camcorder (and an enormous memory chip!), that's what would have been recorded. Genesis, by contrast, offers us more of a portraiture—an artistic rendering of the event in question.

Given our modern proclivities, we may be tempted to conclude that the Genesis account of creation is therefore less true than that of science. But that's not necessarily the case. Reconsider the cartoon. There is, in fact, a great deal of truth to it. To discern its truth claims, we merely need to decipher it by appealing to the common frames of reference which the artist has employed. For contemporary readers, this is a relatively simple task. The scene depicted is a soccer game, a physically competitive, high-contact sport. The players represent an assortment of planetary afflictions, as indicated by the names on their uniforms. Their massive builds and gritty expressions underscore the strength and tenacity of the forces at play. As the soccer ball, Earth is being "kicked" by them. It is taking a beating; it is being pressured, harmed, and abused. In general, the cartoon suggests that the delicate balance and resiliency of our biosphere is being seriously compromised by these particular threats. Indeed, few experts within the scientific community, especially those who monitor global change, would disagree with this assessment.

To some interstellar visitor who knew absolutely nothing about our planet, the caricature may reveal at least as much truth as the photograph—if not more. Their respective truths are just qualitatively different. The photograph communicates the state of the planet relative to its geophysical and atmospheric features, whereas the caricature underscores the stressors which jeopardize its environment.

Now imagine that our interstellar visitor is comparing the two images, side by side. There are, to be sure, definite "contradictions" between them. For starters, their backgrounds are different. In the photograph, the planet is framed against the blackness of space; in the cartoon, it is suspended in the middle of a soccer game. Closer analysis of the world itself reveals a number of additional discrepancies. The photograph has clouds; the cartoon does not. The cartoon has longitudinal and latitudinal gridlines; the photograph does not. The photograph is dominated by a light continent in the middle (Africa) and dark oceans on either side; the cartoon is dominated by a light ocean in the middle (the Atlantic) and dark continents on either side. Comparatively, these contradictions are significant—even irreconcilable. As a consequence, our visitor may be tempted to discard one or the other. But we can recognize that such a comparison is ultimately meaningless, since two very different media are being used to convey two very different types of perspectives. Thus, even despite the evident contradiction of their details, the veracity of both images can still be affirmed. We can apply this exact same principle to the scientific and biblical views of creation.

So if Gen 1 is not describing the geophysical processes that resulted in the creation of the earth (as science is), then what sort of truth claims is it asserting? To answer this question, we need to approach the author's words in the same manner that we approached the political cartoon—the same process by which we ought to approach an overheard conversation. We need to decipher them in light of the prevailing cultural paradigms of their time. But who composed these words, and when and where did they live?

The Historical Context of Genesis 1

The book of Genesis belongs to a subset of five OT books collectively known as the Torah (literally, the Law). Traditionally, the writings of the Torah have been attributed to Moses. However, the general consensus among today's source critics (scholars who specialize in determining from where and from when a given document originated) is that at least four different sources contributed to the composition of the Torah.[4]

[4] These include the Yahwist (J, tenth cent. B.C.E.), the Elohist (E, ninth cent. B.C.E.), the Priestly (P, sixth cent. B.C.E.), and the Deuteronomist (D, seventh cent. B.C.E.). The determination of sources is based on a variety of factors, such as writing style,

Gen 1 belongs to the so-called Priestly (or P) source.[5] Based on the details and types of information that this source supplies, experts deduce that it was most likely written by a member or members of the Judahite priesthood during, or shortly after, the Babylonian exile (ca. 587–539 B.C.E.).

Given this setting, the Priestly author and his contemporaries could hardly have avoided exposure to the cultural and religious belief systems of the Babylonians. (As exiles, the Judahites were, quite literally, a captive audience.) And while the Babylonians had varying traditions concerning the creation of the world, perhaps none of them was as prevalent as the *Enuma Elish.*

The Enuma Elish

This ancient Near Eastern epic predates Gen 1 by at least one thousand years. The saga spans seven tablets, and although some of the text has been lost, that which has survived can be summarized as follows:

> Before the heavens and earth were created, there existed a watery primordial chaos, embodied in Apsu (the male, freshwater deity) and Tiamat (the female, saltwater deity). Their waters mingled together to produce a series of younger gods. However, these younger gods proved to be too noisy for Apsu, so that he could rest neither by day nor by night. Frustrated, Apsu plotted to eliminate his offspring. Having learned of Apsu's intentions towards the younger gods, one of them, Ea, killed Apsu. Enraged by her husband's death, Tiamat fashioned an army of terrible monsters to avenge it. Tiamat then appointed a sympathetic god, Kingu, to be its commander. Word of the army reached the younger gods, who took counsel and elected Marduk to fight Tiamat. Marduk agreed, on the condition that, following his victory, he would be granted absolute authority over all the gods. The younger gods consented and equipped Marduk for the conflict. The battle between Marduk and Tiamat ensued. When Tiamat opened her mouth wide to devour him, Marduk used a mighty wind against her. He blew her up, charged inside, and then stabbed her internal organs, thus killing her. After he

vocabulary, content, and narrative perspective. More comprehensive treatment of these sources can be found in most introductory textbooks. Of those found in the Suggested Reading list in this book, see Barry Bandstra, *Reading the Old Testament: An Introduction to the Hebrew Bible* (2d ed.; Belmont, Calif.: Wadsworth, 1999), 34–48; Lawrence Boadt, *Reading the Old Testament: An Introduction* (Mahwah, N.J.: Paulist Press, 1984), 92–108; Michael D. Coogan, *The Old Testament: A Historical and Literary Introduction to the Hebrew Scriptures* (New York: Oxford University Press, 2006), 21–30; and John J. Collins, *Introduction to the Hebrew Bible* (Minneapolis: Augsburg, 2004), 47–65.

[5] The Priestly label derives its name from the type of material that characterizes it. The P source seems especially interested in cultic and ritualistic matters.

> vanquished the remainder of Tiamat's army, Marduk then split Tiamat apart like an oyster. The top part of her he established as a covering above the earth. He affixed a bolt and stationed guards to prevent her waters from coming forth. Marduk next assigned the gods Anu, Enlil, and Ea to the sky, the atmosphere and earth, and the waters, respectively. Then, Marduk made stations for the gods, setting their images as the stars of the Zodiac. Marduk caused the Moon-god to shine forth, and cleared a path for the Sun-god.[6] Finally, he decided to create human beings, so that the gods might be at ease. For this purpose, he summoned forth the traitorous Kingu and slaughtered him. From Kingu's blood, people were created. The gods then assembled and threw a feast to celebrate.[7]

At first glance, the Babylonian version of creation might not seem to have much in common with Gen 1. But a closer investigation of these two narratives reveals some striking parallels.

Comparative Similarities

From the opening scene of the *Enuma Elish,* two primordial, watery entities exist. Similarly, Gen 1:1–3 appears to describe God not as beginning his creative work "from nothing" (*ex nihilo*) but from a primordial, watery substance: "When God began to create heaven and earth—the earth being unformed and void, with darkness over the surface of the deep and a wind from God sweeping over the water—God said, 'Let there be light'; and there was light" (NJPS).[8] Vestiges of the Babylonian tradition can also be found in the biblical references to the "deep"—the Hebrew of which (תהום, *tehom*) is equivalent to the Akkadian word "Tiamat"—and to God's accompanying "wind" which inexplicably hovers over (subdues?) it.

---

[6] Although the tablet is broken and difficult to read at this point, it appears that Marduk used Tiamat's lower half to create the waters of the earth. The extant text indicates that springs issued from her, and the great Tigris and Euphrates Rivers surged forth from her eyes.

[7] A full translation of this text can be found in Stephanie Dalley, *Myths from Mesopotamia: Creation, the Flood, Gilgamesh, and Others* (rev. ed.; Oxford's World Classics; New York: Oxford University Press, 2000), 228–77.

[8] This translation is also preferred by the New Jerome Biblical Commentary. There is considerable debate over the precise rendering of these verses. Following the Septuagint (LXX), the early Greek translation of the HB, the traditional reading states, "In the beginning God created heaven and earth. And the earth was. . . ." Although this translation is grammatically possible, many scholars today deem it less likely given the literary context. Either translation has implications for *creatio ex nihilo,* or the belief that God created out of nothing. It is safe to say that this doctrine, formulated by Christian theologians some seven hundred years later, wasn't a concern for the Priestly writer.

Of course, one of the most obvious points of contact between these two texts is the division of the primordial water to create the sky and sea and the use of a "firmament" to separate them:[9] "Then God said, 'Let there be a dome [or "firmament"] in the middle of the waters, to separate one body of water from the other.' And so it happened. God made the dome, and it separated the water above the dome from the water below it. God called the dome 'the sky' " (Gen 1:6–7).

Even the overarching sequence of creation as set forth in Gen 1 mirrors that recorded in the *Enuma Elish.* Following the watery chaos and its subsequent division, Genesis mentions land, the heavenly bodies, humanity, and the divine repose in the same order (see Table 1.1).

Similarities between the Enuma Elish and Genesis 1

Feature	*Enuma Elish*	Gen 1:1–2:4a
Opening scene	Chaotic, primordial watery entities	Primordial water
Water named	Tiamat	תהום or *tehom*
Wind	Used by Marduk to defeat the watery Tiamat	God's wind hovers over the primordial water
Sea and sky	Created from division of Tiamat; firmament holds in place	Created from division of primordial water; firmament holds in place
Order of creation	Primordial waters	Primordial waters
		Light
	Waters above/below	Waters above/below
	Land	Land (and plants)
	Bodies of light	Bodies of light
		Birds/fish
	Humanity	Animals/humans
	Divine feast/repose	God rests

Table 1.1

All of these similarities suggest that the author of Gen 1 was influenced by the *Enuma Elish,* or at least by many of the notions expressed in it. However, he was not merely a passive recipient and subsequent transmitter of such traditions. He also sought to assert certain truth claims over and against them. These truth claims are most evident in the

[9] The ancients believed that a storehouse of water lay beyond the sky (thus producing its bluish color). The water was held back by a firmament—a word that typically refers to a section of metal that has been hammered flat. From its gates come forth rain, snow, and other moisture.

differences between the *Enuma Elish* and Gen 1. A number of points of comparison come readily to the fore.

Comparative Differences

First, whereas many gods occupy the stage in the *Enuma Elish,* Gen 1 features only one actor. Clearly, the biblical author is asserting belief in one God (monotheism) over that in many (polytheism).

In the *Enuma Elish,* the preponderance of gods leads to rivalry, violent conflict, bloodshed, and destruction. These are the means, according to the Babylonian epic, by which the world came into being. In contrast, Gen 1 portrays the process of creation as remarkably tranquil. God vocalizes his instructions, and they are immediately carried out.

The divine's relationship to the material world is also different. In the *Enuma Elish,* the creation of the world is inherently related to the creation of the gods. The gods themselves are derived from, and conjoined with, the eternal material. Thus, everything that is in the universe (the sea, sky, sun, moon, stars) either is, or was, a deity. In this way, Marduk doesn't create the world so much as assemble or ordain the natural order by assigning deities to their respective places. The God of Genesis, however, is transcendent. He is above creation and exists independently from it. With one possible exception (the primordial water), what God doesn't simply call into being, he himself "creates" (ברא, *bara'*) or "makes" (עשׂה, *'asah*).

This difference in origins leads to certain implications concerning the quality of the material world. For example, in the *Enuma Elish,* the sky and sea are derived from the corpse of a chaotic mother-god bent on revenge.[10] And human beings are fashioned from the blood of the villainous Kingu. In light of such raw materials, the quality of creation becomes suspect. In the Genesis account, virtually everything is brought into being from scratch by God. Because of its ultimate origin, the biblical author presents God as repeatedly pronouncing it "good."

When it comes to humanity, these accounts vary not only over the origins (and hence, the quality) of people but also over their given roles. In the *Enuma Elish,* human beings are created last, almost as an afterthought, for the primary purpose of serving the gods. They enable the gods to enjoy their lives of ease. Since the natural world is composed of these gods, human beings become subservient to it. For all practical

[10] Notice how even today, we occasionally call both the sky and the sea "angry."

purposes, people occupy the bottom rung in the cosmic hierarchy. Genesis completely reverses this status. Created last, humans become the culmination of God's work. They are the only facet of it that explicitly bears the divine image. As such, they are given broad dominion over the other living creatures. They even get to share in the privilege of God's rest!

This divine repose constitutes yet another point of comparison. In the Babylonian saga, it is Apsu's initial inability to sleep that leads to all of the turmoil. By the story's end, humans have been created so that the pantheon can permanently relax. In this way, the *Enuma Elish* portrays rest as the ultimate aim or objective of the deities. But according to Genesis, the Sabbath rest arises more as a consequence or by-product of creative activity. In other words, God rests because he creates, rather than creates because he desires rest.

Before concluding our analysis, one final difference between the *Enuma Elish* and Gen 1 should be mentioned. Whereas the structure of the *Enuma Elish* follows a narrative form, the Priestly writer has arranged his creation story in a decidedly systematic way. One of the most prominent features of Gen 1 is its heavy reliance on certain repetitious phrases. When these phrases are mapped out according to the verses in which they appear, a distinctive pattern emerges (see table 1.2).

Key Phrases of Genesis 1

Phrase	**Day**					
	1	**2**	**3**	**4**	**5**	**6**
Then God said, "Let there be . . ."	1:3	1:6	1:9 1:11	1:14	1:20	1:24 1:26
And so it happened	1:3	1:6	1:9 1:11	1:15	1:20	1:24 1:29
God saw how good it was	1:4		1:10 1:12	1:18	1:21	1:25 1:31
Evening came, and morning followed—the nth day.	1:5	1:8	1:13	1:19	1:23	1:31

Table 1.2

Notice that the text rarely departs from the regular use of four key phrases. The only major omission occurs on day 2, where there is no mention of God finding the sea and sky "good." (Recall that, according to the Priestly writer, these were the only elements that God didn't create himself. Instead, they were fashioned from the primordial waters. Perhaps that is why they are not explicitly labeled "good.") Of course, these four repetitious phrases would have been useful for transmitting the story orally.

But perhaps even more useful for its oral transmission is the organizational structure of its six days of creation. The first three days of Gen 1:1–13 mirror the second three days of Gen 1:14–31, so that what God creates on days 1, 2, and 3, he then fashions corresponding bodies for on days 4, 5, and 6. This pattern is hardly coincidental (see table 1.3).

Seven-Day Structure of Genesis 1	
Day One Light	**Day Four** Bodies of light
Day Two Sea and sky	**Day Five** Creatures of the sea and sky
Day Three Land (and plants)	**Day Six** Creatures of the land (animals and humans)
Day Seven Rest	

Table 1.3

In essence, then, the one-week structure of Gen 1 functions not as a literal timeline of creation but as a mnemonic device that enabled this tradition to survive. By simply plugging the four key phrases into the parallel three-day pattern, just about anyone could repeat the entire creation story "by heart."[11] To dismiss this narrative as untrue solely on the basis of its timetable, therefore, would be like judging the phrase "Every good boy deserves fudge" to be untrue on the basis of the high caloric content of fudge. The practical validity of the statement is beside the point; its primary function is to help music students remember the musical staff (E-G-B-D-F).

[11] Given this feature, it is not clear whether the tradition of Gen 1 had been passed down orally to the Priestly writer (who edited and recorded it) or whether the Priestly writer created this structure in anticipation of its oral use—perhaps, for example, in a liturgical setting of some sort.

Having completed our survey of the major differences between the *Enuma Elish* and Genesis 1, we can summarize them (see table 1.4).

Differences between the Enuma Elish and Genesis 1

Differences	*Enuma Elish*	Gen 1:1–2:4a
Theological orientation	Polytheistic	Monotheistic
Process of creation	Struggle, violent war	Spoken, tranquil acts
Divine's relationship to material world	Conjoined	Transcendent
Origin and action of creation	Everything is, or was, a deity; Marduk partitions, ordains	Almost everything created by God from scratch
Quality of creation	Suspect	Good
Humanity's place in the cosmic hierarchy	Formed from traitorous Kingu; subservient to the (gods of the) natural world	Bear divine image; given dominion over the natural world
Divine repose	Aim, objective	Consequence; humans also partake
Structure	Narrative style	Key phrases set within a six-day timetable (composed of parallel three-day subsets)

Table 1.4

The Truth Claims of Genesis 1

On the basis of our comparison with one of the most established beliefs of its day, the truth claims of Gen 1 now emerge with greater clarity. The Priestly writer has presented the universe not as the consequence of a violent and chaotic clash between restless parent gods and their noisy offspring but as the deliberate product of a single, transcendent Deity. This Deity exists independently of the material world; however, because most of it originates from him, creation itself is fundamentally good. The author also asserts that human beings occupy a unique position among the earth's inhabitants. Rather than being the nadir, or the low point, of creation, they are portrayed as its zenith, or its culmination.

This status is due primarily to humanity's special relationship to its Creator. Made in the divine image, they are entrusted with God's dominion. Accordingly, they also share in the honor of God's rest.

It is evident, then, that the Priestly writer sought not to compose a textbook detailing the material transactions that produced our biosphere or their precise chronology. Indeed, he had no knowledge of such things. Rather, utilizing both the traditions that he had received and the media of his time, the biblical author set forth certain truth claims about the relationship between God, humanity, and the created order. To read his words otherwise is to miss his intent.[12] Accordingly, Gen 1 need not compete with a scientific perspective. Rather, it can complement it, as a caricature might complement a photograph. Just as science can offer us a perspective that Scripture can't, so too can Scripture offer us a perspective that science can't. In the end, we are surely enriched by both.[13]

---

[12] In this respect, both the scientists who boast that they have "rewritten Genesis" with their models of cosmic evolution and the biblical literalists who would insist on a young-earth cosmology have made equal and opposite mistakes concerning the purpose and function of the Genesis account.

[13] Albert Einstein, the most celebrated scientist of the twentieth century, evidently agreed. He put it this way: "Science without religion is lame, religion without science is blind" (*Science, Philosophy and Religion: A Symposium,* published by the Conference on Science, Philosophy and Religion in Their Relation to the Democratic Way of Life, Inc., New York, 1941).

2

The Second Creation Story—Internal Contradictions?

Focus Text: Genesis 2:4b–25

Attentive readers of the Bible discover something rather unexpected beyond the first chapter of Genesis. The OT contains not one but two stories of creation. As noted in chapter 1, the dilemma posed for the modern believer by the first creation story is primarily external: its truth has been called into question relative to the findings of modern science. But Gen 2 introduces a different problem—one that is primarily internal. The reliability of its account and, by extension, the Bible as a whole, is challenged by the text that immediately precedes it. In other words, Gen 2 contradicts Gen 1.

Genesis 1 vs. Genesis 2: Comparative Discrepancies

Nowhere are the discrepancies between these two creation stories more pronounced than in the sequences of events which they describe, particularly those involving the earth's various life forms. According to Gen 1, it is on day 3 that the planet's vegetation emerges:

> Then God said, "Let the earth bring forth vegetation: every kind of plant that bears seed and every kind of fruit tree on earth that bears fruit with its seed in it." And so it happened. . . . (Gen 1:11)

On day 5, the birds and the fish come forth:

> Then God said, "Let the water teem with an abundance of living creatures, and on the earth let birds fly beneath the dome of the sky." And so it happened.... (Gen 1:20)

On the sixth day, the beasts of the field are produced:

> Then God said, "Let the earth bring forth all kinds of living creatures: cattle, creeping things, and wild animals of all kinds." And so it happened.... (Gen 1:24)

And last (but not least) human beings enter the scene:

> Then God said: "Let us make man in our image, after our likeness.[1] Let them have dominion over the fish of the sea, the birds of the air, and the cattle, and over all the wild animals and all the creatures that crawl on the ground."
>
> God created man in his image;
> in the divine image he created him;
> male and female he created them. (Gen 1:26–27)

Gen 2, however, presents an entirely different order of creation. According to it, God formed man first, "at the time when . . . as yet there was no field shrub on earth and no grass of the field had sprouted. . . ." (Gen 2:4b–5a). It is only after the creation of man that "the LORD God made various trees grow that were delightful to look at and good for food. . . ." (Gen 2:9a).

Following this, God decides that it is not good for man to be alone. Therefore,

> The LORD God formed out of the ground various wild animals and various birds of the air, and he brought them to the man to see what he would call them; whatever the man called each of them would be its name. (Gen 2:19)

[1] The plural pronouns used in this verse (and similarly, in Gen 3:22) often beg the question: To whom is God speaking? The "Christian answer" inevitably involves the Trinity. While such a response may have some doctrinal validity, it cannot be what the original Jewish author had in mind. If Judaism is anything, it is thoroughly monotheistic: God is one. The notion of a trinity would have seemed polytheistic to our author. Alternatively, some suggest that the so-called royal we is being employed here. But again, this is anachronistic. Hebrew knows nothing of a plural of majesty. So how are we to understand the pronouns used here? Scholars advance two possibilities. One is that the plural is appropriate given the self-reflective tone of the passage. This grammatical construction is called a "plural of deliberation." Similar examples can be found in Gen 11:7–8, Isa 6:8, and 2 Sam 24:14. A second possibility is that God is speaking to his assembled heavenly court (i.e., angels, archangels). Although the text has not yet made any explicit reference to them or to their creation, they are evidently in the background since God will station the cherubim to guard the tree of life (Gen 3:24). Descriptions of the "heavenly court" occur throughout the OT (see 1 Kgs 22:19; Job 1:6–7; 2:1–2; 38:7).

The man gave names to all the creatures, but none proved to be the suitable partner for him. So finally,

> The Lord God cast a deep sleep on the man, and while he was asleep, he took out one of his ribs and closed up its place with flesh. The Lord God then built up into a woman the rib that he had taken from the man. When he brought her to the man, the man said:
>
> "This one, at last, is bone of my bones
> and flesh of my flesh;
> This one shall be called 'woman,'
> for out of 'her man' this one has been taken." (Gen 2:21–23)

We can set the sequences of creation side by side in the following table.

Order of Creation in Genesis 1 and Genesis 2

Gen 1:1–2:4a	Gen 2:4b–25
	Man
Plants	Plants
Creatures of the sea and sky Creatures of the land	Animals
Humans	Woman

Table 2.1

From the chart, it becomes evident that the misplaced element in the second creation story is man. Remove him, and the progression of living beings (plants, animals, humans) is basically the same. Yet a simple editorial gloss is hardly possible here, since the entire story line of Gen 2 depends upon man being created first. God purposely holds off making the plants because "there was no man to till the soil" (2:5b). And both the animals and the woman are created specifically for man's well-being (2:18). So whereas Gen 1 portrays the flora and fauna as being established prior to humanity, Gen 2 envisions them subsequent to—and for the benefit of—man. Therefore, it is not simply one link that is mislaid but the entire chain of events that is inverted.

These sequences and their corresponding implications are not the only disparities between Gen 1 and Gen 2. They also differ over the creative act itself. In Gen 1, God simply calls everything into existence: "Then God said, 'Let there be. . . .' And so it happened." In this way, God is portrayed as sort of a sovereign spectator, exerting his power over the cosmos from a position outside of it and then approving the results of his mighty commands. But in Gen 2, God enters completely into the world of his creation. As he "fashions" the man and the animals from the clay of the ground and "forms" the woman from man's rib, we can well imagine God getting his hands dirty. Indeed, the verbs used here lend themselves specifically to this notion. The former (יצר, *yatsar*) is a potter's term (cf. Sam 17:28; Isa 29:16; Jer 18:2, 3, 4), whereas the latter (בנה, *banah*) is typically associated with construction—the building of altars, houses, temples, and cities (e.g., Gen 8:20, 10:11, 11:4, 12:7).

But perhaps the signature difference between these two accounts, and one that is not immediately evident in modern translations of the Bible, is the variation in the names used for God. Gen 1 consistently employs "God" (אלהים, *'elohim*) in English translations, whereas Gen 2 utilizes "Lord God" (יהוה אלהים, *yahweh 'elohim*).

Each of these discrepancies, along with other variations in terminology and narrative style, suggest that Gen 2 was written by someone other than the author of Gen 1 and originally circulated independently from it. On the basis of its preferred designation for God, scholars have labeled this second author the Yahwist (or J) source. The J source is thought to be the earliest and, in many ways, the most primitive of the four that are posited.

The assignment of these two creation stories to different sources doesn't fully resolve the quandary before us. While compiling the book of Genesis, somebody, at some point in time, held both of these creation texts and decided to incorporate both into a new work. Why? Surely the writer could have simply omitted one or the other. Such a move would eliminate any contradictions, making this book (and the beliefs that it espouses) more consistent and plausible. But as it now stands, Gen 2 cannot be true in light of Gen 1. Or can it?

Truth in Contradiction

Recall how in chapter 1, we likened the ancients' conception of truth to a caricature—an artistic rendering of reality. What happens when two such images contradict each other? Can they still be true? To answer this question, we can compare the political cartoon from chapter 1 (the one depicting our planet as a soccer ball) with a second artistic rendering of Earth.

"Hands around the World"

In this scene, the world is again surrounded by people, but this time their number has increased to twenty. Rather than fighting over the world, these individuals join hands as they stand together ringing its outer surface. They wear neither cleats nor jerseys. Instead, their physical features and clothing express multicultural diversity: Middle Eastern kaffiyeh, Chinese coolie hat, Polynesian lei and grass skirt, Native American headband, Indian dupatta, Bavarian lederhosen and Tyrolean hat, Eskimo parka, Mexican sombrero, Asian kimono. Like the soccer players, these figures are also smiling, but their smiles are tranquil and serene, not with teeth clenched in competitive determination.

We can think of these two caricatures as two different sources, or accounts, of the state of our planet. Both of them depict the exact same subject. However, the impressions that they communicate flatly contradict each other: one presents our world in peril; the other portrays our world at peace. So do such contradictions jeopardize their respective truth claims? Not at all! In many ways, our biosphere is suffering from the side effects of human exploitation. And at the same time, planet

Earth is also a place where people are able to transcend vast cultural differences and live together harmoniously. Collectively, then, these two caricatures offer us a richer and more nuanced perspective than either one could individually. Far from diminishing our knowledge of a particular subject, the inherent contradictions of varying sources can serve to enhance it. Evidently, the compiler of the book of Genesis would have agreed.

The Yahwist account opens up a viewpoint on creation and the Creator that is otherwise missing from the Priestly account. For this reason, its truth claims emerge most clearly in comparison with those previously asserted.

The Truth Claims of Genesis 2

Like the Priestly version, the Yahwist champions monotheism over polytheism by portraying God as the sole author of creation. However, they each characterize this Deity quite differently. The Priestly version emphasizes God's transcendence (surpassing detachment) and omnipotence (all-powerfulness). The sun, the moon, and the stars—indeed, the entire universe—instantly materialize at the sound of his voice. In contrast, the Yahwist's narrative emphasizes God's proximity and personal investment in his handiwork. God is decidedly anthropomorphic (human-like), rolling up his sleeves to mold and shape and build his creatures. He even blows into their nostrils! Clearly, this is a Creator who is intimately involved in his creation.

Both Gen 1 and Gen 2 also attribute a special status to humanity. But, as indicated above, they do so in nearly opposite ways. Gen 1 presents humans last, as the culmination of creation. Accordingly, they are entrusted with dominion over virtually all that has preceded them: "over the fish of the sea, the birds of the air, and all the living things that move on the earth" (Gen 1:28). Gen 2, by contrast, introduces man first. As such, he is the primary creature for whose sake everything else—the plants, the animals, and the woman—is created. Man's dominion over creation is thus implied. It is made for him, he names it, and he tends to it.

These varying paradigms lead in turn to the emphasis of different relationships. Gen 1 accentuates the bond between God and people. Created in the divine image, they share in the divine rest. But in Gen 2, man is not cast in God's image.[2] Rather, like the animals, he is fashioned out of the dust of the earth. The ground is his origin, and the ground will be his destiny (Gen 3:19). Even his name underscores the significance of this relationship: "man" (אדם, *'adam*) is derived from the same word as "ground" (אדמה, *'adamah*). In fact, the only living creature not tied directly to the soil is the woman. So how exactly does *she* fit into this picture?

Down through the ages, there has been a tendency to read into Gen 2 a God-ordained hierarchy whereby woman is subordinate to man. There are at least four aspects of this narrative that suggest this relationship. There is, of course, the narrative sequence. Being created first, man has chronological priority over the other creatures. Next, there is the stated function of woman. She is made "for" man, as his "suitable partner." (Other translations have "helper," a word that tends to convey secondary importance, like "assistant.") Then there is the source of the woman's origin. Whereas man seems to originate directly from God, woman originates from man.[3] Finally, man names woman, an act which, as with the animals, connotes dominion.

---

[2]In Gen 2:7 God does blow the "breath of life" into the man's nostrils in order to make him a "living being" (נפש חיה, *nefesh khayah*). But care should be taken not to read the divine imagery of Gen 1 or the modern notion of a human soul into this event. The ancient Hebrews did not distinguish the animating life force found in humans from that found in animals (e.g., Gen 7:22; Ps 104:24–30; Eccl 3:18–20). Thus, although Gen 2 does not explicitly state that God blew life into the other creatures, that act is to be assumed. Accordingly, Gen 1 applies the same phrase used here of man—"living being" (נפש חיה, *nefesh khayah*)—to the rest of earth's inhabitants (Gen 1:20, 21, 24, 30).

[3]In the NT, the apostle Paul uses this argument to support his contention that women in sacred assemblies ought to cover their heads. Paul reasons that a man should not cover his head since "he is the image and glory of God, but woman is the glory of man. For man did not come from woman, but woman from man; nor was man created for woman, but woman for man" (1 Cor 11:7–9). Obviously Paul has fused the two creation stories, resulting in some confusion. Gen 1 presents both genders (not just man) as being created simultaneously in God's image: "God created man in his image; in the divine image he created him; male and female he created them" (1:27). Woman *is* created "from" and "for" man in Gen 2, but since man is made from the dust of the earth in this account, this places her neither further nor closer to God than man. So does this mean that Paul's interpretation of Gen 2 wrong? Not exactly. Like the OT, the NT also needs to be understood in light its historical context. Obviously, the modern methods of biblical scholarship were not available to Paul in the first cent. C.E. Therefore, we ought not to expect him to interpret the OT critically. So while Paul's application of Gen 2 may have been appropriate for his audience in his day, his understanding of this text remains as historically (ir)relevant to a modern audience as the issue of women's head coverings.

So does Gen 2 establish gender hierarchy? Despite appearances to the contrary, the four elements adduced above have different meanings in their original context. For example, God does create man first, but this position doesn't *necessarily* imply superiority. Rather, man's presence acts primarily as a stimulus, an antecedent that prompts God to introduce more creatures. We can liken this situation to first-time parents of a newborn. To comfort and entertain their baby, they buy all sorts of stuffed animals and toys. These things inevitably fail to meet their child's more sophisticated social needs. Therefore, the couple decides to conceive again, hoping that a sibling will prove the suitable companion. In this case, the latter child is in no way inferior to the former; the former simply occasioned the creation of the latter.

Second, although woman is created as a "helpmate" for man, this term (עזר, *'ezer*) is not a subservient one. Rather, it is used throughout the OT to designate an equal or even greater power. In fact, in numerous passages (e.g., Deut 33:7, Ps 33:20; 70:6; 115:9–11) it refers to Yahweh.

Then there is the material from which woman is made. While all the other creatures are formed from the ground, woman is created from man's "side" (צלע, *tsele'*). Being "bone of his bone" and "flesh of his flesh," she is literally the same substance as he. This feature is what ultimately enables these two beings to become one (Gen 2:24).

Finally, while the man does name the woman, he does so in a completely unprecedented way. The name he gives to her is his own. The Hebrew word for "woman" (אישה, *'ishah*) is derived from "husband" or "man" (איש, *'ish*). The man thus sees in the woman more than just a companion. He sees, quite literally, his "other half"—the one who will complete him—and he identifies her accordingly.

In light of these considerations, it appears that the Yahwist author intended neither to establish nor to advance a gender-based pecking order. If anything, he endeavored to present man and woman as profoundly compatible entities. Indeed, the eventual introduction of gender hierarchy as the consequence of sin just one chapter later (Gen 3:16) veritably *requires* this original state of equality between the sexes!

Summary of Findings

Having thus completed our survey of the truth claims of Gen 2, we can illustrate the summary of our findings (see table 2.2).

Summary of Comparison: Genesis 1 and Genesis 2		
	Gen 1:1–2:4a	**Gen 2:4b–25**
Source	***Priestly (P)***	***Yahwist (J)***
Divine name	Elohim	Yahweh Elohim
Order	1 – Light 2 – Waters, sky 3 – Land, plants 4 – Bodies of light 5 – Water, sky creatures 6 – Land creatures 7 – Sabbath rest	1 – Man 2 – Plants 3 – Animals 4 – Woman
Creative act	Spoken into being	Formed out of clay
Truth claims	a) Emphasizes God's nature as 1 – Transcendent 2 – Omnipotent	a) Emphasizes God's nature as 1 – Intimate 2 – Personal
	b) Humans as the culmination of creation	b) Man as the impetus for creation
	c) Stresses the relationship between – Humanity and God	c) Stresses the relationships between 1 – Humankind and the earth 2 – Woman and man

Table 2.2

As mentioned, the Yahwist's portrayal of God and creation in Gen 2 can indeed be said to contradict the Priestly portrayal in Gen 1. However, such contradictions do not necessarily jeopardize their respective truth claims. Like multiple drawings of the same subject, the varying points of view can serve to deepen our understanding of it. On the basis of these two accounts, then, the book of Genesis affirms that God is not only omnipotent; he is also intimate. Humanity is not only the culmination of creation; it is also its impetus. And the most fundamental relationship underlying the human experience is not only that between people and their Creator but also between humankind and the earth and between man and woman.

For the moment, peace and tranquility reign in the garden. But as we shall see, this harmonious existence is about to be shattered. Humanity succumbs to the enticements of sin, and soon, moral degradation prevails. In the brief span of only four chapters, the Almighty comes to regret his decision to make human beings. Because of this, their continued existence will hang perilously in the balance.

3

The Great Flood—Revising History

Focus Text: Genesis 6–9

As morning dawned, bare feet hesitated before the concrete steps of the imposing tower. The valiant lad glanced skyward. He had arrived at his destination. As he stood dwarfed in its shadow, he realized that all he had heard about this legend had failed to do it justice. Success in his quest would now require as much courage as he could muster—and perhaps even more.

The boy swallowed hard and ascended the stairs. Heart pounding, he climbed higher and higher. One story . . . two stories . . . six . . . eight . . . ten. At the top, he stepped cautiously out onto the platform. From its deck, he surveyed the panoramic landscape. The height was dizzying, and the figures below seemed impossibly small. He suddenly felt nauseous, and all his instincts urged him to return the way he came. Instead, the hero drew forward. Taking a deep breath, he squeezed his eyes shut and then, tentatively, thrust himself out beyond the Point of No Return. He plummeted rapidly toward the earth. In less than five seconds, it was all over. The champion sat up. Immediately, he wanted to do it again.

The Point of No Return is a death-defying water slide at the largest water park in America. It is but one of more than forty slides at the seventy-acre site, located in the heart of the Wisconsin Dells. On any given day during the summer season, the complex utilizes more than 5 million gallons of water to accommodate its thousands of guests. The name of this aquatic playland? Noah's Ark.[1]

Noah's Ark: Now and Then

It can be argued that license to appropriate this Old Testament icon ought to be granted to any establishment that can successfully manage volumes of water of such biblical proportions. Point conceded. Equally worthy, no doubt, are the countless animal shelters, welfare associations, sanctuaries, foundations, placement services, and rescue leagues that have also adopted this title. But when it comes to American culture, Noah's ark is far more pervasive than that. From birth, we are inundated with its images. This motif is most commonly featured on baby shower supplies (invitations, cups, plates, napkins, balloons, party favors, and thank-you notes), nursery accessories (crib bedding, wallpaper, lamps and nightlights, mobiles, wall clocks, picture frames, music boxes, and bookends), and children's items (pacifier and rattle sets, pajamas, slippers, step stools, floor puzzles, coloring books, tea sets, and plastic action figures).

The fascination with Noah's ark-themed merchandise can be partially explained by some of this narrative's characteristic features. After all, animals, rainbows, and boats are relatively benign objects with widespread appeal, especially among little ones. But beneath these placid scenes lies a deeply disturbing account of a "pan-icide" (the murder of all) whose killing field far surpasses Mao's, Stalin's, and Hitler's combined.[2] Worse yet, the perpetrator of this act, according to the HB, is none other than God! This claim ought to give us pause. At the very least, we should think twice about commemorating it on sippy cups!

---

[1] The data given has been taken from the Web site: http://www.noahsarkwaterpark.com (accessed March 27, 2008).

[2] This assertion refers primarily to the geographical territory affected, but perhaps also to the total number of lives taken. Population estimates for Noah's time vary widely. According to modern historians, the human census doubled over the third millennium B.C.E., from approximately 15 to 30 million. Biblical literalists, however, note that there are fifteen generations recorded between Adam and Noah and that the average lifespan was around nine hundred years. If each couple produced an average of four children—a modest number by OT standards—and lived to see their grandchildren, the world's population by the fifteenth generation would have exceeded 1 billion people. By comparison, it is estimated that the twentieth-century pogroms in China, the U.S.S.R., and Germany claimed 30, 20, and 11 million lives, respectively.

From a literary standpoint, the saga of Noah's ark (Gen 6–9) presents the modern reader with several formidable challenges. Like Gen 1, its historical legitimacy has been contested by rational science. Like Gen 2, the narrative itself is riddled with internal contradictions. But it is the description of God's behavior and the staggering carnage that results from it that proves to be the most unsettling aspect of this text. How can the biblical account of God's conduct be understood, much less justified, on an ethical/theological level? We shall treat each of these matters in turn.

Historical Considerations

The biblical description of a global deluge has prompted a wide array of questions from modern analysts. For instance, how did Noah and his family build a wooden vessel on such a grand scale—some 450 feet in length with a total floor space of approximately 100,000 square feet—using the knowledge and tools of his time (especially since the technology to create wooden-hulled ships of this size wasn't known until the late nineteenth century C.E.)? How did they gather animals of every species, especially those endemic to widely scattered regions of the planet (such as Australian kangaroos, Arctic polar bears, and Galapagos Island tortoises)? How could the ark, big as it was, possibly accommodate so many creatures? How were predators kept away from their prey? What about the exotic foods and quantities of fresh water needed to sustain all of these creatures over such an extended period of time? How was it collected, and where was it stored? How were the ranges of climates required by such diverse species reproduced? What about the fish—how did freshwater species survive in salt water? As for that matter, where did the enormous amount of water—sufficient to cover even the highest mountains on earth—come from? And where did it go? And if there was such a planetary cataclysm, why doesn't the earth's geological record uniformly corroborate it?

Those seeking to defend a literalistic interpretation of the text offer assorted answers to these questions. Granted, some of their solutions are more plausible than others. But most proponents either suspend the basic laws of physics or fall back upon supernatural intervention. Understandably, such explanations don't "hold water" with the majority of today's scientists. Nor, for that matter, have the well-publicized but poorly substantiated claims that the ark itself has been found.[3]

The problem of historicity is rather easily overcome if one approaches Gen 6–9 in the same way that we approached Gen 1–2: as a painting rather than a photograph. The intention of the original author(s) was not to answer the questions of twenty-first-century scientists but to communicate to their own contemporaries something about the nature and character of God. Recognizing this, we can table our queries about the logistics of the event itself and focus instead on the truth claims underlying this work. To identify those truth claims, we first need to acknowledge and resolve some of the internal contradictions of Gen 6–9.

Internal Contradictions

As with the creation stories of Gen 1–2, the flood story of Gen 6–9 demonstrates numerous inconsistencies. For instance, God specifically commands Noah to take two of all living creatures, one male and one female, into the ark with him (Gen 6:19–20; 7:14–16; 8:19; 9:10). But then God instructs Noah to take seven pairs of every clean animal and one pair of every unclean animal (7:2–3, 8–9; 8:20).[4] Noah is given seven days to gather the animals into the ark (7:4, 10). But according to Gen 7:13–16, this happens in one day. Two different chronologies are also at play here. One envisions the flood as a forty-day event (7:4, 12, 17; 8:6), while the other stretches it out over the span of a year (7:11, 24; 8:3–4, 13–14). There is even variation in the means by which the world is flooded. On the one hand, the deluge is attributed to a heavy, forty-day rain (7:4, 12). On the other, it is the gates of the firmament—the one God fixed in place to separate the waters above from the waters below (1:6)—that give way, causing the waters to both rise from the ground and fall from sky (7:11; 8:2). Finally, Noah's departure from the ark is prompted by two different causes. In Gen 8:6–12, Noah determines for himself that the flood waters have receded by sending forth birds. But in Gen 8:15–19, God simply commands Noah to come ashore.

[3] Most such ark-aeological expeditions have concentrated on the mountain range near the border of eastern Turkey. The mainstream scientific community has yet to recognize any definitive evidence establishing the existence of this relic.

[4] This instruction is decidedly anachronistic, since the distinction between "clean" and "unclean" isn't made until Moses' time.

Along with these discrepancies, we can note another striking peculiarity of this text. Key aspects of the story line are duplicated. Twice, the narrative is introduced; humanity's wickedness is described; God announces his decision to destroy the earth; Noah's righteousness is acknowledged; God instructs Noah about the ark and animals; Noah's obedience to God's instructions is verified; Noah, his family, and the animals enter the ark; the waters come; all creatures on earth are destroyed; the waters recede; Noah opens the hatch; and God vows never to destroy the earth again.

The literary disagreements and numerous repetitions are readily resolved if we take Gen 6–9 to be the product of two originally independent sources. Unlike Gen 1–2, where the creation stories are set side by side, Gen 6–9 weaves the two sources together. By teasing them apart, we can identify their similarities and differences more precisely (see table 3.1).

Scholars assign the material in the left column to the Yahwist author, the same one who penned Gen 2. In fact, many of the terms and motifs found there reappear again here. God is referred to as Yahweh (יהוה, *yahweh*). The plot revolves around a single man, this flood account being described primarily from Noah's point of view. Once more, God is portrayed anthropomorphically and as intimately connected to his creation. Thus, God "regrets" making humans and his heart is "grieved" (6:6), he personally closes the ark's door (7:16), and he is moved by the savory aroma of Noah's sacrifice (8:21). Drawing upon some of the same imagery as Gen 2, this flood version acknowledges the corresponding relationship between man and the ground (אדם, *'adam;* אדמה, *'adamah* [Gen 6:6–7; 7:23; 8:21]) and between the male and the female (איש, *'ish;* אישה, *'ishah* [Gen 7:2]). It also refers to living creatures and as having the "breath of life" in their "nostrils" (Gen 7:22).

The material in the far right column derives from the Priestly source, the same one responsible for Gen 1. As in his creation story, the Priestly writer consistently refers to God as Elohim (אלהים, *'elohim*). He emphasizes God's omnipotence and sovereignty by describing the flood entirely from God's perspective. He again appeals to a calendar-based structure, this time fitting the flood episode within a one-year period. Other allusions to Gen 1 also occur here, including references to the waters of "the abyss" (7:11; 8:2) and to people as the "image of God" (9:6).

Despite their differences, there is obviously considerable agreement between the Yahwist and Priestly accounts. To be sure, their points of departure are relatively minor compared to what they both affirm. And

Flood Narratives: Genesis 6–9
The Yahwist and Priestly Accounts Compared

Lord = יהוה (Yahwist Account)	**God = אלהים (Priestly Account)**
6:5–8	
Introduction	
Humanity's wickedness described	
God "regrets," "heart grieved"	
God announces decision to destroy	
Noah's righteousness acknowledged	
	6:9–22
	Introduction
	Noah's righteousness acknowledged
	Humanity's wickedness described
	God announces decision to destroy
	Specific dimensions of ark given
	Covenant described
	1 pair of all animals
	Noah did as God commanded
7:1–5	
7 pairs clean, 1 pair unclean animals	
7 days to gather animals	
Noah did as God commanded	
	7:6
	Noah's age: 600 years
7:7–10	
Noah and family enters ark with clean/unclean animals	
After 7 days	
	7:11
	600 years, second month, 17 days
	The firmament breaks; waters rise from below and fall from above
7:12	
Rains 40 days/nights	
	7:13–16a
	On same day as flood begins,
	Noah and family enters ark with animals

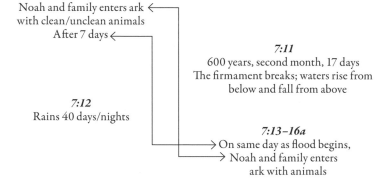

Flood Narratives: Genesis 6–9
The Yahwist and Priestly Accounts Compared, continued

Lord = יהוה (Yahwist Account)	**God = אלהים (Priestly Account)**
7:16b–17a Flood lasts 40 days/nights	
	7:18–21 Waters rise All creatures destroyed
7:22–23 All creatures destroyed	
	7:24–8:5 Flood lasts 150 days God remembers Noah Fountains and floodgates closed Water recedes Seventh month, seventeenth day, ark lands on Mt. Ararat
8:6–12 After 40 days Noah opens window Sends forth raven, dove, dove 7 days between flights	
	8:13–19 601 year, first month, first day Noah opens cover Drying begins Second month, twenty-seventh day, dry land Noah, family, animals told to exit Animals breed and multiply
8:20–22 Noah builds altar Sacrifices clean holocaust God smells the sweet aroma God promises not to destroy again	
	9:1–17 Noah and family told to multiply Given dominion, animals to eat Covenant established God promises not to flood again Rainbow = sign of the covenant

Table 3.1

yet, it is *precisely* what they both affirm that turns out to be the most problematic feature of this text. Both the Yahwist and Priestly writers attribute the great flood and its desired outcome to God. Such an assertion raises some rather serious ethical/theological concerns.

Ethical/Theological Concerns

Why would God obliterate his own handiwork? To answer this question, it may help to return to the beginning of Genesis. The first two chapters had established a fully positive view of creation. The world and all its inhabitants were derived from God's own hands (Gen 2), and God had deemed everything he made to be "good" (Gen 1). But from there, things began to deteriorate. Gen 3 describes humanity's fall from grace as Adam and Eve consume the forbidden fruit from the tree of knowledge. Gen 4 records the first homicide, with Cain killing his brother Abel in a fit of jealousy over divine favoritism. By Gen 6, we learn that corruption and lawlessness are so pervasive that God "regrets" having made human beings at all.[5] Therefore, he decides to wipe them off the face of the earth (7:4).

Even in light of its literary context, God's decision seems surprising. Prior to Gen 6, God had tailored individual punishments to suit their respective crimes. In this way, Adam, Eve, and Cain all learn the errors of their ways.[6] Given that strategy, the wholesale destruction of humanity makes one question the level of justice involved. For example,

---

[5] Scholars disagree as to whether the enigmatic episode involving the Nephilim (literally, "fallen ones") in Gen 6:1–4 represents a further example of moral decay. Some argue that when these "sons of heaven" (6:2)—members of the divine court—had sexual relations with women (6:4), it thoroughly corrupted the human race, thereby compelling God to destroy it. The position of this account right before the flood seems to suggest this interpretation, as do later Jewish traditions which evolved around it (e.g., *1 Enoch* 1–36 and *Jubilees*). In its original context, however, this interpretation may be a bit of a stretch. The flood account makes no mention of these Nephilim, nor does it serve to eliminate them (so Gen 6:4; Num 13:33). Instead, Gen 6:1–4 functions primarily to explain the origins of the heroes of ancient mythology and the limits of the human lifespan. It is a descriptive passage which appears to withhold judgment on the "sons of heaven."

[6] Adam had to toil in the fields among the weeds to produce food (Gen 3:17–19a). Eve had to suffer the pangs of childbirth and was made subservient to her husband (3:16). Both were also expelled from Eden and barred access to the "tree of life" (3:22–24). As for Cain, his very livelihood—tilling the soil—was taken away from him, forcing him to become a "restless wanderer" of the earth (4:10–14).

if Cain committed premeditated murder but was allowed to live, what could Noah's contemporaries have possibly done to deserve this sort of death? And since we are told that all perished except for those in the ark, wouldn't that necessarily include infants and children? Why condemn these innocent ones? Equally baffling is God's decision to annihilate the animals, birds, and plants as well (6:7, 13). Up until this point, the reader has been given little reason to believe that they are complicit in, or corrupted by, human depravity.[7]

Indeed, even the ultimate effectiveness of the flood can be called into question. Gen 6:5 explains that God resolved to obliterate humankind because he saw "how no desire that his heart conceived was ever anything but evil." Yet God concedes that "the desires of man's heart are evil from the start" (8:21) just before promising never to submerge the earth again. From all appearances, he seems to acknowledge that the flood was a terrible idea from the beginning! So how are we to comprehend the portrayal of God in Gen 6–9? Once again, the premises of the original authors prove invaluable.

Literary Background

More than a thousand years before our biblical writers lived, stories of a great flood circulated widely among the ancient Near Eastern people.[8] Two of these stories, both from the region of Mesopotamia, have a particular bearing on our discussion. The first is the Gilgamesh Epic, a Mesopotamian myth dating from about 2300 B.C.E. and surviving in its most complete form today in Old Babylonian written on twelve clay tablets dating from about 1000 B.C.E. This epic commemorates the life of Gilgamesh, ruler of the ancient city of Uruk. Its plot can be summarized as follows.

---

[7] The serpent is the only animal whose involvement in human sin is documented (Gen 3:1–6). But accordingly, the serpent is made to suffer the specific consequences of his behavior (3:14–15). As for the plants, it is true that the pleasing fruit trees of Eden were replaced by "thorns and thistles" in the aftermath of the original sin (3:18). But this is simply in accordance with God's punishment of Adam.

[8] Scholars have recovered and identified nearly three hundred ancient flood stories from around the world. They are nearly as prevalent as, and often associated with, primal creation stories. Their popularity ought not to surprise us. Recent history, including the tsunami in Indonesia (December 2004) and Hurricane Katrina along the Gulf Coast in the United States (August 2005), demonstrates both the frequency and the dramatic impact of such cataclysmic events. Furthermore, numerous firsthand accounts of these floods have attributed personal survival to divine intervention of some sort.

The Gilgamesh Epic

The first nine tablets detail the exploits of Gilgamesh and his close companion, Enkidu. When this duo's unbridled adventures earn the disdain of the gods, the latter decree that one of the former must die. Enkidu is chosen, and in the wake of his death, Gilgamesh becomes despondent over his own mortality. Desperate, he turns (in the tenth tablet) to Utnaphishtim for help. Specifically, Gilgamesh seeks to learn how Utnaphishtim, a legendary mortal who has joined the assembly of the gods, was granted immortality. In the eleventh tablet, Utnaphishtim recounts for Gilgamesh the story of the great flood. According to Utnaphishtim, when the gods decided to inflict the flood, one of them, Ea, secretly revealed their plan to Utnaphishtim. Ea instructed him to tear down his hut and build a boat whose length and width were of equal measure. He also enjoined him to keep living beings alive with him in the boat. Consequently, Utnaphishtim employed carpenters, reed workers, children, and even the infirm to assist him in his project. In seven days, they constructed a boat whose dimensions measured 120 by 120 cubits. The boat had six decks and was waterproofed with bitumen and pitch. Into the boat, Utnaphishtim brought all of his silver and gold, varieties of living creatures, his family members, and assorted craftsmen. Then the storm began. Its severity overwhelmed the earth's inhabitants and frightened even the gods, who now regretted their decision. After seven days, the storm abated. When Utnaphishtim opened a hatch and witnessed the destruction, he wept. His boat came to rest on Mt. Nimush (or Nisir), and after seven more days, Utnaphishtim sent forth a dove. The dove returned, so he released a swallow. This, too, returned, so he freed a raven. When the raven failed to return, Utnaphishtim dismissed all of the boat's occupants and offered a sacrifice. Smelling its sweet aroma, the gods gathered like flies around the offering. The creator goddess Ishtar vowed to be as mindful of the day as the lapis lazuli (beads) that hung around her neck. When Enlil (or Ellil), the god who had orchestrated the flood, arrived at their gathering, he saw the boat and became furious. The other gods, however, deprived Enlil of the sacrifice and criticized him for killing so indiscriminately. They reasoned that the violation should be charged only to the violator, and that instead of a flood, people could be diminished by carnivorous beasts, famines, or pestilences. Duly chastened, Enlil approached Utnaphishtim and inducted him into the assembly of the gods (an honor Gilgamesh ultimately failed to achieve).[9]

The second related narrative is the Story of Atrahasis. Although our earliest extant copy is from Babylonia (ca. 1700 B.C.E.), the story itself dates back to Sumerian times. In fact, Atrahasis is listed as one of the antediluvian (pre-flood) rulers of Shuruppak in one of the Sumerian king-lists. Accordingly, many scholars believe that the Atrahasis legend

[9] The complete translated text of the Gilgamesh Epic can be found in Stephanie Dalley, *Myths from Mesopotamia: Creation, the Flood, Gilgamesh, and Others* (rev. ed.; Oxford's World Classics; New York: Oxford University Press, 2000), 39–153.

may have been the source of the flood material in the Gilgamesh Epic. At any rate, its storyline (to the extent that it is preserved) is as follows.

The Story of Atrahasis

Before men had been created, the lesser gods (Igigi) did the work of the greater gods (Anunnaki). They toiled constantly, digging out the great riverbeds of the Tigris and the Euphrates. After thirty-six hundred years, they had had enough. Dissatisfied with their lot, they burned their tools and revolted. To appease them, the greater gods sacrificed one of the lesser gods and mixed his flesh and blood with clay. From this, the creator goddess Nintu (or Mami) formed offspring to bear the load of the disgruntled gods. The humans fashioned new tools and dug irrigation canals to grow food for themselves and the gods. Contentment reigned until, after twelve hundred years, the humans had grown so numerous that their noise drove Enlil (or Ellil), the earth god, to distraction. At Enlil's command, a plague was sent to reduce their numbers. Atrahasis, the "exceedingly wise" leader of Shuruppak, appealed to the freshwater god, Enki (or Ea) for help. Enki advised Atrahasis and his people to ignore all the other gods and to shower only the god responsible—in this case, Namtar, the plague god—with attention. Enki's plan worked, and Namtar relented. Two more twelve-hundred-year cycles ensued. Each time, as the human population rebounded, their escalating noise grew unbearable to Enlil. First he ordered a drought and then a general embargo on all of the gods' natural gifts. Both times, however, Atrahasis and his people circumvented extinction with the aid of Enki. Fed up, Enlil demanded that Enki completely flood the earth. To this Enki complied, but not before revealing the threat to Atrahasis. Enki instructed Atrahasis to dismantle his house and to construct a boat. This Atrahasis did, using bitumen as waterproofing. He filled the boat with his family and every type of animal. Then the deluge came. The gods grew nauseous with fright, and Nintu wept over the victims. The flood lasted for seven days, during which time the gods, without their human servants, grew thirsty and hungry. Once the waters subsided, Atrahasis offered a sacrifice. As the gods gathered around it like flies, Nintu swore by her lapis lazuli necklace that she would remember the flood. Enlil arrived, spotted Atrahasis's boat, and became irate. Enki defended his actions and persuaded Enlil to adopt a more reasonable approach to the population/noise problem. Accordingly, Enlil and Nintu decreed that from that point onward, various female priestesses would remain celibate, other women would be barren, and some infants would die at birth.[10]

Obviously, there are numerous parallels between these older flood stories and Gen 6–9. A comparison of them (see table 3.2) makes it fairly evident that the biblical writers knew of, and were influenced by, these types of earlier traditions.

---

[10] The complete translated text of the Story of Atrahasis can be found in Dalley, *Myths from Mesopotamia*, 1–38.

Ancient Near Eastern Flood Narratives Compared

	Gilgamesh Epic	Story of Atrahasis	Gen 6–9
Individuals			
Human hero	Utnaphishtim	Atrahasis	Noah
Creator god(dess)	Ishtar	Nintu/Mami	Yahweh (J)/Elohim (P)
Sympathetic god	Ea	Ea/Enki	Yahweh (J)/Elohim (P)
Destructive god	Enlil/Ellil	Enlil/Ellil	Yahweh (J)/Elohim (P)
Purpose			
Reason for flood	?	Too noisy	Widespread wickedness
Object			
Object built	Boat	Boat	Ark
Materials used	Dismantled house, bitumen, oil, asphalt	Dismantled house, bitumen	Gopherwood, bitumen
Dimensions	120 x 120 cubits	?	300 x 50 x 30 cubits (P)
Number of decks	6	?	3 (P)
Time to complete	7 days	7 days	7 days (J)
Taken aboard	Family, silver and gold, animals, craftsmen	Family, animals	Family, 2 of all animals (P), 7 pairs clean, 1 pair unclean (J)
Time			
Duration of storm or flood	7 days	7 days	40 days/nights (J) 1 year (P)
Final destination	Mt. Nimush/Nisir	?	Mt. Ararat
Birds sent	Dove, swallow, raven	?	Raven, dove, dove (J)
Time before flights	7 days	?	7 days (J)
Aftermath			
Post-flood sacrifice	Food over reeds, pine, myrtle	Food, smoke offering	Clean holocaust (J)
Divine response	Smell sweet odor	Smell sweet odor	Smells sweet odor (J)
	Gather like flies	Gather like flies	
Commemorating god(dess)	Ishtar	Nintu/Mami	Yahweh (J)/Elohim (P)
Promise of god(dess)	Never to forget	Never to forget	Never to doom the earth (J) To recall the covenant never to flood the earth again (P)
Sign	Lapis lazuli necklace	Lapis lazuli necklace	Rainbow (P)
Hero's reward	Granted immortality	?	Given dominion, long life

Ancient Near Eastern Flood Narratives Compared

	Gilgamesh Epic	Story of Atrahasis	Gen 6–9
Result			
Divine conclusion	Charge offender with offense; limit population with wild animals, famines, pestilences	Charge offender with offense; limit population with barrenness, stillbirths, celibacy	Capital punishment for capital crimes; humans are told to "be fruitful and multiply" (P)

Table 3.2

The great flood, therefore, was a fact of life for the OT authors. So how could they account for it? In the Mesopotamian accounts, the roles of creator god, destroyer god, and sympathetic god are each played by different deities. Given their monotheistic belief system, the Yahwist and Priestly authors had little choice but to subsume them all into one. Paradoxical as it might seem, then, the God who created humans would now also be bent on destroying them.

What the biblical authors needed, therefore, was some rationale to account for God's destructive behavior. The Gilgamesh Epic offers no motive for the gods' decision.[11] As for the Story of Atrahasis, the root cause given—noise—proved too insignificant to incur God's wrath. Left to their own devices, the Hebrew writers evidently reasoned that a just God would not destroy his world unless it had become so thoroughly corrupted that it was otherwise beyond repair. This is precisely the situation that they describe.

Beginning with their presuppositions, then, we get a glimpse into the thought processes of the biblical authors. Already widely attested, the great flood was their starting point. They reasoned that if there was a great flood, God must have caused it. And if God caused it, then the inhabitants of the earth must have done something terrible to deserve it. But how, then, did anyone survive it?

Here, the Genesis account again diverges from its predecessors. In those accounts, the divine council intended to eradicate humanity. There were to be no survivors. Humanity's endurance is due only to the (happy) accident of Ea's defiance. But in Genesis, the creator God/destroyer God becomes the sympathetic God as well. By deliberately

[11] The conclusion to the narrative seems to suggest that, like the Story of Atrahasis, population control may have had something to do with it.

choosing someone to save, God's justice is tempered by his mercy. Given the moral justification of the flood, the one selected must be someone righteous, someone qualitatively different from his wicked peers, and someone deserving of deliverance. Someone like Noah.

God thus commands Noah to build the ark and gather the animals—two of every type. For the Yahwist writer, a post-flood sacrifice as found in the earlier traditions would require additional members lest Noah inadvertently kill off an entire species. For this reason, Noah takes extra pairs of clean (sacrifice-appropriate) animals. The story continues accordingly. The flood comes. Life is wiped out. The waters subside. The ark comes to rest on a mountain. Noah thrice releases birds. Noah, his family, and the animals disembark. Noah offers a sacrifice. God smells it and is pleased. With a beautiful, necklace-like object (a rainbow), the creator God promises to remember the flood and the destroyer God vows never to do it again. His covenant with Noah confirms this and establishes a system of justice whereby only capital crimes will merit capital punishment (Gen 9:5–6).

At this point, the most noteworthy departure of Genesis from the Mesopotamian legends is to be found in God's attitude toward humanity. Whereas both the Gilgamesh Epic and the Story of Atrahasis conclude with the gods formulating strategies to limit the population, the God of the Hebrew Bible encourages it (twice): "Be fertile and multiply and fill the earth" (9:1, 7). Comparatively speaking, then, Genesis (and more specifically, the Priestly writer) envisions humanity not as a problem to be suppressed but as a blessing to be promoted.[12]

Generally speaking, then, our ethical and theological concerns about the biblical flood story can be somewhat mitigated by the premises that originally gave rise to it. That which we modern readers are rightfully inclined to perceive as morally objectionable represents, in its historical context, an ethical improvement over the earlier traditions. Using such traditions as their starting points, the authors of Gen 6–9 have endeavored to uphold God's monotheistic character while simultaneously upholding his justice and his mercy. Considering what they had to work with, we can, at the very least, appreciate their labors.

[12] This lesson is hardly intended to encourage or to endorse overpopulation in the modern world. Nor is it necessarily a viewpoint shared by the Yahwist author, who describes humanity's inclinations as being evil from the start (Gen 8:21). Rather, relative to his historical context, the Priestly writer is simply reaffirming the inherent goodness of humanity.

Summary/Conclusion

To conclude this chapter, we can affirm that the popular commercialization of Noah's ark-themed merchandise and the cheery sentiments associated with it stand in stark contrast to the disturbing account of Gen 6–9. Like the creation stories, the great flood is not meant to be taken literally. The biblical authors never intended to reproduce history photographically, for the analysis of twenty-first-century inquiry, but impressionistically, for the spiritual instruction and edification of their contemporaries. And while the truth claims of Gen 6–9 vary somewhat according to the special emphases of the Yahwist and Priestly authors, thus explaining this text's internal contradictions and repetitions, it is in comparison with the earlier Mesopotamian flood stories that they emerge most clearly. In contrast to these polytheistic traditions, the biblical authors assert their belief in one God. This assertion forces them to position God in numerous and even conflicting roles within the flood story. Nevertheless, the biblical authors adapt their versions to justify God's wrath and to credit him for humanity's survival. In this way, their accounts not only maintain God's justice and his mercy but also represent an ethical improvement over the former traditions. Thus, while we may object to the abhorrent act of genocide attributed to God in Gen 6–9, we can acknowledge the efforts the biblical authors made to frame this event within the parameters of their belief systems. Of course, whether such efforts deserve to be memorialized on diaper bags—that remains a matter of debate!

4

The Abraham Narratives —Middle East Implications

Focus Text: Genesis 12–22

On November 7, 2001, the Country Music Association (CMA) held its thirty-fifth annual awards show at Nashville's elegant Grand Ole Opry House. The evening had a somber, patriotic mood to it. This was, after all, less than two months after the tragic events of September 11. Nevertheless, neither the live audience nor the estimated 39.2 million CBS television viewers were quite prepared for what they were about to witness when country songwriter Alan Jackson stepped out onto the stage.

Just ten days prior to the show, Jackson had awoken at 4 a.m. with a new set of lyrics running through his head. Feeling compelled, he rose from his bed and sang them into a small recorder at his home. A few days later, Jackson had the song tracked in a Nashville studio. Now he prepared to debut his latest project for the entire world. The entertainer picked up his guitar and began singing: "Where were you when the world stopped turning, that September day. . . ."[1]

When Jackson finished, those attending the CMA awards, many of whom were visibly moved, gave him a standing ovation. On the heels of its premiere, Jackson's fledgling inspiration soared in popularity.[2]

---

[1]The full lyrics to this song can be found online at http://www.azlyrics.com/lyrics/alanjackson/wherewereyouwhentheworldstoppedturning.hmtl (accessed March 27, 2008).

[2]Nine days after its debut, U.S. Congressman Mac Collins had the words to Alan Jackson's song entered into the official *Congressional Record*. "Where Were You" not

Without a doubt, its phenomenal success was due to the song's ability to so poignantly capture the raw emotional experience of September 11. As its lyrics imply, the sheer gravity and unexpected nature of the attacks have branded its surreal moments into the permanent memories of most Americans. Those who watched the disaster unfold, or even those who learned of it later, will forever recall precisely where they were when they heard the news.[3]

The Foreground: The 9/11 Attacks and Their "Justification"

In the aftermath of this tragedy, considerable analysis has concentrated on the who, what, when, where, and how of the attack. Almost immediately, the U.S. government implicated Osama bin Laden and his al-Qaeda organization.[4] As a retaliatory measure, America launched its so-called war on terror. First, it invaded Afghanistan in an effort to break up the al-Qaeda strongholds established there under the Taliban regime. Next, it invaded Iraq, presumably to end the state-sponsored

---

only went on to win single and song of the year honors at the 2002 Country Music Association Awards; it also earned *Drive* (the album on which it was released) the Album of the Year and Jackson the Male Vocalist and Entertainer of the Year awards. Furthermore, it netted the country star his first Grammy for Best Country Song at the forty-fifth annual Grammy awards in February 2003.

[3]To recap, at 8:46 a.m., American Airlines Flight 11 struck the North Tower of New York City's World Trade Center (WTC1) between the ninety-third and ninety-ninth floors. Approximately seventeen minutes later (9:03 a.m.), United Airlines Flight 175 slammed into the South Tower (WTC2) between the seventy-seventh and eighty-fifth floors. As attention focused on New York, reports came in that American Airlines Flight 77 had battered the Pentagon building in Washington, D.C., at 9:37 a.m. and that United Airlines Flight 93 had crashed in a field outside of Shanksville, Pennsylvania, presumably en route to the U.S. Capitol building, at 10:03 a.m. After burning for almost an hour, the 110–floor WTC2 imploded and collapsed at 10:05 a.m. WTC1 followed suit at 10:28 a.m. An estimated 2,976 individuals perished in these events. Perhaps the most disconcerting aspect of this statistic is that nearly all of the victims, aside from some of the military personnel who died at the Pentagon, were ordinary citizens going about their ordinary lives.

[4]On September 16, 2001, bin Laden publicly denied any involvement in the attacks. However, in a subsequent series of videotapes which surfaced between November 2001 and May 2006, bin Laden admitted knowing about the attacks ahead of time, praised those who carried out the attacks, acknowledged al-Qaeda's involvement and his own direct role in the attacks, and claimed he had personally directed the nineteen hijackers.

terrorism of Saddam Hussein and to destroy any weapons of mass destruction (WMD) that he may have possessed.[5]

But one of the factors largely overlooked in the public discourse on September 11, and subsequently unaddressed by the response, has been the question of why. Why did nineteen foreigners hijack four commercial airliners and fly them on suicide missions into prominent targets in America? Why did bin Laden and his al-Qaeda organization spend more than two years to plan and upwards of $500,000 to orchestrate their assault? Even today, when I ask my students this question, the prevailing assumption seems to be that al-Qaeda was motivated by a deep disdain for the lifestyles, freedoms, and opportunities that most Americans enjoy. As widespread as it is, this assessment hardly coincides with the reasons given by bin Laden.

The impetus for al-Qaeda's campaign was initially set forth in a *fatwa* (a religious edict issued by an Islamic authority) drafted by bin Laden in 1998. In it, bin Laden lists three transgressions of America: its support of Israel, its occupation (via military bases and installations) of the Arabian Peninsula, and its hostility toward the Iraqi people as demonstrated by America's so-called Operation Desert Storm in 1991. In a videotaped message broadcasted on December 27, 2001, bin Laden subsequently lauded the September 11 attacks in light of what he perceived to be the U.S.'s most grievous sin: "Terrorism against America deserves to be praised because it was a response to injustice, aimed at forcing America to stop its support for Israel, which kills our people."[6] By "our people," bin Laden meant Muslims, particularly those of Arab descent residing in the Middle East.

Of course, most moderate and liberal Muslims vehemently oppose bin Laden's terrorist response toward America and its allies. However, many also protest the U.S.'s major role in establishing and supporting—politically, economically, and militarily—the state of Israel.[7] The clearest

---

[5] To date, no such WMD ever surfaced. Ironically, none of the 9/11 hijackers were citizens of Afghanistan or Iraq. The vast majority of them (fifteen out of nineteen) were Saudi Arabian.

[6] British Broadcasting Corporation, "Bin Laden Video Condemned," online at http://news.bbc.co.uk/1/hi/world/middle_east/1729740.stm/ (posted on December 27, 2001; accessed December 1, 2007).

[7] Prior to Israel's independence, Great Britain had been assigned management of the region of Palestine by the Allied forces following their defeat of the Ottoman Empire in WWI. In 1914, the estimated population of Palestine was 690,000, including 535,000 Muslims (78%) and 85,000 Jews (12%). By 1946, those numbers had swelled

demonstration of their position was witnessed on May 15, 1948, the day after Israel declared its sovereignty. That morning, the armies of Syria, Lebanon, Transjordan (now Jordan), Iraq, and Egypt invaded Israel from all sides. Israeli troops repelled them and eventually managed to even expand their own borders. But while Israel's statehood created a refuge for Holocaust survivors and Sephardic Jews from hostile regions throughout the world, at the same time it also caused the displacement of nearly 1 million Palestinians, the vast majority of whom were Muslims, who had previously called this area home.[8] With no place to go, some 650,000 of them ended up settling in one of the fifty-three refugee camps set up by the UN in Jordan, the Gaza Strip, Lebanon, and Syria. Many of their descendants remain there, in poverty and misery, to this day. Thus, it isn't a Jewish homeland per se that Israel's Arab neighbors oppose. Rather, it is its location in the Middle East.

So why, of all places, has the U.S. endeavored to maintain a Jewish state in the middle of Palestine? In other words, why not establish Israel in New York or in Florida? Why not carve out space for this nation in Texas or in Alaska? Here is where the Old Testament comes into play. Israel's claim to this particular territory can be traced historically all

---

to 1,269,000 Arabs and 678,000 Jews (figures taken from "Palestine," *Encyclopædia Britannica,* 15th ed., vol. 25 [Chicago: Encyclopædia Britannica, 2003], 407–25). In the aftermath of WWII and in light of the horrors of the Jewish Holocaust, the UN drafted a resolution calling for the creation of a Jewish homeland. Specifically, it called for partitioning Palestine into separate Arab and Jewish states. All of the Islamic Asian countries opposed the resolution, in part because it assigned 55% of the land to the minority Jews. Nevertheless, the resolution passed in the UN General Assembly, thanks largely to U.S. brokering. Great Britain refused to implement the resolution on the grounds that it had not been agreed to by both sides. On the same day that Great Britain withdrew the last of its forces (May 14, 1948), Israel declared its statehood. In the decades since, Israel's history has been marred by violence and other atrocities committed by both sides. On several occasions, its very survival was at stake. Were it not for its strong economic and military relationship with the U.S., Israel would almost certainly cease to exist.

[8]It is in the displacement of so many Muslims that some consider *jihad* against America as especially justified. The Koran is cited as proof: "And fight in the way of God with those who fight with you, but aggress not: God loves not the aggressors. And slay them wherever you come upon them, and expel them from where they expelled you; persecution is more grievous than slaying. . . . Fight them, till there is no persecution and the religion is God's; then if they give over, there shall be no enmity save for evildoers. The holy month for the holy month; holy things demand retaliation. Whoso commits aggression against you, do you commit aggression against him like as he has committed against you" (*The Koran Interpreted,* trans. A. J. Arberry [New York: Touchstone, 1996], 53–54).

the way back to Genesis. Specifically, it is rooted in the figure and story of Abraham. Many readers of the Old Testament are probably already familiar with the terms of the covenant on which Israel's claim to the Holy Land is based. But what they may not realize is that the record of this covenant is derived from multiple traditions. Moreover, while some of these traditions attest to (and arguably, promote) interfamilial conflict in the Middle East, others offer a potential blueprint for peace and reconciliation. Given all that is premised upon these narratives, then, it is only fitting that we turn now to consider some of the premises that lie behind them.

The Background: The Abraham Narratives of Genesis 12–21

As mentioned in chapter 3, the great flood proved ineffective at eradicating the evil inclinations of the human heart. The response of Noah's sons to his drunkenness (Gen 9:18–27) and the construction of the tower of Babel (Gen 11:1–9) both exemplify this. In Gen 12, therefore, God begins a new strategy. In short, he calls Abraham forth from his father's house in order to establish a covenant—an everlasting pact—with him.[9] God leads Abraham on to the land of Canaan (the region later known as Palestine, or modern Israel), which he promises to the patriarch and to his descendants as a permanent possession. Furthermore, God vows to render Abraham exceedingly fertile, with offspring as numerous as the stars in the sky and the sands on the seashore. God offers to live in special relationship with these children of Abraham, so that through them, all the communities of the earth will find blessing in him.

As the story unfolds, Abraham fathers his first son, Ishmael, with his wife's maidservant, Hagar. (Hagar had been given to Abraham by his wife, Sarah, when the latter was thought to be barren.) Abraham eventually has a second son, Isaac, with his (miraculously fertile) wife Sarah.

In many respects, the rivalry that would arise between Abraham's two children, Ishmael and Isaac, foreshadows the modern conflict

[9] A covenant is a legally binding contract or agreement. Also called a testament, the Abrahamic covenant is where the Old Testament ultimately derives its name.

between Arab Muslims and the Jewish people of Israel. Judaism traces its ancestral line through Isaac. Not surprisingly, then, the Hebrew writings portray God as specifically sanctioning his covenantal promises with Isaac, Abraham's first legitimate son (17:19; 25:5).[10] But many Arab Muslims, including Muhammad himself, trace their roots back to Ishmael. And according to Islamic tradition, Abraham married Hagar. Presumably, then, this would make Ishmael and his descendents the rightful heirs.[11]

When presented with this reasoning, some Jews and Christians argue that the Islamic scriptures, beginning with the Qur'an (Koran) in the seventh century C.E., are comparatively late, revisionist attempts to champion Arab agendas. Many Muslims argue that the Jews and Christians have corrupted God's revelation and strayed from the true path, thus necessitating the correction of the prophet Muhammad and the religion of Islam. Our purpose here is not to resolve this dispute but to understand the Old Testament texts as they were intended by their original authors. To this end, we find that the text of Gen 12–21 is not nearly as straightforward as the preceding summary might suggest.

Duplications and Contradictions

We encounter in the Abrahamic narratives, as we have in the stories of creation and the great flood, a host of duplications and internal contradictions. Scholars attribute such literary discrepancies to the compilation of originally independent sources. By teasing them apart, as we have done with the Noah narratives, we can gain a better insight into the truth claims they sought to advance (see table 4.1).

---

[10] By legitimate, I mean relative to the covenantal inheritance, not relative to Abraham's paternity. This notion of legitimacy seems to underlie a curious description of Isaac in the testing of Abraham. There, God commands Abraham to "Take your son Isaac, your only one, whom you love . . ." and offer him up as a sacrifice (Gen 22:2). In Islamic tradition, this matter is presented differently. According to the Koran, it is Ishmael—not Isaac—whom Abraham nearly slaughters. The stone altar on which this purportedly transpired is enshrined within the Dome of the Rock (*Qubbat As-Sakhrah*), the third-holiest Muslim site, located on the former Jerusalem Temple Mount. Muslims further commemorate this event with the annual Feast of the Sacrifice (*Eid Al-Adha*).

[11] I say "presumably" because the Koran never explicitly mentions the land of Canaan/Palestine or even the covenant associated with it.

The Abraham Narratives Compared

Yahwist Account	Gen 12–21	Priestly Account
Call of Abram Go to land Make a great nation Blessing for all people	12:1–4a	
	12:4b–5	Abram = 75 years old Abram sets out for Canaan
Sarai as Abram's "sister" Taken by Pharaoh Abram given flocks, etc. Pharaoh smitten by God Sarai returned to Abram	12:9–20	
Identifies "promised" land Offspring like dust	13:14–17	
Offspring like stars Covenant ritual Fire and smoke pass between the two halves of the split animals	15:1–21	
Sarai gives Hagar to Abram as wife Hagar (pregnant with Ishmael) departs Abram disinterested God's promise to Hagar that Ishmael will be numerous, a wild ass, against everyone, in opposition to all his kin God has heard Hagar = "Ishmael"	16:1–16	
	16:15–16	Announcement of Ishmael's birth Abram = 86 years old
	17:1–14	Abram = 99 years old Abram to be father of many Abram's name changed to Abraham Covenant (verbal) Sign of covenant = circumcision
	17:15–22	Sarai's name changed to Sarah Sarah's offspring predicted Abraham laughs = "Isaac" Abraham's concern for Ishmael God promises to bless and make a great nation of Ishmael
	17:23–26	Circumcision of Ishmael and Abraham's household
Three visitors Sarah's offspring predicted Sarah laughs = "Isaac"	18:1–15	
	20:1–18 (E)	Sarah as Abraham's "sister" Taken by king Abimelech Sarah returned Abraham given flocks, etc. Abimelech's household smitten
	21:1–5	Isaac born Named Isaac Isaac circumcised
	21:8–21 (E)	Hagar and Ishmael depart Abraham distressed God has heard boy cry = "Ishmael" God's care for Ishmael

Table 4.1

Literary critics assign the column on the left primarily to the Yahwist (J) source while the material on the right derives mostly from the Priestly (P) source. (Material from the Elohist [E] source has also been interjected.[12]) As evidenced by the chart, there are numerous instances in which their contents overlap.

Sarah Added to the Harem

In Gen 12:9–20 and Gen 20:1–18 we find twin accounts in which Abraham, a stranger in a strange land, declares his wife, Sarah, to be his sister. In both cases, the monarch of the region (first Pharaoh and later Abimelech) finds Sarah very beautiful and adds her to his harem. Because of this action, the unwitting sovereign and the members of his household are smitten by God. The king subsequently discovers the truth about Sarah and eagerly returns her to Abraham. In both instances, Abraham's deception nets him a rather generous payout.

The Names of Abraham's Sons

Two pairs of corresponding stories serve to explain the origins of the names of Abraham's two sons. The first pair involves the derivation of the name "Ishmael" (lit., "God has heard"). According to Gen 16:11, it is Hagar whom God hears speaking in the wilderness; in Gen 21:17, however, it is the boy himself whom God hears crying. The second pair accounts for the name "Isaac" (from צחק, *tsakhaq,* "to laugh"). In Gen 17:17, it is Abraham who chuckles to himself when God predicts the birth of the boy. But according to Gen 18:12–15, it is Sarah who does so at the announcement of Abraham's visitor.

The Ratification of the Covenant

Genesis also offers dual descriptions of God's covenant with Abraham: the Yahwist version in 15:1–21 and the Priestly version in 17:1–14. Both agree on that which is promised—land and descendants—but they

---

[12] This source, E, derives its name from its exclusive use of the word *Elohim* for God. Scholars judge it to be the product of northern Israel, written some time during the mid-ninth cent. B.C.E. For the sake of simplicity and comparison, the chart above divides the narratives into two major groupings only, indicating with (E) those sections which predominantly belong to the Elohist. It does not account for smaller literary inclusions, such as single verses or half-verses, within the given subsets.

differ on just about everything else. Because of the rather unusual and potentially confusing symbolism that they employ, we shall examine the details of these accounts a little more closely.

In the Yahwist account, Abraham queries God concerning his "reward" by asking

> "O Lord God, what good will your gifts be, if I keep on being childless and have as my heir the steward of my house, Eliezer? . . . See, you have given me no offspring, and so one of my servants will be my heir." (Gen 15:2–3)

God reiterates his promise of descendants and land (15:5–7), but Abraham continues to press him: "O Lord God, how am I to know that I shall possess it?" (15:8). God thus tells Abraham to gather a heifer, a goat, a ram, a turtledove, and a pigeon. Abraham does so and then splits the animals in two, placing each half opposite the other. When the sun had set,

> There appeared a smoking brazier and a flaming torch, which passed between those pieces. It was on that occasion that the Lord made a covenant with Abram, saying: "To your descendants I give this land, from the Wadi of Egypt to the Great River [the Euphrates]." . . . (Gen 15:17–18)

To most modern readers, this ritual seems bizarre. But to the Yahwist and his contemporaries, it would have been commonplace. In ancient Near Eastern times, when two parties sought to make a contract, they would split large animals in two and then walk between their halves. Why? Remnants of this practice can be found, conceptually speaking, in the oaths many children make to each other even to this day. One popular rhyme goes: "Cross my heart; hope to die. Stick a needle in my eye."

Of course, no one who utters these words harbors any desire to impale their corneas with sharp, metal implements—much less court a premature death! But in an effort to appear as sincere as possible, they swear harm upon themselves should they prove to be unfaithful to their word. It is for this same reason that the ancients passed between the butchered beasts. The carnage that surrounded them served as a powerful visual reminder of what would become of them if they should fail to comply with the terms of their agreement.[13]

[13] This meaning is alluded to in Jer 34:18: "The men who violated my covenant and did not observe the terms of the agreement which they made before me, I will make like the calf which they cut in two, between whose two parts they passed."

According to Gen 15, a smoking brazier (i.e., a pan for holding burning coals) and a flaming torch advance between the carcasses. What do these represent? According to Jewish tradition, no one could see the face of God and live.[14] Therefore, when the OT describes God as appearing in physical form (called a theophany), he is typically portrayed in the form of smoke and/or fire.[15] But notice that it is *only* God who passes between the pieces, not Abraham. In this respect, the scene emphasizes God's role in the covenant. So confident is he of his pledge to Abraham that he calls down upon himself the brutal fate of the sacrifice, pending his failure to deliver.

The ceremonial ritual of Gen 15 stands in sharp contrast to the verbal contract between God and Abraham in Gen 17. There, it is not Abraham who moves God to action, but God who moves Abraham. There is little dialogue between these two parties. Instead, God simply announces his plans for Abraham and dictates to him the terms of his agreement:

> "On your part, you and your descendants after you must keep my covenant throughout the ages. This is my covenant with you and your descendants after you that you must keep: every male among you shall be circumcised. Circumcise the flesh of your foreskin, and that shall be the mark of the covenant between you and me. . . . Thus my covenant shall be in your flesh as an everlasting pact. If a male is uncircumcised . . . such a one shall be cut off from his people; he has broken my covenant." (Gen 17:9–11, 13–14)

Following God's declaration, we are told that Abraham and every male member of his household were circumcised that day (17:23–27).

To briefly summarize, then, both descriptions of the covenant agree that God will provide Abraham with abundant offspring and the land of Canaan. Both covenants also involve the shedding of blood, albeit in very different ways. In the first (Yahwist), animals are split in two to signify God's intention to follow through on his obligation. In the second (Priestly), Abraham and his male successors are circumcised to physically identify them as partners in the covenant as the people to whom God has extended his special promise. As divergent as these two accounts are, they are easily reconciled. Taken together, they demonstrate the tremendous investment both parties have in their commitment to each other.

---

[14] So, e.g., Gen 32:31; Exod 20:19; Deut 4:33; Judg 13:22.

[15] Other well-known examples include the burning bush (Exod 3), the pillars of smoke and fire (Exod 13:21–22), the clouds and lightning on Mt. Sinai (Exod 19:16–18), and the fireball on Mt. Carmel (1 Kgs 18:30–40).

Two Takes on Hagar and Ishmael

Last, but certainly not least, we find in Gen 16:1–14 and Gen 21:8–21 parallel stories of Hagar and Ishmael's departure from Abraham's household. The two versions contain numerous points of agreement. Both incidents are triggered by Sarah's discontent. She presents her case to Abraham, who subsequently capitulates. As a result, Hagar and Ishmael set out for the wilderness. There, near a spring, God encounters them. He announces that he has "heard" one of them. After making certain predictions concerning Ishmael, God then sends them on their way.

But it is not the similarities that prove to be so compelling. Rather, it is their differences. Through them, two radically distinct and even opposing attitudes toward Hagar and Ishmael emerge. Consider Gen 16:1–14. According to this, the Yahwist's version, Hagar is the troublemaker. It is she who, now pregnant with Abraham's child, begins to look upon Sarah with disdain (16:4). When Sarah demands satisfaction from Abraham, the patriarch is apathetic about Hagar (and the baby—*his* baby—developing within her): "Your maid is in your power. Do to her whatever you please" (16:6). Thus empowered, Sarah abuses Hagar, who then flees from her mistress. When God finds Hagar, he offers her no sympathy whatsoever. Instead, God orders her to return to Sarah and to submit to her mistress's maltreatment. He then predicts a profusion of offspring for Hagar and characterizes them in this description of her son Ishmael:

> "He shall be a wild ass of a man,
> his hand against everyone,
> and everyone's hand against him;
> in opposition to all his kin
> shall he encamp." (Gen 16:12)

Clearly, this episode presents a negative portrayal of the origin and reputation of the Ishmaelites, the predecessors of modern-day Arab Muslims. According to it, they are destined for nothing but conflict in their relationships with their Semitic relatives, the modern-day Jewish people. Moreover, this tradition lays the blame for such conflict squarely upon the shoulders of Ishmael's progeny.

The departure of Hagar and Ishmael in Gen 21:8–21, which originates from the Elohist source, is remarkably different. This time, it is Sarah, not Hagar, who disturbs the peace. One day she notices Ishmael "laughing."[16] Consumed with anger, Sarah demands that Abraham expel Hagar and Ishmael from their midst, insisting that "no son of that slave is going to share the inheritance with my son Isaac!" (21:10). In response, Abraham is "greatly distressed, especially on account of his son Ishmael" (21:11). God intervenes and assures Abraham: "Do not be distressed about the boy or about your slave woman. . . . I will make a great nation of him also, since he too is your offspring" (21:12–13). Thus consoled, Abraham sends the pair forth, but not without personally securing provisions of bread and water for them. Carrying Ishmael on her back, Hagar wanders aimlessly in the wilderness until her water supply gives out. Alone and helpless, she places Ishmael under a shrub and sits a short distance away from him, not bearing to watch him die. Ishmael begins to cry, and the sound of the child's anguish prompts God to respond.[17] From heaven, the Lord's messenger tenderly encourages Hagar:

> "Don't be afraid; God has heard the boy's cry in this plight of his. Arise, lift up the boy and hold him by the hand; for I will make of him a great nation." (Gen 21:17–18)

God then directs Hagar to a nearby well, where she and Ishmael are refreshed. The narrative concludes on this note:

> God was with the boy as he grew up. He lived in the wilderness and became an expert bowman, with his home in the wilderness of Paran. His mother got a wife for him from the land of Egypt. (Gen 21:20–21)

---

[16] Or literally, "Isaacing." In the original Hebrew, the description of this account is somewhat ambiguous because neither a preposition nor a direct object is supplied (i.e., Ishmael is not laughing at anything or with anyone). As such, Ishmael's act of "Isaacing" suggests that he may have been emulating Isaac. This interpretation would help to explain Sarah's reaction. Unfortunately, in an effort to improve the text, the LXX eliminates the Hebrew word play. There, Ishmael is "playing with Isaac" (παίζοντα μετὰ Ισαακ, *paizonta meta Isaak*). Some commentators ascribe negative connotations to Ishmael's "playfulness" (so, e.g., Gal 4:29), but this is pure conjecture, designed primarily to justify Sarah's outrage.

[17] This scene, which comes from the Elohist source, envisions a much younger Ishmael than the narrative story line—from the Priestly source—requires. According to the chronology of the latter, Ishmael was thirteen when Isaac was first conceived (Gen 17:25). Furthermore, this episode takes place after Isaac's weaning (21:8), which likely would have occurred around age three. Minimally, then, Ishmael would have to be at least sixteen years old. The Elohist hardly intends to portray an adolescent male being carried by his mother, placed under a shrub, and wailing inconsolably! More likely, this independent tradition was inserted anachronistically into the narrative.

In contrast to its parallel, Gen 21:8–21 depicts Hagar much more sympathetically. She is no longer the brazen, headstrong slave but the pitiable victim of unjust circumstances. Both Abraham and God demonstrate great concern not only for her welfare but also for that of her son, Ishmael. In fact, God's promise to "make a great nation" of Ishmael echoes an earlier conversation—this time, from the Priestly source—between God and Abraham (Gen 17:15–22).

When Abraham first learns about Isaac's birth, he suggests that God instead let Ishmael remain in his favor. God insists on establishing the covenant through Isaac. Nevertheless, God declares:

> "As for Ishmael, I am heeding you: I hereby bless him. I will make him fertile and will multiply him exceedingly. He shall become the father of twelve chieftains, and I will make of him a great nation." (Gen 17:20)

These episodes demonstrate that both the Elohist and the Priestly authors perceived in God's special treatment of Ishmael an affirmation of his esteem as Abraham's son.

To briefly summarize, therefore, Genesis provides us with two very different portrayals of Hagar and Ishmael. Unlike the two accounts of the Abrahamic covenant, however, these depictions are a little more difficult to reconcile. One tradition, from the Yahwist source, condemns Ishmael and his descendents as disregarded by Abraham and accursed by God. Another tradition, represented in the Priestly and Elohist sources, commends them as cherished by Abraham and blessed by God. In light of our preceding discussion, then, we can affirm that the origin of the conflict between Arab Muslims and Jews goes back even further than the book of Genesis. Traces of this clash can be found in the very sources that engendered this work.

Conclusion: The Choice before Us

As previously noted in the introduction, Abraham possesses unwavering faith in God. He who would withhold not even his own son from the Almighty now serves as the basis of three of today's major world religions: Judaism, Christianity, and Islam. We find in Genesis a rich amalgamation of traditions surrounding this patriarch. And for thousands of years, such traditions have spurred both hope and conflict among believers.

Obviously, the Old Testament's presentation of the Abrahamic covenant represents a decidedly Jewish (and by extension, Christian) point of view. Accordingly, God's promises regarding the land of Canaan and the "chosen-ness" of offspring are applied primarily and somewhat exclusively to Isaac's descendents. There is, to be sure, some variation in the two portrayals of the covenant ratification. But these differences only underscore both parties' extraordinary level of commitment to the terms of their agreement. Indeed, so steadfast is their commitment that it continues to underlie Israel's claim to the Holy Land to the present day.

As for the ancestors of those now competing for this same territory, the traditions in Genesis convey somewhat opposite attitudes. Such attitudes are easily transposed upon our contemporary situation: The Yahwist perspective sees the Middle Eastern conflict as inevitable, attributing the problem to the inherently contentious nature of Arab Muslims. According to such an outlook, peace will never be achieved; the best one can hope for is to contain, expel, or oppress these unruly people. Alternatively, there is the Elohist/Priestly approach. This standpoint embraces the biological and spiritual descendents of Ishmael as stepchildren in the Abrahamic tradition, acknowledges the patriarch's personal concern for their safety and well-being, and treats them as objects of divine mercy and affection.

Since 1946, Americans have ceased to be innocent bystanders in Middle Eastern affairs. As 9/11 demonstrates, we are all considered active participants—whether we like it or not. And while we can't undo the past, we can influence the future. For this reason, our particular opinions about this issue are becoming significantly more important. Either attitude we choose to adopt is bound to color our behavioral treatment of, political stance toward, and personal relationships with Arab Muslims. Ultimately the decision rests with us. But if we chose wisely, carefully, and deliberately—and act accordingly—then perhaps it might one day be possible for all communities of the earth to finally find blessing, rather than endless conflict, in Abraham's name.

5

The Torah—Beyond the Ten Commandments

Focus Texts: Exodus, Leviticus, Numbers, and Deuteronomy

Reportedly, the wearing of fake moustaches so as to cause laughter in church is legally prohibited in the state of Alabama.[1] In Tombstone, Arizona, anyone over eighteen must have at least one tooth visibly missing when smiling. An unmarried woman who parachutes on Sundays in Florida risks jail time. And it is considered a misdemeanor to feed alcohol to moose in Fairbanks, Alaska.

These are just a few examples of curious legislation that has been enacted in our country over the years. To these, we can add still more, some of which (allegedly) have yet to be repealed and therefore remain on the books to this day (see list 5.1).

- Animals are to be banned from mating publicly within fifteen hundred feet of a tavern, school, or house of worship (California).
- Tomatoes may not be used in the production of clam chowder (Massachusetts).
- Beer and pretzels can't be served at the same time in any bar or restaurant (North Dakota).

[1] All of the unusual laws mentioned in this chapter were found (among others) online at http://www.dumblaws.com/index.php (accessed March 27, 2008).

- One-armed piano players must perform for free (Iowa).
- It is illegal to take a French poodle to the opera (Chicago).
- It is illegal to mispronounce the name "Joliet" (Joliet, Illinois).
- No man is allowed to make love to his wife with the smell of garlic, onions, or sardines on his breath. If his wife so requests, the law mandates that he must brush his teeth (Alexandria, Minnesota).
- No monkey may smoke a cigarette (South Bend, Indiana).

The United States is hardly alone when it comes to such ordinances. Similar regulations can be found throughout the world as well. In France, for instance, no pig may be addressed as "Napoleon" by its owner. Israel forbids bringing bears to the beach. An Australian mandate prohibits the wearing of hot pink pants after midday on Sunday. And in England, any person found breaking open a hard-boiled egg at its pointed end is to be sentenced to twenty-four hours in the village stocks.

At first glance, such laws seem rather odd, perhaps even a bit whimsical. In part, this is because we have little firsthand knowledge of the contexts that originally gave rise to them. After all, who among us has ever witnessed the mayhem caused by a drunken moose? Or a bear at the beach? Or, worse still, by hot pink pants on someone traipsing around town on Sunday night? But legislative peculiarities can often be rendered quite sensible in light of their historical settings. And quirky or not, virtually all legal codes offer us valuable glimpses into the ideologies and fears of the cultures which produced them. In this respect, the Torah is no exception.

The Torah Defined

In previous chapters, we have used the word "Torah" (תורה, *torah*) in reference to the first five books of the Hebrew Bible. This word is derived from the verb ירה (*yarah*), meaning to direct, to teach, or to instruct. In its noun form, then, it literally means direction, teaching, or instruction. Since many of the instructions in the Torah allegedly originate from God, they assumed the status of commandments or laws.

Ask most Christians how many commandments are contained in the Torah, and they'll typically answer ten: namely, those listed in Exod 20:1–17 and Deut 5:6–21. This figure is derived from those that were explicitly written upon the stone tablets at Mt. Horeb/Sinai

(Exod 34:27–28; Deut 4:13). However, as every good Jew knows, the Torah contains considerably more commands than that. Jewish tradition puts the total at 613, and to this day, Orthodox Jews still keep the majority of them.[2] According to the HB, observance of the Torah is a key aspect of the covenantal agreement between Yahweh and the children of Abraham.

Narrative History: From Abraham to Moses

Having left off at the Abrahamic covenant in the previous chapter, we can now fill out the story of its subsequent evolution. According to the narrative history of the OT, God's sacred promise descended from Abraham to Isaac to Jacob and his sons. Through his wives, Leah and Rachel, and their maidservants, Zilpah and Bilhah, Jacob fathered twelve sons.[3] At the occasion of his name change—from Jacob to Israel—these twelve brothers became the ancestors of the twelve tribes of Israel. It was Joseph, Jacob's favorite son, who ultimately brought his siblings to Egypt. There, they and their descendents resided, growing both in prosperity and in number. Over time, relations with the Egyptians soured, and the Hebrew foreigners found themselves enslaved. They cried out to God for deliverance, and God responded. Using Moses as his spokesperson, God confronted Pharaoh with a series of plagues. Pharaoh remained obstinate, until the last of the plagues—now commemorated as Passover—took the life of his firstborn. The slaves' exit (or exodus) from Egypt thus ensued. Deprived of his laborers, Pharaoh soon recanted. His chariots pursued the Hebrew slaves and caught up to them at the Red Sea. Dramatically, God parted its waters to allow the children of Israel safe passage. But when Egypt's chariots followed, the sea returned and engulfed Pharaoh's troops. Safe from the Egyptians, Moses led the Israelites to Mt. Horeb/Sinai. It was here, according to tradition, that Moses first received the Torah from God.

---

[2] Their respective positions toward the Law are primarily what distinguish the three major branches of contemporary Jewish faith. The spectrum of formal adherence—from strict to moderate to liberal—is represented by the Orthodox, Conservative, and Reform branches, respectively.

[3] They include, in order of their appearance, Reuben, Simeon, Levi, and Judah (to Leah); Dan and Naphtali (to Bilhah); Gad and Asher (to Zilpah); Issachar and Zebulun (to Leah); and Joseph and Benjamin (to Rachel).

The Gift of the Torah

To modern readers, the prospect of following 613 rules may seem daunting, overly restrictive, or even oppressive.[4] This may be especially true in the U.S., a nation where the immortal words of Revolutionary War heroes Patrick Henry ("Give me liberty or give me death!") and General John Stark ("Live free or die!") still ring loud and clear. But Judaism approaches the Torah from an entirely different perspective. It frames these instructions against the backdrop of God's initial covenant, when he promised: "I will be their God" (Gen 17:8). The Torah regulations speak to the corollary aspect of that relationship: "and you will be my people" (Lev 26:12). The commandments are intended to spell out the specific terms of the covenant—to define for Abraham's descendants precisely what it means to be God's people. In this respect, the Torah regulations can be thought of more as relational guidelines than laws. If we can conceive of the Abrahamic covenant as the inaugural marriage between God and his people (an analogy the HB often employs), then the precepts of the Torah would function as its postnuptial vows. They establish the obligations involved for a long-term, mutually beneficial, harmonious relationship.

If the notion of adhering to so many rules still seems too imposing, consider this: theoretically, God could have established his covenant with anyone—the Egyptians or the Ammonites, the Philistines, the Moabites, the Sidonians, the Midianites, or any other of the ancient tribes. But according to the OT, he didn't. He chose the Israelites. And with privilege comes responsibility. These directives, therefore, are the means by which God sets this nation apart as his special possession, dearer to him than all others (Exod 19:5). For this reason, the Jewish tradition regards them not as a tedious burden to be suffered but as an inestimable gift to be celebrated.[5]

---

[4] For a humorous, firsthand account of one man's endeavor to keep these laws for a whole year, see A. J. Jacob, *The Year of Living Biblically* (New York: Simon & Schuster, 2007).

[5] Perhaps nowhere is the Torah more celebrated than in Ps 119, the longest by far in the Psalter. Ps 119 is an acrostic work devoted exclusively to the praise of God's law. The psalm proceeds alphabetically. Each stanza consists of eight lines which all begin with words using the same Hebrew letter. (Thus, each line of vv. 1–8 begins with an א [an *alef*], the first consonant of the Hebrew alphabet; each line of vv. 9–16 begins with a ב [a *bet*], the second consonant of the Hebrew alphabet, etc.) As a rule, each line of every stanza also contains at least one of eight different synonyms for Torah. (Techni-

Unwrapping the Gift: The Torah Decoded

So what exactly does this gift entail? Space forbids us here from undertaking an in-depth examination of all 613 laws. But by subsuming them into eight broader categories, we can delve into this corpus much more efficiently.

WORSHIP GOD ALONE

Of all the statutes and ordinances in the Torah, the most prominent is the prohibition of idolatry. Its primacy is indisputable—no single statute precedes its appearance in the Ten Commandments (Exod 20:2–6; Deut 5:6–10) or appears more frequently (more than twenty times). But what exactly does it mean to "worship God alone"?

The ancient Israelites were surrounded by nations that practiced polytheism. It was not only their gods that proved attractive but also their precious idols, their shrines, their practices, and even their followers. The God of Israel claimed to be a jealous God with no tolerance for divided loyalties. He expected his people to love him with all their heart, all their soul, and all their strength (Deut 6:5). Therefore, anything remotely associated with rival deities was to be expelled from the community and from the land that it occupied.

The Torah specifically forbids the Israelites from crafting idols (Exod 20:23; 34:17; Lev 19:4) in the form of any figure on the earth or in the heavens (Deut 4:15–19; 5:8), erecting them for worship (Lev 26:1), or bowing low before them (Exod 23:24; Deut 5:9). They were not even supposed to possess the precious metals from which the idols were once made (Deut 7:25–26). In fact, the Torah prohibits inquiring about other gods altogether (Deut 12:30), and even speaking their names (Exod 23:13). Ancillary practices associated with pagan religions were likewise banned. For this reason, the Israelites could not pierce or tattoo their bodies, clip the hair at their temples, or trim the edges of their beards (Lev 19:27–28)—all customs of the Canaanite nations in the land promised to them upon their departure from Egypt.

---

cally, v. 90 has a ninth synonym and v. 122 has none at all.) English Bibles translate these words variously (e.g., law, statute, ordinance, decree, command, precept, dictate, and injunction). Given the twenty-two consonant letters of the Hebrew alphabet, and the eight stanzas assigned to each letter, this psalm contains a total of 176 verses all with a single focus: celebrating the goodness of God's law.

As for punishments, the Torah stipulates that those who sacrificed (Exod 22:19) or dedicated their children (Lev 20:1–5) to other gods, practiced sorcery (Exod 22:17), or worshiped the sun, moon, or stars (Deut 17:2–5) were to be put to death. So, too, were any false prophets, family members, friends, or other inhabitants of the land who promoted foreign gods (Deut 13:2–19). Those who consulted the dead or practiced fortune telling, soothsaying, divination, or spell casting were to be driven out, as were all those who listened to (heeded) them (Deut 18:10–14).

Since the Abrahamic covenant dedicated the land of Canaan to the Israelites and the Israelites to God, the land itself was to be purged of all things pagan. Once they arrived there, the Israelites were commanded to demolish all of the idols, sacred pillars, altars, and shrines they could find (Exod 23:24; Num 33:52; Deut 7:5). They were even obligated to drive out the land's previous occupants: the Amorites, Canaanites, Hittites, Girgashites, Perizzites, Hivites, and Jebusites. The Israelites were forbidden from entering into marriages or any other political alliances with them, for fear that they would entice God's people away from him (Exod 23:27–33; 34:11–16; Deut 7:1–4; 20:17–18).

Support Israel's Religious Establishment

According to the Torah, God's presence was to abide among the Israelites. Therefore, numerous ordinances pertain to the religious establishment which would minister to it. There are, for example, detailed instructions for the construction of God's tabernacle and its furnishings, statutes describing the special responsibilities and privileges of its ministers, and an impressive array of ordinances relating to sacrificial offerings.

God commanded the Israelites to build him a temporary sanctuary, so that he might physically dwell among them as they traversed the wilderness (Exod 25:8).[6] From there, God could be present to his people, to comfort and guide them. God's dwelling would have three successive levels of holiness. The most inner sanctuary was called the holy of holies. This small area (15 x 15 feet) housed the golden ark of the covenant, between whose cherubim God's presence would reside (Exod 25:10–22). None were permitted to enter the holy of holies except the

[6] Once they became established in the promised land, the temporary sanctuary served as the model for the permanent temple in Jerusalem.

high priest, once a year, on the Day of Atonement (Lev 16:2). The holy of holies was separated by a curtain from its slightly larger (30 x 15 feet) antechamber, the holy place. The holy place contained a small altar of incense (Exod 30:1–10), a seven-branched lamp stand (Exod 25:31–40), and a table (Exod 25:23–30), all made of gold. On the table, twelve cakes of showbread were to be placed and replaced each Sabbath (Lev 24:5–9). These and the lamps (Lev 24:1–4) were to be maintained by the priests. Together, the holy of holies and the holy place formed the tabernacle, or the tent of meeting. Surrounding this free-standing structure was a much larger courtyard (150 x 75 feet), which was enclosed by linen cloth hung on bronze columns (Exod 27:9–19). In this courtyard were two items. One was a large bronze altar (7.5 x 7.5 x 4.5 feet), on which sacrifices would be made (Exod 27:1–8). The other was a bronze wash basin, used by the priests for purification before entering the holy place (Exod 30:17–21). Any Israelite who was ritually clean was granted access to the courtyard.

From among the Israelites, God chose the members of the tribe of Levi to be special ministers. They—specifically, the twenty-five-to-fifty-year-old males (Num 8:24–25)—were the custodians of the sanctuary. They were responsible for all of its furnishings and were charged with the work of disassembling, transporting, and setting it back up (Num 1:50–51). When it was stationary, they were even required to camp around it (Num 1:52–53). Because of their responsibilities, the Levites were held to higher standards of purity than other Israelites. But in exchange for their efforts, they also received certain privileges. They received mandatory tithes (Lev 18:21–24) and portions of various sacrificial offerings. Once the promised land was settled, they were also given designated cities in which to dwell (Num 35:1–8), since their roles at sanctuaries throughout the region precluded them from occupying a discrete tribal territory.

From among the Levites, God chose his priests. Not all Levites could be priests. Only the descendents of Aaron (Moses' brother) qualified, and of these, only males without any physical defects could serve (Lev 21:18–21). While the Levites were charged with the work surrounding the tabernacle, the priests were responsible for the ministrations within it. They alone approached the altars, handled its sacred vessels, and presided over the sacrifices (Lev 18:1–3). Accordingly, they were held to even higher purity standards than the Levites (Lev 21:1–15) and were granted even larger portions of the cultic sacrifices.

As for the sacrifices, the Torah describes five major types: holocausts (Lev 1:1–17), cereal/grain offerings (Lev 2:1–16; 6:7–16), peace offerings (Lev 3; 7:11–21), sin offerings (Lev 4:1–5:13; 6:17–23), and guilt offerings (Lev 5:14–26; 7:1–10). It covers their occasions for use, distinguishes between acceptable and unacceptable victims, and provides instructions for the ritual processes involved. The Torah also introduces the tithe, an annual contribution of one-tenth of one's livestock and/or agricultural harvest. According to Deut 14:22–29, the tithe should be brought to the sanctuary and consumed in revelry with one's family. It was, in effect, a required party![7] Nor was it the only one. A variety of offerings were also associated with the celebration of various holy days. These constitute our third category.

Observe the Holy Days

Of all the holy days mentioned in the Torah, none receives as much attention as the Sabbath. The command to commemorate it as a day of rest is repeated a dozen times. Work was strictly prohibited. This applied to both the master and the mistress of the house, their children, their slaves, their animals, and even the foreigners among them; none were permitted to labor on that day (Exod 20:9–11; Deut 5:12–15). Violation of this law was punishable by death (Exod 31:12–17; Num 15:32–36).

The notion of Sabbath rest extended beyond just the weekly cycle. Every seven years, the Israelites were required to observe a sabbatical (a tradition we have happily incorporated into academia). For six years, they could plow their fields and prune their vineyards, but during the seventh, they were required to let their land rest. This practice raises the question, how would they survive that year? According to Lev 25:18–22, God promised to bless the harvest of the sixth year so abundantly that it would sustain them throughout the seventh, eighth, and even ninth years. During the sabbatical year, the Israelites were also admonished to relax any outstanding debts that might be owed to them by their neighbors (Deut 15:1–6).

The year following seven sabbaticals (7 x 7 = 49 years) constituted the Jubilee Year. It was during this fiftieth year that any tribal lands

---

[7] The injunction from the book of Deuteronomy reminds the celebrants, almost as an aside, not to forget to include the Levites in their celebration. This is somewhat at odds with the description of the tithe in Num 18:21–24, which puts the bounty entirely in the hands of the Levites. Eventually, it would be usurped by the monarchy (1 Sam 8:15–17).

that had traded hands were to be returned to their original owners (Lev 25:13–28). Furthermore, any Israelite who had been sold into slavery was to be set free (Lev 25:39–43).

The Torah enjoins the Israelites to observe a host of other holy days. Every spring, they were to commemorate their exodus from Egypt with Passover and its associated Feast of Unleavened Bread. They were to celebrate their summer harvest during the Firstfruits festival (also called Pentecost or Weeks). Around September-October, they were to mark the beginning of the New Year festival with the Feast of Trumpets (Rosh Hashanah). Nine days later, they were to offer a communal sacrifice for their sins on the Day of Atonement (Yom Kippur). Five days after that, they were to offer thanks for the fall harvest during the Feast of Booths (Sukkoth).

Remain Ritually Pure

Proper fellowship with God, whether in the courtyard of the sanctuary, during the observance of the holy days, or even within the Israelites' camp, required that one strive to remain as ritually pure as possible. The Torah describes a number of conditions and situations that could render one unclean. Should they be encountered, it also prescribes the measures necessary to return to a state of purity.

Ritual impurity could be contracted in a variety of ways. Many involve bodily fluids, especially blood. Thus, for example, a woman's menstruation would render her unclean for a period of seven days. During this time, not only would the woman herself become unclean, but so too would any object on which she sat or lay (Lev 15:19–27). Anyone who came into contact with these would also become defiled. For this reason such women were to be quarantined outside of the camp (Num 5:2–3).[8] Identical standards applied to any male who was afflicted with a chronic flow from his genitalia (Lev 15:1–15). Since the process of childbirth involves even more blood, the period of impurity was considerably longer. Mothers of newborn males were to wait forty days for their purification; the mothers of newborn females were to wait eighty days (Lev 12:1–8).

Blood was not the only bodily fluid that had the potential to defile. Semen, whether produced by a nocturnal emission or sexual intercourse,

[8] It is this period of quarantine that gave rise to the tradition of the red tent, popularized by novelist Anita Diamant.

caused those whom it contacted to become unclean (Lev 15:16–18; Deut 23:11–12). And excrement was considered to be highly contaminating. The Torah strictly confined it to a designated latrine area outside the camp and required that it be buried deep under the ground. Should anyone's fecal matter be found within the camp, God threatened to part company with the Israelites (Deut 23:12–15)!

Beyond corporeal by-products, disease and death also had the power to pollute. Foremost among the maladies that the Torah concerns itself with is leprosy. The book of Leviticus offers detailed instructions for the identification and treatment of leprosy in people (Lev 13:1–46), clothing (Lev 13:47–59), and homes (Lev 14:33–57). Individuals who were infected with the disease were required to dwell outside of the camp, neglect their personal appearance, and cry out, "Unclean, unclean!" as a warning to others of their status (Lev 13:45–46).

When an individual died, everyone and everything in that person's tent became unclean for seven days (Num 19:14–15). So, too, did anyone in the open country who touched a corpse or a grave (Num 19:16). By extension, soldiers who had experienced combat in war (i.e., who had touched those slain in battle), had to submit themselves and their belongings to a seven-day process of purification (Num 31:19–20).

Finally, the violation of virtually any of God's dictates could render one unclean. For those who broke them unintentionally, the Torah sets forth a variety of sin and guilt offerings (Lev 4:27–35, 5:1–26). However, no such sacrifice exists for the one who deliberately disobeyed them (Num 15:30–31).

Keep Kosher

Closely related to the subject of ritual purity (but broad enough to warrant its own category) are the dietary regulations of the Torah. According to the OT, God gave certain creatures to the Israelites to eat. These were considered kosher, or acceptable. Those that were not kosher, or unacceptable, were considered unclean.

Within four broader categories (animals, fish, birds, and insects) certain simple guidelines distinguish kosher beings from their non-kosher counterparts. Among animals, for instance, only those that have cloven hooves and chew the cud are kosher (Lev 11:1–8; Deut 14:3–8). This includes sheep, goats, cattle, deer, gazelle, and oxen. All others are not, including pigs, rabbits, camels, horses, mice, lizards, dogs, cats, and so on. Of the creatures that live in the water, only those that have both fins and scales are kosher (Lev 11:9–12; Deut 14:9–10). This includes most varieties of fish. Those that lack either fins or scales, including shark, octopus, eels, and most shellfish, are not. Nearly all birds are kosher. The exceptions include a short list of scavengers (vultures, buzzards, gulls, crows) and predators (eagles, hawks, falcons, owls) found in Lev 11:13–19 and Deut 14:11–18. As for insects, virtually all are not kosher, with the exception of those that have jointed legs for leaping on the ground, such as locusts, grasshoppers, katydids, and crickets (Lev 11:20–23).

In preparing kosher meats, the Israelites were obliged to first drain away the animal's blood. Because blood was thought to contain life, the Israelites were instructed to "pour it out onto the ground like water" (Lev 7:26; 17:10–14; 19:26; Deut 12:15–16, 22–25). This act prevented the animal's life from mingling with that of the one consuming it.[9]

The Israelites were also forbidden from eating any animal, including a kosher one, which had died naturally. Their bodies were to be considered unclean (Exod 22:30; Lev 11:39–40; 17:15–16; Deut 14:21), capable of contaminating not only those who touched or ate them, but in some cases, even objects which came into contact with them (Lev 11:31–38).

Finally, the Torah contains three injunctions against boiling a kid (a young animal) in its mother's milk (Exod 23:19; 34:26; Deut 14:21). Whether this deed was forbidden because of its Canaanite associations or because it was considered excessively cruel—much like harvesting both a mother bird and her chicks (cf. Deut 22:6–7)—is unclear. At any rate, it became the basis for the modern Jewish practice of separating meat meals and their accompanying utensils and table service from dairy meals and *their* accompanying utensils and table service.

Avoid Sexual Immorality

Also related to the purity laws (but again, large enough to justify its own category) are the numerous statutes differentiating legitimate

---

[9]In general, the Torah demonstrates a tendency against mingling. The Israelites were commanded not to cross-breed their animals, sow two different types of seed in the same field, and weave their garments with different types of threads (Lev 19:19). Given this tendency, the mingling of life forces (via blood) becomes the ultimate taboo.

sexual relations from illegitimate ones. Throughout the OT, infidelity to God's covenant is likened to marital infidelity.[10] To some extent, then, one's sexual discretion reflected one's covenantal commitment and vice versa.

It should be noted that most of the sexually-based ordinances are framed from a masculine perspective. Thus, a man was forbidden from consummating any relationship involving an immediate family member, including his mother, stepmother, or mother-in-law (Lev 18:7–8; 20:11, 14), his sister, stepsister, half-sister, or sister-in-law[11] (Lev 18:9, 16, 18; 20:17, 21), his stepdaughter, granddaughter, or daughter-in-law (Lev 18:10, 15, 17; 20:12; Deut 23:1), and his aunt (Lev 18:12–14; 20:19–20). For the most part, these types of relationships were considered incestuous.

In addition to these, the acts of adultery (Exod 20:14; Lev 18:20; 20:10; Num 5:11–31; Deut 5:18; 22:22), homosexuality[12] (Lev 18:22; 20:13), bestiality (Exod 22:18; Lev 18:23; 20:15–16), rape (Deut 22:23–27), and prostitution (Lev 19:29; Deut 23:18) were also forbidden. Violation of most of these mandates was considered a capital crime, punishable by death.

According to the Torah, premarital sex was not a capital crime unless one of the parties was already betrothed to someone else. However, it did involve a penalty. Assuming the couple was discovered, the man involved was required to pay the bridal price to the woman's father and then take her as his wife. Furthermore, he was forbidden from divorcing her for as long as he lived (Exod 22:15–16; Deut 22:28–29).[13] If their activity remained undiscovered, it could spell even more trouble for the woman if and when she eventually married. Upon failing to provide her

[10] Numerous examples could be adduced, but some of the most memorable come from the prophets: Ezek 16 and Hos 1–3.

[11] Although sex with the wife of one's brother was forbidden while he was alive, it was *required* if one's brother died and left his wife childless. In that case, a man was obligated to sleep with his sister-in-law in order to produce children on behalf of his dead brother, thereby ensuring the continuity of the family bloodline (Deut 25:5–10).

[12] It should be noted that while the Torah forbids homosexual activity, it says nothing about homosexual orientation (the deep-seated sexual predisposition toward members of one's own gender). Thus, one strategy of contemporary Jewish and Christian ethicists is to condemn the former but not the latter.

[13] Generally speaking, divorce is permitted by the Torah. The primary restriction pertaining to it involves remarriage. If a man divorces a woman and she marries another, she cannot, on the occasion of a subsequent divorce or the death of her second husband, remarry the first (Deut 24:1–4).

new husband with evidence of her virginity, the woman could be stoned to death (Deut 22:13–21).

ACT WITH JUSTICE

In addition to right relationship with God, some of the Torah directives also encourage a just relationship to society. In this respect, they bear the closest resemblance to the legal codes of their ancient Near Eastern neighbors as well as to our own justice system today.[14] Thus, for instance, the Torah prescribes the installation of judges throughout the community (Deut 1:15–17; 16:18–20). Justice, and justice alone, was to be their aim (Deut 16:20). They were to arbitrate fairly, and their decisions were final (Deut 17:8–13).

Justice, of course, is predicated upon truth. Therefore, the Torah condemns all types of deceit. These includes lies (Lev 19:11), fraudulent reports against one's neighbor (Exod 20:16; Deut 5:20), dishonest testimony in court (Exod 23:1–2; Deut 19:16–21), undue favoritism (Exod 23:3; Lev 19:15), accepting bribes (Exod 23:8), making false vows (Lev 19:12; Num 30:2–17; Deut 23:22–24), utilizing imprecise measuring tools or weights (Lev 19:35–36), and moving landmarks or boundary lines (Deut 19:4).

All sorts of civil matters are covered in the Torah. Many of these pertain to business transactions and associated property rights. Various regulations cover loans and collateral (Exod 22:25–26; Deut 24:6, 10–13), interest charges (Exod 22:24; Lev 25:36–37; Deut 23:20–21), entrusted assets (Exod 22:6–14), wages (Lev 19:13; Deut 24:14–15), and inheritances (Num 27:5–11; 36:1–9; Deut 21:15–17). The Torah further explains how to reclaim or redeem various possessions, including land (Lev 25:23–28), houses (Lev 25:29–31), and even fellow kinsmen working as indentured servants (Lev 25:47–55).

The Torah also treats a host of civil cases involving property damage and personal injury. If intentional, the Torah invokes the well-known standard of *lex talonis:* life for life, limb for limb, eye for eye, and tooth for tooth (Lev 24:17–22). If the injury was unintentional, the outcomes were more variable, depending on whether the harm was sustained to animals (Exod 21:33–36; 22:13–14), neighboring fields

[14] For a comparison of some ancient Near Eastern laws with the Torah, see Appendix B.

(Exod 22:4–5), slaves (Exod 21:20–21, 26–27, 32), thieves (Exod 22:1–3), women (Exod 21:22–25; Deut 25:11–12), or the population at large (Exod 21:18–19, 28–31).

Beyond civil matters, the Torah advocates justice with respect to criminal activity. It describes a variety of crimes and establishes their associated punishments. Chief among such transgressions are adultery (Exod 20:14; Lev 18:20; 20:10; Num 5:11–31; Deut 5:18; 22:22), murder[15] (Exod 20:13; 21:12, 14; Num 35:16–21; Deut 5:17; 19:11–13), theft (Exod 20:15; 21:37; Lev 19:11; Num 5:5–8; Deut 5:19), and kidnapping (Exod 21:16; Deut 24:7). With the exception of theft, each of these was considered a capital crime. Assuming a sufficient number of witnesses could attest to the wrongdoing (Num 35:30; Deut 17:6–7), the guilty party was to be executed.

Show Mercy and Respect

As a corollary to justice, the Torah also promotes the practice of mercy. Scattered among the 613 laws are repeated admonitions to care for the poorer and more vulnerable members of society, especially the resident aliens (immigrants), orphans, and widows. Given an agriculturally-based economy, these groups were at a distinct disadvantage, since they rarely possessed land and consequently had little means of supporting themselves. Since these groups were of unique concern to God, the Israelites were enjoined to pay special attention to their well-being (Exod 22:20–23; 23:9; Lev 19:33–34; Deut 10:17–19).

Institutionalized welfare systems were unheard of in the ancient Near East, but some of the precepts of the Torah function to create a sort of safety net for those who might otherwise fall through the cracks. So, for example, landowners could harvest their fields, their trees, and their vines once, but they were enjoined not to do so repeatedly. Whatever produce remained was to be left for the aliens, orphans, and widows to glean (Deut 24:19–22). Similarly, crops could be gathered from within fields, and produce could be picked from vines and trees, but the

[15] Here, we can distinguish, as the Torah does, between murder (intentional killing) and manslaughter (unintentional killing). Although the former is a capital crime requiring the death of its perpetrator, the latter was to be handled differently. The Torah called for the creation of several cities of asylum, to which those guilty of manslaughter could flee. In this way, they could avoid the wrath of the relatives of the one whom they had killed. Their period of exile was to last until the death of the reigning high priest (Num 35:22–28; Deut 4:41–43; 19:1–7).

outer edges of properties (Lev 19:9; 23:22) and any fruit that fell to the ground (Lev 19:10) were to be surrendered to the poor and needy. These individuals were also permitted access to crops on dormant sabbatical lands (Exod 23:10–11).

Beyond the aliens, orphans, and widows, the Torah espouses mercy toward one's neighbor in general. Assistance is to be readily offered to those facing financial hardships (Deut 15:1–11) or physical danger (Lev 19:16b). It even extends to animals that are lost or overburdened (Exod 23:4–5; Deut 22:1–4). The Israelites were enjoined to honor their parents (Exod 20:12; Lev 19:3; 20:9; Deut 5:16; 21:18–21), respect the aged (Lev 19:32), and not mock the handicapped (Lev 19:14). In all things, God's people were called to love their neighbors as themselves. This meant that they were to bear no hatred, take no revenge, or cherish no grudge against their countrymen (Lev 19:17–18).

Summary and Conclusion

Having completed our overview of the 613 commands of the Torah, we can summarize our survey (see table 5.1).

At the outset of this chapter, we noted that legal codes can offer us valuable insights into the ideologies and fears of the cultures that produce them. The Torah is no exception. Its laws are far from whimsical, though some of them may seem so at first. Emanating from the Divine, they set forth practical guidelines that enable the children of Abraham to honor God with single-minded fidelity. As we have seen, most of the behaviors regulated (esp. numbers 1–5 in the table on the next page) are directly concerned with ritual purity and cultic participation. Even the more socially-based laws (numbers 6–8) are nevertheless tied to one's relationship with the Divine. Therefore, unlike our laws today, or even those of Israel's ancient neighbors, the primary goal of the Torah is not to establish a fair and harmonious society. Rather, it is to forge a people who, in all aspects of their lives, would constitute a chosen nation set apart and uniquely dedicated to the God of Abraham. It is this ideal that distinguishes this particular law code and its adherents from all others.

To reinforce this notion, the Torah concludes by emphasizing that the future of this people is entirely predicated upon its obedience to God. For those willing to embrace their unique heritage as the children of Abraham, God promises his blessings. For those who stray from this covenant, more dire consequences loom:

The Torah Summarized	
Principle	**Examples**
1. Worship God alone	Idolatry forbidden Pagan influences expelled from the land No foreign alliances or marriages
2. Support Israel's religious establishment	Construction of the sanctuary Guidelines for Levites Guidelines for priests Sacrificial offerings
3. Observe the holy days	Sabbath/sabbatical/Jubilee Passover New Year (Rosh Hashanah) Day of Atonement (Yom Kippur)
4. Remain ritually pure	Avoid bodily fluids Treatment of leprosy Death Inadvertent sin
5. Keep kosher	Guidelines for animals Guidelines for fish Guidelines for birds Guidelines for insects Pour out blood
6. Avoid sexual immorality	Incestuous relationships Capital offenses Premarital sex
7. Act with justice	Judges False witnesses Business transactions/property rights Property damage/personal injury Crime and punishment
8. Show mercy and respect	Care for resident aliens, orphans, and widows Assist those in need Respect your elders Love your neighbor

Table 5.1

"Here, then, I have today set before you life and prosperity, death and doom. If you obey the commandments of the LORD, your God, which I enjoin on you today, loving him, and walking in his ways, and keeping his commandments, statutes and decrees, you will live and grow numerous, and the LORD, your God, will

> bless you in the land you are entering to occupy. If, however, you turn away your hearts and will not listen . . . I tell you now that you will certainly perish; you will not have a long life on the land which you are crossing the Jordan to enter and occupy." (Deut 30:15–18)

In sum, therefore, the biblical model is not to "Live free or die," but rather, to "Live faithfully or die." So how did the Israelites fare in light of this challenge? Their narrative history continues in the prophetic literature.

Part II נביאים

The Prophets (Nevi'im)

The second section of the Hebrew Bible consists of the Prophets. While the term is a familiar one, there are significant differences among the Jewish and Christian canons regarding the classification of such books.[1]

Judaism divides the Prophets into two categories: the Former Prophets and the Latter Prophets. The Former Prophets consist of the books of Joshua, Judges, 1 and 2 Samuel, and 1 and 2 Kings. (These books include episodes about some of Israel's earliest prophets, such as Elijah and Elisha.) Nowadays, scholars refer to this collection as the Deuteronomistic History, so named because of the pervasiveness of the reward/punishment theology set forth in Deuteronomy. Narratively speaking, the works begin with the Israelites' securing of the promised land and end with their forfeiture of it. In light of this big picture, then, they tend to have a rather negative assessment of the people's covenant fidelity. Christians include these titles in their canons as well, but they categorize them as historical books.

The Latter Prophets designate the Writing Prophets, or those seers who have specific works attributed to them. This group includes Isaiah, Jeremiah, Ezekiel, and The Twelve: Hosea, Joel, Amos, Obadiah, Jonah, Micah, Nahum, Habakkuk, Zephaniah, Haggai, Zechariah, and Malachi. In the Christian canons, the prophets are very similar, except

[1] For a comparative view of the Jewish, Roman Catholic, Protestant, and Eastern Orthodox canons, see Appendix C.

that Daniel is added to the major prophets and Lamentations (and for Catholics, Baruch) to the minor prophets. These terms refer not to a prophet's importance but to length of his book.

This second section will concentrate primarily on the Latter or Writing Prophets of the Old Testament. Chapter 6 will survey these prophets' messages vis-à-vis our modern notions of prophecy and the historical settings of their time. Chapter 7 will focus more exclusively on the book of Jonah. There it will be maintained that the ironic juxtaposition of this prophet's experience over and against that of his colleagues is essential for grasping the point of this work. Chapter 8 will consider the book of Daniel as an example of Old Testament apocalyptic literature—an offshoot of the prophetic genre. Utilizing a modern case study for the sake of comparison, this chapter will investigate the method of Daniel's predictions and illuminate their purpose in light of their original setting.

6

The Prophets —God's Spokespersons

FOCUS TEXTS: THE LATTER PROPHETS

Prophecy: Modern Conceptions

Prophecy. What sorts of images does this word conjure up for you? A mysterious gypsy woman peering intently into a crystal ball? An elderly man with a long white beard proclaiming "The End Is Near!" on a makeshift sign? Perhaps a palm reader plying her trade in a tiny, back-alley shop—the one right next to the tattoo parlor? For many of us, the notion of prophecy suggests the ability to see into the future or to experience premonitions of events yet to come.

While tarot cards, Ouija boards, and other tools of divination may be vestiges of a bygone era, their electronic makeovers and online proliferation demonstrate that our generation remains no less fascinated by the prospect of precognition. Just how widespread is our interest? Consider this. A recent Google search found that some 19.5 million Web sites correspond to the keyword "psychic," 29.2 million to "astrology," and 40.4 million to "horoscope." To put these numbers into perspective, the keywords "Old Testament" and "New Testament" matched only 2.58 and 6.78 million websites, respectively.[1]

[1] This survey was taken on August 3, 2007. For the record, the keyword "Bible"—a decidedly more generic designation—matched some 98.4 million sites.

Indeed, our enchantment with prescience is reflected across a broad spectrum of multimedia outlets. Recent prime-time television lineups have featured programs about clairvoyants, such as *Medium* (NBC) and *Psychic Detectives* (Court TV); "spirit messengers," such as *The Ghost Whisperer* (CBS) and *Crossing Over with John Edwards* (Sci-Fi); and the ability to alter history, such as *Quantum Leap* (NBC), *Early Edition* (CBS), and *Journeyman* (NBC). To such shows, we can add a slew of Hollywood films, including *Back to the Future, Groundhog Day, Premonition, Minority Report, Frequency, The Sixth Sense,* and *The Celestine Prophecies,* to name just a few. Best-selling books claim to anticipate the future in rather creative ways, from Nostradamus's medieval quatrains to Michael Drosnin's *The Mysterious Bible Code.*[2] And then there are the telephone services (remember Dionne Warwick's infamous Psychic Friends Hotline?), now adapted for the latest instant text-messaging technologies. Throw in the pop-culture kitsch—Chinese fortune cookies, Magic 8–Balls, supermarket tabloids—and the prevalence of "prophecy" is practically unavoidable.

Why are we so captivated by prospective insights into the future? What makes knowledge of the yet-to-come so alluring? Well, consider the following scenarios. Although a few details have been modified, all are drawn from real life (see list following).

- A high school athlete is heavily recruited by several colleges and universities. He chooses one primarily on the basis of its financial incentives and legendary sports reputation. However, he soon finds himself overwhelmed by his coursework and academically ineligible to play. Discouraged, he falls behind his classmates and withdraws from school. Lacking a degree, he faces limited career choices. Ultimately, he regrets his decision.
- An adolescent female finds herself emotionally torn between her longtime boyfriend and a new love interest. Hoping for more adventure in her life, she chooses the latter. After a torrid affair, she's left heartbroken, pregnant, and alone.
- A young married couple invests their life savings in a "can't miss" technology stock. Three weeks after its initial public offering (IPO), the stock hasn't budged from its $8 a share price. Nervous, they sell back their shares. The next week, the stock soars to $24

[2] We'll examine Drosnin's work more closely in chapter 8.

a share. They buy back in. One month later, the stock has plummeted to $2 a share—and it remains there for good.

- Two friends hop in a car and head out for a night on the town. On the freeway, the driver becomes distracted and nearly misses his exit. He overcorrects and hits an on-ramp at a high rate of speed. The vehicle jumps the embankment and crashes into a tree. Both men are killed.

Clearly, mistakes were made in each case. Some are unfortunate; some downright tragic. Had the individuals known these outcomes ahead of time, they certainly would have opted for different choices. In much the same way, information about our futures, were it possible to obtain, would enable us to avoid similar errors in judgment. It is little wonder, then, that present-day diviners tend to concentrate on our most significant and difficult decisions: romance, careers, personal finances, and health issues. If only they worked![3]

Prophecy: Ancient Role

In contrast to our modern take on prophecy, the prophets of the Hebrew Bible were not focused on romance, career choices, personal finances, or health issues. Nor were they primarily interested in predicting the future. Rather, their principal role is connoted by their title. The Greek word προφήτης (from whence we derive our English word "prophet") literally means "one who speaks on behalf of another." Thus, the primary duty of OT prophets was to speak on God's behalf—to bridge the gap between divinity and humanity. The Hebrew word for prophet, נביא, *nabi'*, comes from the root word נבא, *naba'*, which means to announce, to inform, to call, to bubble up, to pour forth, or to

[3]The fact that they don't is recognized by a variety of state and local ordinances that render it illegal to pass off fortune telling as a legitimate service. In the state of New York, for instance, such activity qualifies as a class B misdemeanor under Statute 165.35: "A person is guilty of fortune telling when, for a fee or compensation which he directly or indirectly solicits or receives, he claims or pretends to tell fortunes, or holds himself out as being able, by claimed or pretended use of occult powers, to answer questions or give advice on personal matters or to exorcise, influence or affect evil spirits or curses; except that this section does not apply to a person who engages in the aforedescribed conduct as part of a show or exhibition solely for the purpose of entertainment or amusement. However one should use his intelligence and wisdom while visiting fortune tellers."

proclaim. In this respect, we can think of the prophets as fountainheads or springs from which God's words "bubble up" and "pour forth."[4] But to whom were these men sent, and what did they say?

The Prophets' Place in Old Testament History

In order to establish the historical setting of the Writing Prophets, we need to fill in the narrative gap from our last chapter.[5] After settling into the promised land, the Israelites soon struggled in the absence of any centralized authority. Therefore, they demanded a king to help unify and consolidate their disparate tribes. Saul, David, and Solomon each in turn (and with varying degrees of success) fulfilled this role. But following the death of Solomon, a political schism put an end to the united monarchy. Ten tribes banded together in the North under Solomon's general, Jeroboam. They established their capital at Samaria and were collectively known as Israel (and henceforth, Israelites). The two remaining tribes, Judah and Benjamin, merged together in the south under the leadership of Solomon's son, Rehoboam. They retained the capital city of Jerusalem and were collectively known as Judah (and henceforth, Judahites). From this point on, these two nations had completely independent histories, including their own succession of kings. According to the OT records, these kings, with a few exceptions, fared poorly. Indeed, it is during this crisis of leadership that the golden age of prophecy emerged. When the monarchy failed to heed him, God sent his prophets to speak to his people on his behalf. The vast majority of biblical prophecies, therefore, pertain either to the northern kingdom of Israel or to the southern kingdom of Judah.[6]

---

[4] In fact, the prophet Amos describes the absence of prophetic words as a famine, or drought (Amos 8:11–13). These definitions also coincide well with the analogy of the "watchman" (Ezek 3:17–21; 33:1–9; Hos 9:8; Mal 7:4)—a sentinel stationed on a high point who could announce to those below that which he saw coming. In much the same way, the OT prophets were charged with the task of communicating that which God intended to do.

[5] For a narrative timeline from the united monarchy to Greek rule, see Appendix D.

[6] The approximate dates of the Writing Prophets can be found in Appendix E. It should be noted that the prophets also spoke against the surrounding nations and their major cities as well. Prime examples can be found in Isa 13–23; Jer 46–51; Ezek 25–32; Amos 1–2; Zeph 2:4–15; and Zech 9:1–8. To these, we can also add

The Message of the Prophets

It makes sense that God's spokespersons would primarily address the Israelites and the Judahites. But what, specifically, was their message? The prophetic literature contains more than 230 chapters of text, about 20% more than the Torah. Therefore, any survey of such a massive amount of material runs the risk of oversimplification. With that caveat in mind, we can group the content of their pronouncements into four major categories: a call to fidelity and justice; an indictment of guilt; punishment; and mercy and restoration. We shall examine these categories in turn.

CALL TO FIDELITY AND SOCIAL JUSTICE

Virtually all of the prophets take God's people to task for their failure to live up to their end of the covenantal agreement.[7] In this respect, they act as the collective consciences of their communities. Of course, because the terms of the covenant are so extensive (613 commands), so too are their possible infractions. However, of all the crimes cited by the prophets, idolatry easily tops the list. With well over one hundred references, no violation even comes close to being mentioned so frequently.

When it comes to idolatry, the prophets are quite detailed about the types of practices that provoke God's wrath. There is, for instance, the initial creation of the idols—the fashioning of images out of wood, stone, iron, silver, or gold. Such objects were often adorned with finely dyed clothing and expensive perfumes. Then they were placated with oil, incense, food, flour, honey, wine and drink libations, bread and grain offerings, and other sacrifices. Free-standing altars, sacred poles, and sanctuaries were also erected for these gods, most typically on "lofty mountains" and "under leafy trees." Such shrines became the sites of

---

the entire books of Obadiah (against Edom) and Nahum (against Nineveh). In fact, few of Israel's immediate neighbors escape condemnation. Babylonia, Egypt, Assyria (Nineveh), Moab (Kir Hareseth, Heshbon), Edom, Phoenicia (Tyre, Sidon), Ammon, Philistia (Ashkelon, Gaza, Ekron, Ashdod), Aram/Syria (Hamath, Damascus), Ethiopia/Cush, Elam, and Arabia are all implicated at one point or another—mostly in that order of frequency. These instances aside, the prophets' principal concern remained Israel and Judah.

[7] Generic references to covenant violation include Isa 24:5; 42:24; 58:2; Jer 6:9; 9:12; 11:1–8; 16:11–13; 22:9; 44:10, 23; Ezek 20; Amos 2:4; Hos 4:6; 8:1, 12; Hab 1:4; Zeph 3:4; Zech 7:12; Mal 2:5–10.

illicit rituals, including divination and soothsaying, fertility rites (including prostitution), self-mutilation, and even child sacrifice.[8]

Occasionally, the OT prophets mention the rival gods involved. Thus, for example, the people stand accused of swearing by Milcom (Zeph 1:5), invoking the name of Ba'al (Hos 2:19), baking cake offerings for Ishtar, "the queen of heaven" (Jer 44:1–28), weeping for Tammuz (Ezek 8:14), sacrificing sons and daughters to Molech (Ezek 16:20–21), worshiping Sakkuth and Kaiwan (Amos 5:26), bowing to the sun (Jer 8:2; Ezek 8:16), and adoring the stars (Zeph 1:5). Because devotion to these deities spread to Israel and Judah from foreign countries, the prophets adamantly denounced partnerships with such people, especially political alliances and mixed marriages.[9]

Beyond idolatry, the prophets' second most frequently cited transgressions are *not* the more prominent commands of the Decalogue: disrespecting one's elders, murder and bloodshed, adultery, theft, bearing false witness, or coveting. While such offenses are mentioned, they are done so only in moderation.[10] Nor do violations against the formal worship of God assume a very prominent position. Honoring the Sabbath and sabbatical rules, keeping kosher, observing ritual and sexual purity laws, celebrating the feast days, offering acceptable prayers, fasts, sacrifices, and tithes, and supporting the temple establishment all merit some attention, but not nearly as much as one might assume.[11] In fact, most of the prophets deliberately subordinate such cultic concerns to an even higher priority: justice for the poor.

In this respect, the prophetic corpus shows a certain departure from tendencies found in the Torah. Both place their greatest emphasis on

---

[8] The passages pertaining to idolatry are too numerous to list, but for representative texts, see Isa 2:6–8; 44:6–20; 57:3–13; Jer 2:4–28; 7:16–20; 10:1–16; 11:9–13; 44:1–28; Ezek 6:1–14; 8:3–18; 16:15–21; Hos 2:4–18; 4:12–19; 8:4–11; Hab 2:18–19.

[9] On foreign alliances, see Isa 30:1–22; 31:1–6; Jer 42:7–22; Ezek 23:1–45; Hos 7:8–12. Mal 2:10–16 discusses mixed marriages.

[10] In the book of Habakkuk, for example, the chief crime is violence and bloodshed. Zechariah takes issue with thieves and perjurers (Zech 5:1–4). And other prophets list, in whole or part, violations of the Ten Commandments (see Jer 7:9; Ezek 22:1–12; Hos 4:2).

[11] Texts pertaining to each include the Sabbath (Isa 58:13–14; Jer 17:19–27; Ezek 46:1–6); sabbatical rules (Jer 34:8–20); keeping kosher (Isa 65:4; 66:17); observing ritual and sexual purity laws (Ezek 22:10–11; 43:10–31); celebrating the feast days (Ezek 45:18–25); offering acceptable prayers (Isa 43:22), fasts (Joel 2:15–17), sacrifices (Isa 43:23–24; Mal 1:7–14; Ezek 45:13–17), and tithes (Mal 3:7–12); and supporting the temple establishment (Ezek 44:4–9; Zech 8:9; Hag 1:1–11).

fidelity to God alone. But when it comes to secondary concerns, the Torah devotes far more space to the institutional worship of God than to the care of the destitute (presumably reflecting the relative importance of these duties). The prophets, however, do just the opposite. According to them, compassion for the marginalized takes precedence over the observance of religious traditions. If the former is neglected, then no amount of the latter will ever prove effective. Their bold rhetoric leaves little doubt as to God's stance on this matter:

> What care I for the number of your sacrifices? says the LORD. "I have had enough of whole-burnt rams and fat of fatlings; in the blood of calves, lambs and goats I find no pleasure. When you come in to visit me, who asks these things of you? Trample my courts no more! Bring no more worthless offerings; your incense is loathsome to me. New moon and sabbath, calling of assemblies, octaves with wickedness: these I cannot bear. Your new moons and festivals I detest; they weigh me down, I tire of the load. When you spread your hands, I close my eyes to you; though you pray the more, I will not listen. Your hands are full of blood! Wash yourselves clean! Put away your misdeeds from before my eyes; cease doing evil; learn to do good. Make justice your aim: redress the wronged, hear the orphan's plea, defend the widow." (Isa 1:11–17)[12]

According to the prophets, Israel and Judah have fared no better toward the indigents of their society than they have toward God. Their track record is filled with incidents of neglect, abuse, and exploitation.[13]

INDICTMENT OF GUILT

Of course, the prophets did more than simply accuse the people of their crimes. They also pleaded for reform. They held out the hope that if the guilty were to return to God wholeheartedly, then their punishment could be avoided or at least mitigated. No prophet extends this invitation more frequently than Jeremiah,[14] and perhaps none more earnestly than Ezekiel:

> Therefore I will judge you, house of Israel, each one according to his ways, says the Lord GOD. Turn and be converted from all your crimes, that they may be no cause of guilt for you. Cast away from you all the crimes you have committed.

---

[12] For more on the importance and meaning of the prophetic notion of justice, see Appendix F.

[13] In addition to the texts found in Appendix F, see also Jer 5:26–28; 22:1–5; Amos 2:6; 4:1; 5:7–15; 8:4–6.

[14] See, for example, Jer 3:12–16, 22; 4:1–2; 7:3; 18:1–11; 25:4–7; 26:2–3; 36:2–3, 6–7.

> . . . Why should you die, O house of Israel? For I have no pleasure in the death of anyone who dies, says the Lord God. Return and live! (Ezek 18:30–32; similarly, 14:6–8; 18:21–23; 33:10–11)

These prophets were scarcely alone. Isaiah, Hosea, Joel, Zephaniah, Zechariah, and Malachi also tendered this offer.[15] Unfortunately, their entreaties were largely ignored.

God's only recourse, then, was to bring charges against his own people—to enter into a lawsuit, as it were, for their breach of the covenant contract.[16] Among those indicted by the prophets are the leaders of the people—the kings, princes, judges, elders, cult prophets, priests, and Levites—as well as the general populace: the men, the women, and even the children of Israel and Judah.[17] To illustrate the seriousness of their crimes and the pervasiveness of their corruption, the prophets drew upon an assortment of vivid analogies.

The most common portrayal of Israel and Judah is that of the adulteress—the unfaithful spouse who has forsaken her husband to pursue a life of harlotry and prostitution. Adding insult to injury, she utilizes all the good things he has bestowed upon her to arouse the passions of others and attract lovers to herself.[18] The prophets also liken Israel and Judah to rotten figs (Jer 24:8–10), wild grapes (Isa 5:1–7; Jer 2:21), briers and thorns (Mic 7:4), stubborn cows (Hos 4:16), senseless doves (Hos 7:11), charred vines (Ezek 15:1–8), rusted cookware (Ezek 24:1–14), shattered pottery (Jer 19:1–13), and broken wine flasks (Jer 13:12–14). But by far the most striking comparison involves the prophet Jeremiah's decomposed underwear (Jer 13:1–11)!

To demonstrate the status of his people, God instructs Jeremiah to purchase and wear a linen loincloth for himself. Shortly thereafter, God asks Jeremiah to remove the undergarment and stash it in a rocky crag. Following a long interval, God has Jeremiah retrieve it. The prophet discovers that "it was rotted, good for nothing!" (Jer 13:7). God then explains that:

---

[15] Cf. Isa 31:5–6; Hos 5:4–6; 12:6–7; 14:2–9; Joel 2:13–14; Zeph 2:3; Zech 1:3; Mal 3:7b.

[16] Examples of the lawsuit terminology can be found in Isa 3:13–15; Hos 4:1–3; 12:2; Mic 6:1–2.

[17] Although numerous texts mention these groups specifically, some group them collectively, as in Isa 9:13–17; 59:1–15; 64:4–6; Jer 5:1–5; 6:11–14; 7:16–19; 8:1–6; 9:1–5; 32:32; Ezek 7:10–14; 22:24–31.

[18] Although the imagery of the adulteress is found throughout the prophets, the most notable examples occur in Jer 2–3; Ezek 16, 23; Hos 1–3.

> As close as the loincloth clings to a man's loins, so had I made the whole house of Israel and the whole house of Judah cling to me, says the Lord; to be my people, my renown, my praise, my beauty. But they did not listen. (Jer 13:11)

For this reason, God concludes, his people have become like the decaying underwear. Once they were intimately close to him; now they are destined for nothing but destruction.

Punishment

Serious crimes call for serious penalties. When the prophets' appeals for reform were repeatedly ignored, God sought to get his people's attention through a variety of lesser calamities: famine, drought, crop failure, plague, pestilence, and war.[19] None of these achieved their desired goal. It seems that the guilty were no more likely to change their ways than a leopard change its spots (Jer 13:23). The evils that they continued to commit could no longer be ignored. For the sake of his name, God was left with no alternative. Not even Moses or Samuel (Jer 15:1), Noah, Daniel, or Job (Ezek 14:12–20) could save them now. God would consign his people to destruction:

> Therefore thus says the Lord God: Because you have been more rebellious than the nations surrounding you, neither living by my statutes, nor fulfilling my ordinances . . . See, I am coming at you! I will inflict punishments in your midst while the nations look on. Because of all your abominations I will do with you what I have never done before, the like of which I will never do again . . . I swear to cut you down. I will not look upon you with pity nor have mercy. A third of your people shall die of pestilence and perish of hunger within you; another third shall fall by the sword all around you; and a third I will scatter in every direction, and I will pursue them with the sword. (Ezek 5:7–12)[20]

Like a jilted lover, God would enact the death penalty against his adulterous spouse (Ezek 23:46–48).[21] He vowed, like a panther, to stalk his prey; like a bear robbed of its young, to savagely attack;

---

[19] These phenomena are variously described in Jer 3:3; 14:1–10; Amos 4:6–11. To these passages we can add the entire book of Joel, which treats a massive plague of locusts as a foreshadowing of the Day of the Lord.

[20] Similarly, Ezek 14:21–23 and Jer 15:1–4, which both add a fourth punishment: the attack of wild animals.

[21] In the context of this analogy, the prophets are somewhat inconsistent concerning the adulteress's future. In Ezekiel, infidelity calls for the death penalty (Ezek 23:46–48). Jeremiah only suggests that an eventual "remarriage" is out of the question (Jer 3:1). But in Isaiah and Hosea, the husband redeems the adulteress and takes her back as his wife (Isa 54:5–10; Hos 3).

and like a lion, to tear apart and devour his people (Amos 13:7–8). There would be no leniency. When the sword passed through the land, children would be dashed to pieces, and expectant mothers would be ripped open (Hos 14:1).

God used two instruments for such brutality. The nation of Assyria attacked and destroyed the northern kingdom of Israel in 722 B.C.E. The defeated Israelites were deported to other conquered lands throughout the Assyrian Empire, and vanquished peoples from afar were in turn settled in Israel. The ten tribes were no more. The southern kingdom of Judah narrowly escaped the Assyrian onslaught. But it did not take its lesson to heart. It lasted until 587 B.C.E., when the Babylonian army invaded, laid siege to Jerusalem, and destroyed it.[22] The few who remained—forty-six hundred by Jeremiah's count (Jer 52:28)—were rounded up and led off to captivity in Babylon.[23] Had Nebuchadnezzar, the Babylonian king, decided to slaughter them instead, the story of Judaism, for all practical purposes, would have ended here. But destruction was not to be the prophets' final word.

Mercy and Restoration

The prophets insisted that, as harsh as God's punishment would be, it would not spell the end of the covenant relationship. God could no more forsake his people than a mother could forsake her newborn or a pregnant woman the child within her womb (Isa 49:15). Rather, as a metalworker purifies silver or gold, God would use the furnace of their affliction to purify his people.[24] Like a forgiving husband, God would re-embrace his bride with great tenderness and enduring love (Isa 54:5–10; Hos 3). God would rescue the exiles from their captors and carry them home as a shepherd gathers his sheep and carries his lambs (Isa 40:11). He would bind up their wounds and heal them of all their afflictions.[25] God would crush their enemies and once again prove himself their Savior and Redeemer.

---

[22] The book of Lamentations, which Christian Bibles include among the prophets, mourns the loss of Jerusalem, the destruction of the temple, and the end of national sovereignty.

[23] This number accounts for the able-bodied inhabitants who had not managed to escape the siege. Technically, at least two other groups of Jews survived. One was a small contingent that managed to take refuge in Egypt (see Jer 41:11–44:28). Another was the non-able-bodied citizens who were left behind in Judah.

[24] Isa 48:10; Jer 9:6; Ezek 22:17–22; Zech 13:9; Mal 3:3.

[25] Jer 30:17; 33:6; Ezek 34:16; 37:26; Hos 14:5.

In addition to resettling them in their land, God also promised his people a series of "new things"—things that would far surpass the "things of old." Thus, for example, the prophets envisioned a "new covenant."[26] Whereas the former was written on stone tablets, this one would be written upon the hearts and the souls of God's people.[27] Coinciding with this new covenant, God vowed to regenerate his people (Ezek 37:1–14) and to gather them back from wherever they had been scattered.[28] He would endow them with new hearts and new spirits of obedience (Ezek 11:19–20; 36:26–27). He would restore and reunite Israel and Judah as one nation (Ezek 37:15–22). It would be given a new name (Isa 62:2) and a new leader to shepherd it justly.[29] Under this king, God's "anointed one"—in Hebrew, the משיח (*mashiakh*), or messiah—there would be everlasting peace and prosperity.[30] There would also be a new "Zion" or Jerusalem[31] and a new temple (Ezek 40:1–41:26) in which God's glory would find a permanent dwelling place (Isa 4:5; Ezek 43:1–9). There, all the nations of the earth would come to worship him.[32] In effect, these changes would usher in a new world order—a new heaven and a new earth (Isa 65:17; 66:22)—wherein joy and happiness reigned (Isa 65:18–20). Under this new order, all creation would co-exist in perfect harmony:

> The wolf shall be a guest of the lamb, and the leopard shall lie down with the kid; the calf and the young lion shall browse together, with a little child to guide them. The cow and the bear shall be neighbors, together their young shall rest; the lion shall eat hay like the ox. The baby shall play by the cobra's den, and the child lay his hand on the adder's lair. There shall be no harm or ruin . . . for the earth shall be filled with knowledge of the LORD, as water covers the sea. (Isa 11:6–9)

Historical Aftermath

Historically, these prophecies saw only partial fulfillment. The Persians defeated the Babylonians in 538 B.C.E. At that time, the Persian

---

[26] Isa 55:3; 61:8; Hos 2:20–25.

[27] In other words, fidelity to God would be so ingrained within them, that it would be a natural rather than a learned response (Jer 31:31–34).

[28] Isa 66:20; Jer 31:7–11; Hos 11:10–11; Zech 9:11–12.

[29] Frequently, but not always, this new leader is patterned after David. Cf. Isa 9:6–7; Jer 3:18; 23:5–6; 30:9; 33:14–18; Ezek 34:23–24; Hos 3:5; Mic 5:1–4.

[30] Isa 60:1–22; Mic 4:3–4.

[31] Isa 62:6–12; 66:7–13; Jer 33:6–9; Zech 12:1–9; 14:1–21, among others.

[32] Isa 56:1–8; 66:18; Jer 3:17; Mic 4:1–2; Zech 8:22–23.

ruler, King Cyrus, issued a decree permitting the Judahite captives to return to their homeland. This decree marked the official end of their seventy-year-long exile.

Once they returned to Judea, the people (henceforth referred to as Jews) restored the city walls of Jerusalem under the leadership of Nehemiah. Under Joshua and Zerubbabel, Jerusalem's temple was rebuilt. There was even a program of religious reform initiated by a scribe named Ezra.[33] But the dream of a self-governing, independent nation would have to wait. The yoke of the Persians gave way to that of the Greeks, and this was eventually exchanged for that of the Romans. In fact, it would be nearly twenty-five hundred years before Israel would achieve its statehood. The city of Jerusalem has survived, but its magnificent temple has long since been destroyed. And as for the promised messiah, his appearance continues to be a matter of debate. While Christians believe that he came in the person of Jesus of Nazareth, Jews argue otherwise. Their argument is based, in part, on the absence of a new world order and everlasting peace—components of the messianic reign that remain largely unaccounted for.

Despite these issues, history has largely vindicated the prophets. And while they may disagree over the precise application of their words, both Jews and Christians have incorporated them into their canon of sacred Scriptures. There they stand alongside the Torah as authentic witnesses to God's revelation in human history.

Conclusion

In light of our preceding analysis, perhaps our contemporary notions of prophecy can now be adjusted. If the indications of the OT prophets are correct, then successful decisions and bright futures are not predicated upon the alignment of the stars, the lines on our hands, messages in cookies, or even the turn of the die in an oversized liquid-filled plastic pool ball. ("It is decidedly so.") As entertaining as these may be, they offer no real assistance for practical decision making and even less for glimpsing that which is to come. Rather, according to God's spokes-

---

[33] Most of these achievements are described in the historical books of Ezra and Nehemiah. (Although they appear in this order in the Bible, the evidence suggests that Nehemiah's efforts preceded Ezra's.) Among the Writing Prophets, the books of Haggai and Zechariah both pertain to the rebuilding of the temple.

persons, the best predictor of a happy and peaceful existence is a vibrant, covenant-based faith life. Such a faith life is chiefly characterized by undivided loyalty to God and a deep and demonstrable commitment to justice for the poor. The prophets assure their readers that once these things are in place, then whatever the future holds—no matter how unforeseen—it can be faced with confidence and hope rather than fear and apprehension. In short, this is God's word and God's promise to his people.

7

The Book of Jonah —Prophecy Parodied

Focus Text: Jonah

Jonah's Whale

Try this exercise. Engage some unsuspecting people on the street in a game of free association. As prompts, use the names of biblical prophets. No doubt you'll receive some totally random and probably humorous responses to Amos, Obadiah, Nahum, Habakkuk, or Zephaniah. But try this with Jonah, and you're likely to encounter just the opposite. A consistent, indelible image is forever paired with God's reluctant spokesperson: the whale, that denizen of the deep whose rare encounters over the centuries have spawned yarns that send chills down the spines of even the most stalwart and salty of seamen. Indeed, there is something about Jonah's whale that quickens our pulse, stirs our senses, and fires our imagination—especially if we dare to place ourselves in his position:

> We have been completely abandoned on the high sea, cast adrift amidst the cavernous swells of the open ocean. The tempest's fury rages all around us. Billowing storm clouds meet the roiling black abyss, obliterating both horizon and hope. Our feeling of abject desolation quickly gives way to something entirely worse, however, as our gaze is drawn to a colossal swirl that distorts the water's veneer just a dozen yards away. A primal fear wells up within us, instilled by a primordial creature unfathomably larger and more powerful than ourselves. It's the helpless realization that we are no longer the predator, but the prey. The murky

> depths prove to be both a blessing and a curse by masking the true size of what is slowly circling below us. We are left to our remaining faculties to imagine its proportions. Suddenly, our silent foreboding is violently shattered by a frenetic act of ingestion. In that moment, we meet the great behemoth, eye to eye. It is only then that we discover just how vastly we have underestimated its enormity. In the acrid, stygian darkness into which we are engulfed, we immediately reconsider our "good fortune" of having somehow evaded the fatal crush of the monster's teeth. . . .

Questions surrounding the historicity of this event continue to dominate most discussions about Jonah.[1] Could Jonah really have been swallowed by a whale or some other large fish? Proponents typically suggest that the cetacean in question was a whale shark, a great white shark, or a sperm whale. Of these, the whale shark (*Rhindodon typhus*) appears to be the least likely candidate. Although it is the largest of all sharks—growing up to 12 meters (42 feet) long and weighing in at 12 tons (25,000 pounds)—it possesses a very narrow throat. It is well-designed to process the zooplankton, krill, and tiny fish that it subsists upon, but it would have great difficulty handling anything larger. Furthermore, although whale sharks inhabit most of the world's warmer waters, they are conspicuously absent from the Mediterranean or Adriatic Seas. However, great white sharks do ply the Mediterranean. In fact, specimens over 6 meters (20 feet) long and weighing up to 3 tons (6,600 pounds) have been caught there. But whether or not the notorious *Carcharodon carcharias* could or would swallow a man whole remains to be seen—the *Jaws* movies notwithstanding! Finally, there is the sperm whale (*Physeter macrocephalus*). Fully grown males, whose range includes the Mediterranean, can exceed 18 meters (59 feet) in length and weigh up to 45 tons (nearly 100,000 pounds). Understandably, these leviathans are the subject of many legendary tales, from *Moby Dick* to *Pinocchio,* and have become the leading contender for the Jonah story as well.

Of course, questions of historicity involve more than simply identifying a suitable species. Could a man really survive inside a whale for three days? How could he breathe? And what effect would the digestive acids have upon him? If only something like that were to occur in modern times! Has it? Anecdotal stories from nineteenth-century

---

[1] For a solid, balanced survey of these discussions, see the "Fact or Not?" section of Tim Spalding's "Jonah on the Web" site, http://www.isidore-of-seville.com/jonah/literalism.html (accessed March 27, 2008).

English whaling expeditions include claims of finding hapless sailors alive in the bellies of sperm whales. However, recent research into such reports has found them to be largely unsubstantiated.[2] The answers to these questions, therefore, continue to be hotly contested.

It is easy to allow a preoccupation with the whale to consume our attention and to thus overshadow the principal points of this biblical work. Perhaps the following observation can help keep things in perspective. Out of Jonah's forty-eight verses, the whale appears in only three of them (Jonah 1:17; 2:1, 10). That's a scant 6.25% of the text. There is, in other words, an additional 93.75% of content in which the whale does not appear. And as scholars have long known, it is therein that the real lessons of this document emerge.

The Biblical Story

As we shall see, Jonah's lessons are drawn most sharply in comparison to the typical experiences of the OT prophets. Those experiences form the presuppositions on which this book is based. In light of them, Jonah is presented as a study in contrasts—an example of prophecy parodied.

Jonah 1

> This is the word of the LORD that came to Jonah, son of Amittai. . . .
> (Jonah 1:1)

Of the prophetic books, only Ezekiel begins with the same word as Jonah. As an opening line, "And it happened . . ." (ויהי, *wayhiy*) usually introduces historical narratives (e.g., Judg 1:1; Ruth 1:1; Esth 1:1). This signal may be significant, for although the book of Jonah is officially classed among the Latter (or Writing) Prophets, it is essentially a story

---

[2]One of the most famous incidents involves James Bartley, a sailor aboard the *Star of the East.* In February 1891, while whaling near the Falkland Islands, Bartley purportedly fell overboard and was swallowed by a whale which the crew had harpooned and was struggling to subdue. Once the whale was overcome, it was butchered on the deck of the ship. Bartley was eventually discovered in the whale's stomach, alive but traumatized, his skin forever blanched by the gastric juices. Edward B. Davis thoroughly researched this event and judged it to be pure fabrication ("A Whale of a Tale: Fundamentalist Fish Stories," *Perspectives on Science and Christian Faith* 43 [1991]: 224–37).

about a prophet. In this respect it bears a much closer resemblance to the legendary accounts of the Former (or Non-Writing) Prophets.

In fact, it is in the Former Prophets that we find a brief reference to "Jonah, son of Amittai." According to 2 Kgs 14:25, Jonah prophesied in Israel during the reign of Jeroboam II (786–746 B.C.E.). This would make Jonah a contemporary of Amos and may explain the proximity of their books in the OT canon.

> "Set out for the great city of Nineveh, and preach against it; their wickedness has come up before me." (Jonah 1:2)

Here, in only the second verse of the book, the narrative drops a bombshell, especially for its ancient readers. God's prophet is sent neither to Israel nor to Judah but to Nineveh: the capital city of the dreaded Assyrian Empire.[3] Assyria was Israel's nemesis. It would eventually prove to be its exterminator as well. Throughout the ancient Near East, its savage atrocities earned this nation a fearsome reputation. Assyria's royal archives attest to its ruthlessness. To assert its dominance, expand its territories, and add to its wealth, Assyria would attack neighboring countries, pillage and burn their cities, and impale their survivors on stakes. At other times, it would behead its enemy's soldiers and erect a massive pyramid of skulls in grotesque commemoration of its victory. One vanquished king had his cheek pierced with a spear and a ring set through his jaw. He was then chained to the east gate of Nineveh as a humiliating spectacle for its citizens' entertainment. In the wake of their conquests, the Assyrian kings demolished foreign idols and altars and erected in their places images of themselves and of their patron gods.[4]

Not surprisingly, the OT prophets despised the Ninevites. Zephaniah, for instance, relishes the city's desolation:

> [God] will stretch out his hand against the north,
>   to destroy Assyria;
> He will make Nineveh a waste,
>   dry as the desert.
> In her midst shall settle in droves
>   all the wild life of the hollows;
> The screech owl and the desert owl
>   shall roost in her columns;

[3]Technically, Nineveh didn't become the capital of the Assyrian Empire until the reign of Sennacherib (704–681 B.C.E.). This transpired after Jonah's career and the demise of Israel (722 B.C.E.).

[4]For the records of these incidents and others, see *ANET,* 274–301.

Their call shall resound from the window,
the raven's croak from the doorway.
Is this the exultant city
that dwelt secure;
That told herself,
"There is no other than I!"
How has she become a waste,
a lair for wild beasts?
Whoever passes by her
hisses, and shakes his fist! (Zeph 2:13–15)

Zephaniah's prediction would see its fulfillment when Nineveh fell to the Babylonians and the Medes in 612 B.C.E. Nahum also speaks against Nineveh, but with even greater vehemence and disdain. In fact, the book of Nahum is devoted exclusively to its destruction:

Woe to the bloody city, all lies,
full of plunder, whose looting never stops!
The crack of the whip, the rumbling sounds of wheels;
horses a-gallop, chariots bounding,
Cavalry charging,
The flame of the sword, the flash of the spear,
the many slain, the heaping corpses,
the endless bodies to stumble upon!
For the many debaucheries of the harlot,
fair and charming, a mistress of witchcraft,
Who enslaved nations with her harlotries,
and peoples by her witchcraft:
I am come against you,
and I will strip your skirt from you;
I will show your nakedness to the nations,
to the kingdoms your shame!
I will cast filth upon you,
disgrace you and put you to shame;
Till everyone who sees you runs from you, saying,
"Nineveh is destroyed; who can pity her?
Where can one find any to console her?" (Nah 3:1–7)

Such sentiments are hardly limited to the prophetic literature. The authors of the OT are fairly consistent with regard to their contempt for the Assyrians and Ninevites.[5] Jonah's reference to it as a "great" city thus refers to its size and might—not its reputation!

[5]The following passage from Tobit is representative: "But before [Tobiah] died, he heard of the destruction of Nineveh and saw its effects. He witnessed the exile of

> But Jonah made ready to flee to Tarshish away from the LORD. He went down to Joppa, found a ship going to Tarshish, paid the fare, and went aboard to journey with them to Tarshish, away from the LORD. (Jonah 1:3)

According to 2 Kgs 14:25, Jonah was from Gath-hepher, a town in the region of Galilee. Nineveh, located on the eastern bank of the Tigris River (near the modern city of Mosul, Iraq), lay 500 miles to the northeast. Instead of going to Nineveh, Jonah went in the exact opposite direction. He immediately set out for Joppa (or Joffa), a port city southwest of Gath-hepher. While early readers of this book would have been sympathetic to Jonah's decision, it would nevertheless have struck them as an unusual one. No biblical prophet had ever demonstrated such blatant disregard for his divinely appointed task.

From Joppa, Jonah "paid the hire" of a ship bound for Tarshish.[6] "Ships of Tarshish," a designation that could refer either to their point of origin or their route of travel, are frequently mentioned throughout the OT.[7] From these references, we know that it was an active, well-known, and fairly distant trading port, popular with importers and merchants alike. The exact location of Tarshish remains unknown to us today (most scholars favor the coast of Spain). Nevertheless, this destination clearly conveys Jonah's intent: get as far away from Nineveh—and from God—as possible!

> The LORD, however, hurled a violent wind upon the sea, and in the furious tempest that arose the ship was on the point of breaking up. (Jonah 1:4)

The Hebrew Bible typically portrays God as the one who subdues the sea. But now, in an effort to rein in his errant prophet, God becomes its agitator. The storm is an especially strong one, and it causes the ship to literally "consider cracking up" (חשבה להשבר, *khishebah*

---

the city's inhabitants when Cyaxares, king of Media, led them captive into Media. Tobiah praised God for all that he had done against the citizens of Nineveh and Assyria. Before dying he rejoiced over Nineveh's destruction, and he blessed the Lord God forever and ever. Amen" (Tob 14:15). Written around the second cent. B.C.E., this text suggests that animosity toward the Ninevites prevailed long after the Assyrian Empire had collapsed.

[6] The Hebrew construction is somewhat ambiguous here, leading some scholars to theorize that Jonah commissioned the ship to take him to Tarshish, rather than wait for one traveling in that direction. This could account for the haste of the departure, as well as the lack of fellow passengers.

[7] So 1 Kgs 22:49 // 2 Chr 20:36; 1 Kgs 10:22 // 2 Chr 9:21; Isa 23:1; 14; 60:9; Ezek 27:25.

lehishaber, a clever Hebrew onomatopoeia that sounds like creaking wooden planks). The mariners are afraid. This is a Gentile crew, and each one cries out to his own god(s). We can imagine waves breaking over the bow and seawater flooding the deck. To keep their ship from sinking, the sailors begin dumping its cargo (1:5).

Meanwhile, Jonah is asleep in the hold. The captain rouses him and begs him to pray. As the storm continues, the seamen become desperate. Attributing the gale to divine wrath, they cast lots to determine the guilty party. The results implicate Jonah, who confesses that he is fleeing the Lord, "the God of heaven, who made the sea and the dry land" (1:9). Jonah's solution is simple. To silence the squall, the sailors must throw him overboard (1:12). At first, Jonah's suggestion seems so outlandish that the shipmen ignore it. Instead, they redouble their efforts to row back to shore. But the bad weather only intensifies. Terrified for their lives, they are left with no alternative.

> Then they cried to the Lord: "We beseech you, O Lord, let us not perish for taking this man's life; do not charge us with innocent blood, for you, Lord, have done as you saw fit." Then they took Jonah and threw him into the sea, and the sea's raging abated. Struck with great fear of the Lord, the men offered sacrifice and made vows to him. (Jonah 1:14–16)

One might recall from earlier chapters that the greatest affront to God, as far as the Law and the Prophets are concerned, is idolatry. Yet the book of Jonah presents the idolatrous sailors as wholly righteous. They go to great lengths to spare Jonah's life. Even when faced with no other choice, they beg God's forgiveness for tossing a (not so) "innocent man" into the sea. The storm miraculously subsides, and the idolaters immediately convert.[8] They literally "sacrifice sacrifices" and "vow vows" to the Lord. Their efforts to appease God contrast sharply with Jonah's, who has sought only to avoid him.

Scholars debate the intention behind Jonah's offer. Was he so concerned for the lives of the mariners that he was willing to lay down his own? At first glance, it might appear this way. But was such a dramatic

[8] The entire episode bears a striking similarity to Ps 107:23–30: "Some went off to sea in ships, / plied their trade on the deep waters. / They saw the works of the Lord, / the wonders of God in the deep. / He spoke and roused a storm wind; / it tossed the waves on high. / They rose up to the heavens, sank to the depths; / their hearts trembled at the danger. / They reeled, staggered like drunkards; / their skill was of no avail. / In their distress they cried to the Lord, / who brought them out of their peril, / Hushed the storm to a murmur; / the waves of the sea were stilled. . . ."

act really necessary? Jonah divulged his secret to the crew. Why didn't he come clean before God? Surely God would have honored a heartfelt confession and a nautical u-turn! In light of such reasoning, many commentators contend that Jonah's solution marks the prophet's stubborn refusal to do what God has asked of him. In other words, Jonah would rather drown than preach to the Ninevites.

Jonah 2

> But the Lord sent a large fish, that swallowed Jonah; and he remained in the belly of the fish three days and three nights . . .
>
> Then the Lord commanded the fish to spew Jonah upon the shore.
>
> (Jonah 2:1, 11)

The creature in question is simply a large "fish" (דגה, *dagah*). Technically, the ancient Hebrews had no term for "whale." Thus, any attempt to determine the exact species on the basis of this word is pure conjecture. Popular conception of the whale stems from the Greek translation of the text, which employs the word κῆτος (*kētos*), or "sea monster." The fish serves God's purpose by delivering Jonah from certain death and putting him back on track in the direction of Nineveh.

> From the belly of the fish Jonah said this prayer to the Lord, his God:
> Out of my distress I called to the Lord,
> and he answered me;
> From the midst of the nether world I cried for help,
> and you heard my voice.
> For you cast me into the deep, into the heart of the sea,
> and the flood enveloped me;
> All your breakers and your billows passed over me.
> Then I said, "I am banished from your sight!
> yet would I again look upon your holy temple."
> The waters swirled about me, threatening my life;
> the abyss enveloped me;
> seaweed clung about my head.
> Down I went to the roots of the mountains;
> the bars of the nether world
> were closing behind me forever,
> But you brought my life up from the pit,
> O Lord, my God.
> When my soul fainted within me,
> I remembered the Lord;
> My prayer reached you
> in your holy temple.

Those who worship vain idols
forsake their source of mercy.
But I, with resounding praise,
will sacrifice to you;
What I have vowed I will pay:
deliverance is from the LORD. (Jonah 2:2–10)

As far as scholars are concerned, one of the most contentious passages in this work is Jonah's prayer in the belly of the fish. Actually, the prayer is more of a hymn, a pastiche of phrases that bear a remarkable resemblance to various passages in the Psalms.[9] Did it originally belong in the narrative, or was it an independent and/or later addition to the text? The matter might seem trifling, but it has a significant effect on the portrayal of Jonah. Its inclusion or exclusion leads to two opposite—and to some extent, diametrically opposed—characterizations of the prophet. If, for example, this prayer is original, then we are presented with a contrite and pious figure. Here is a man who has completely reversed his former ways. He no longer seeks to avoid God; he calls directly upon him. Perhaps his near-death experience prompted a change of heart? At any rate, Jonah's devotion now rivals the seamen: he pledges to offer sacrifices and to make good on his vows. Obviously, he is grateful for God's merciful intervention. Such is the story line as we presently have it.

But many literary experts (I daresay most) suspect that this prayer was inserted into an already integral plot. There are good reasons to support this contention. Aside from the arguments based on style, grammar, and vocabulary, the psalm is conceptually inconsistent with the rest of the narrative. For example: (1) The psalmist blames God for casting him into the sea. There is no acknowledgement either of Jonah's own guilt or of the sailors' actions. (2) The psalmist's "deliverance" is in response to his plea for help. Yet according to the narrative, God sent the fish on his own accord. There is no reference to Jonah's request for assistance. (3) The psalmist holds in high regard God's "holy temple," the typical designation for Jerusalem's sanctuary. Yet as a resident of Israel, Jonah would not have worshiped there, since Jerusalem and its temple belonged to the southern kingdom of Judah. (4) The tone of the prayer is deferential, pious, and appreciative toward God. Its speaker

---

[9]Jack Sasson (*Jonah* [AB 24B; Garden City, N.Y.: Doubleday, 1990], 168–201) lists more than three dozen "illustrative passages" that correspond to Jonah's prayer. The vast majority of these are from the Psalms.

seems eager to please. Nowhere else in this narrative is Jonah portrayed as such. (5) The psalmist, in the tradition of the Law and the Prophets, condemns idolaters. But as we have noted, the idolaters are, so far, the only righteous characters in the book! (6) The psalmist joyfully celebrates his "deliverance." Yet according to the story line, Jonah is still entombed within the bowels of the fish. From there, a favorable outcome remains quite a presumption. (7) Finally, the psalmist seeks to escape death. As previously discussed, Jonah seems to court it.

Without the prayer, we have a different take on Jonah. He has sought to elude God and his divine charge by ending his life, but he has obviously underestimated the Almighty. God has trumped every one of Jonah's evasive maneuvers. He has proven impossible to dodge.[10] Having been vomited back onto the shore, Jonah is no doubt exasperated and resentful. Thus defeated, he is approached by God a second time.

Jonah 3

> The word of the Lord came to Jonah a second time: "Set out for the great city of Nineveh, and announce to it the message that I will tell you." So Jonah made ready and went to Nineveh, according to the Lord's bidding. Now Nineveh was an enormously large city; it took three days to go through it. Jonah began his journey through the city, and had gone but a single day's walk announcing, "Forty days more and Nineveh shall be destroyed." (Jonah 3:1–4)

In addition to its syllabic spelling, ancient cuneiform texts employ a rather curious combination of symbols to denote the city-name of Nineveh. One resembles the sign of an enclosure (i.e., a temple or a house). Within that appears the mark of a fish. Scholars have speculated over the relationship (if any) between the etymological roots of the city's name and the emergence of later traditions such as Jonah. However, there is little consensus on this matter.

What we do know is that, at the peak of the Assyrian Empire, Nineveh was indeed a large city. Its walls encompassed an area 7.75 miles in circumference, 1,850 acres in all. Therefore, the population given in Jonah 4:11 ("more than 120,000 individuals") appears entirely

---

[10] In this respect, Jonah's experience resonates closely with Ps 139:7–10: "Where can I go from your spirit? / from your presence where can I flee? / If I go up to the heavens, you are there; / if I sink to the nether world, you are present there. / If I take the wings of the dawn, if I settle at the farthest limits of the sea, / even there your hand shall guide me, / and your right hand hold me fast."

plausible.[11] Of course, compared with the world's megalopolises of today, such statistics are fairly negligible. But relative to pre-exilic Jerusalem—125 acres and a citizenry under 25,000—Nineveh's dimensions would have been staggering. The text literally describes it as עיר־גדולה לאלהים (*'ir-gedolah le'lohim*), "a city great to God."

As formidable as Nineveh must have seemed, it is difficult to account for the supposed three-day journey needed to traverse it. Given its historical dimensions, Jonah should have been able to completely circumnavigate Nineveh in under three hours, let alone cross it in three days! Various explanations for this discrepancy have been offered. Perhaps Jonah was including Nineveh's suburbs as well? Perhaps he was stopping along the way to chat with those whom he met? Or maybe, in his effort to be especially thorough, Jonah became lost and disoriented while taking a circuitous path through Nineveh's narrow and winding streets? While such explanations are reasonable, they are incompatible with the Jonah portrayed by the text. With his curt, five-word declaration, the prophet's contempt for his assignment is evident. This is the shortest OT prophecy on record. Unlike his contemporaries, Jonah provides no explanation for God's wrath and extends no invitation to repent. He merely announces a time frame in which Nineveh will be "overthrown."[12] This is hardly a man intent on expanding the scope of his mission, understanding Nineveh's inhabitants, or even communicating his message with due diligence.

The three-day span, therefore, is most likely the product of historical aggrandizement. By the time Jonah was written, Nineveh may have existed only as a distant memory, its size and reputation now the stuff of legends. Nevertheless, the temporal reference serves an important narrative purpose: it underscores the swiftness of the people's response.

> The people of Nineveh believed God; they proclaimed a fast and all of them, great and small, put on sackcloth.
>
> When the news reached the king of Nineveh, he rose from his throne, laid aside his robe, covered himself with sackcloth, and sat in the ashes. Then he had this

[11] According to Simo Parpola, chief editor of the State Archives of Assyria project, the population of Nineveh just prior to its collapse could have exceeded 300,000 (Sasson, *Jonah,* 311–12).

[12] Some of the texts have "three days" instead of "forty." While the former would parallel Jonah's sojourn in the whale and better account for the Ninevites' quick response, it is most likely an editorial gloss. Elsewhere in the OT, the verb "overthrown" (מהפכה, *maheppekah*) is applied almost exclusively to Sodom and Gomorrah (cf. Deut 29:22; Isa 1:7; 13:19; Jer 49:18; 50:40; Amos 4:11).

> proclaimed throughout Nineveh, by decree of the king and his nobles: "Neither man nor beast, neither cattle nor sheep, shall taste anything; they shall not eat, nor shall they drink water. Man and beast shall be covered with sackcloth and call loudly to God; every man shall turn from his evil way and from the violence he has in his hand. Who knows, God may relent and forgive, and withhold his blazing wrath, so that we shall not perish." (Jonah 3:5–10)

Yet again the story of Jonah radically departs from the tradition of the HB. To Israel and Judah, God sent a number of prophets on multiple occasions with detailed indictments, threats of impending punishment, and repeated calls for reform—all to no avail. Now a solitary, tight-lipped spokesperson barely utters five words a third of the way through an infamous city, and the entire populace, from least to greatest, immediately repents. Even its animals participate![13] The Ninevites, those bloodthirsty heathens of the ancient Near East, become models of humility and obedience. This study in contrasts marks the apparent fulfillment of God's words to Ezekiel:

> Not to a people with difficult speech and barbarous language am I sending you, nor to the many peoples [with difficult speech and barbarous language] whose words you cannot understand. If I were to send you to these, they would listen to you; but the house of Israel will refuse to listen to you, since they will not listen to me. (Ezek 32:5–7)

It is worth noting that Jonah portrays the king of Nineveh as having an instrumental role in the city's conversion. The OT tends to portray the Assyrian kings just the reverse. Haughty and boastful, they mock and ridicule the power of God.[14]

In the book of Jonah, it is the king's hope that God will change his mind and spare the city of Nineveh. Indeed, such hope is well-founded. According to a story repeated in 2 Kgs 20:1–6, 2 Chr 32:24–26, and Isa 38:1–6, the Israelite king Hezekiah was able to successfully (if only

---

[13]While this detail seems embellished, it may be rooted in historical practice. During ancient festivals and celebrations, domesticated animals were often decorated with colorful garlands. Similarly, during periods of mourning, they bore appropriate signs of grief (see Jdt 4:9–12).

[14]So, e.g., Isa 10:5–37; 2 Kgs 18:13–36; 19:1–37. An intriguing parallel to Jonah's story line has been found among the Assyrian archives. An instruction to one of the governors from an unknown monarch (reigning sometime between the ninth and eighth centuries B.C.E.) reads: "Over a three-day period, you and your district's citizen should pray and perform a public weeping before the god Adad. Purge all your land and fields, and offer many burnt-sacrifices. The purification of the *nakarkanu*-house should be undertaken within one full day, so that you many bring about the reconciliation of Adad" (cited in Sasson, *Jonah,* 245).

temporarily) avoid an Assyrian invasion through prayer, humility, and faithful conduct. In the book of Joel, fasting, sacrifices, and pleas for mercy stir God to pity the Judeans and deliver them from a devastating plague of locusts (Joel 2:12–18). And through the prophet Jeremiah, God explains that "if that nation which I have threatened turns from its evil, I also repent of the evil which I threatened to do" (Jer 18:8).

As promising as these examples may seem, God's compassion is hardly automatic. A complementary tradition in the HB affirms God's unwavering commitment to justice: "God is not man that he should speak falsely, nor human, that he should change his mind. Is he one to speak and not act, to decree and not fulfill?" (Num 23:19; similarly, 1 Sam 15:29). This tradition insists that God's course of action, especially when it involves chastising the wicked, cannot be influenced by lobbying or swayed by manipulative conduct. For instance, to punish King David for his murderous affair with Bathsheba, God pledged to take the life of their child. In a desperate appeal for the child's life, David donned sackcloth and fasted continuously for seven days. Nevertheless, the child died (2 Sam 12:13–18). Because the OT frequently and simultaneously affirms God's mercy *and* justice, Nineveh's fate hangs perilously in the balance.

> When God saw by their actions how they turned from their evil way, he repented of the evil that he had threatened to do to them; he did not carry it out. (Jonah 3:10)

Though either of God's actions toward Nineveh would have been justified, his ultimate decision demonstrates that his mercy is greater than his wrath. This notion accords well with the numerous OT passages which extend God's condemnation to the third or fourth generation but his mercy down to the thousandth (e.g., Exod 20:5–6; 34:6–7; Num 14:18; Deut 5:9–10; Jer 32:18).

Jonah 4

> But this was greatly displeasing to Jonah, and he became angry. "I beseech you, Lord," he prayed, "is not this what I said while I was still in my own country? This is why I fled at first to Tarshish. I knew that you are a gracious and merciful God, slow to anger, rich in clemency, loathe to punish. And now, Lord, please take my life from me; for it is better for me to die than to live." (Jonah 4:1–3)

God's pronouncement does not sit well with Jonah, nor would it have sat well with Jonah's original audience. We now learn the real reason why Jonah sought to avoid his calling. Jonah knew that God's kindness surpassed his indignation. Therefore, as the Lord's spokesperson, Jonah suspected that he might be made the instrument of the Ninevites' deliverance. Clearly Jonah prefers their annihilation—and if not theirs, then his!

Here again we encounter another prophetic irony. After Israel and Judah failed to repent and met their respective ends, the prophets remained optimistic and comforted the survivors with encouraging words of hope. But when Nineveh succeeds at repenting and avoids its destruction, Jonah despairs to the point of death! His request that God take his life acknowledges his own failure to do so in Jonah 2.

Despite God's words, Jonah clings to the possibility that he will change his mind about Nineveh. Jonah takes his position outside the city, presumably in anticipation of its ruin. There, the prophet soon learns the reason for God's forbearance.

> Jonah then left the city for a place to the east of it . . . to see what would happen to the city. And when the LORD God provided a gourd plant that grew up over Jonah's head, giving shade that relieved him of any discomfort, Jonah was very happy over the plant. But the next morning at dawn God sent a worm which attacked the plant, so that it withered. And when the sun arose, God sent a burning east wind; and the sun beat upon Jonah's head till he became faint. Then he asked for death, saying, "I would be better off dead than alive." But God said to Jonah, "Have you reason to be angry over the plant?" "I have reason to be angry," Jonah answered, "angry enough to die." (Jonah 4:5–9)

God creates a plant which provides Jonah considerable relief from the hot sun. Jonah literally "rejoiced . . . with great joy" (וישמח . . . שמחה גדולה, *wayyismakh . . . simkhah gedolah*) over the vegetation. But when it wilts, Jonah once again despairs unto death.[15] God has cleverly channeled the negative emotion that Jonah had just expressed regarding the Ninevites' salvation into what he now feels in the aftermath of the plant's demise.[16] Jonah's sentimental shift enables God to drive home his point:

---

[15] The similarity between Jonah under his castor-bean plant and Elijah under the broom tree (1 Kgs 19) is probably deliberate. Both prophets are discouraged and prefer death over life. Ironically, though, Elijah despairs over his failure to turn the heart of heathens to God, whereas Jonah despairs precisely because he has done so.

[16] The correspondence between people's lives and fragile greenery, especially grass, is a common motif in the OT (e.g., 2 Kgs 19:26; Job 5:25; 8:12; Ps 37:2; 90:5; 102:11; 103:15; 129:6; Isa 37:27; 40:6–8; 44:4; 51:12). On numerous occasions, the HB also likens Israel to a vine. But had the author of Jonah intended that comparison, he would

> Then the Lord said, "You are concerned over the plant which cost you no labor and which you did not raise; it came up in one night and in one night it perished. And should I not be concerned over Nineveh, the great city, in which there are more than a hundred and twenty thousand persons who cannot distinguish their right hand from their left, not to mention the many cattle?" (Jonah 4:10–11)

In essence, God makes an emotional appeal to Jonah. As much as Jonah abhorred his assignment, loathed the Ninevites, and resented the loss of the plant, so does God abhor, loathe, and resent the demise of the Ninevites—even exponentially more. Therefore, God has decreed their continued existence. God has a great deal invested in them!

The concluding emphasis on God's mercy and salvation matches up with the events at the end of Jonah 2. In fact, with hindsight, one can discern a parallel symmetry which encompasses the entire book of Jonah (see table 7.1).

The Parallel Symmetry of the Book of Jonah

Part 1 (Jonah 1–2)	**Part 2 (Jonah 3–4)**
Jonah is commissioned to go to Nineveh	Jonah is commissioned to go to Nineveh
Jonah disobeys	Jonah obeys
A notorious group of Gentiles (idolatrous sailors) proves to be meritorious	A notorious group of Gentiles (violent Ninevites) proves to be meritorious
They appeal to God and escape destruction	They appeal to God and escape destruction
Jonah courts death	Jonah courts death
God's response: sends fish	God's response: sends plant
Emphasis on God's mercy/salvation	Emphasis on God's mercy/salvation

Table 7.1

Jonah's Original Audience and the Purpose of This Book

From our preceding analysis, it should be fairly clear by now that the story of Jonah really isn't about the whale. But what is its point? The

---

have used the standard word for it, rather than the highly unusual קִיקָיוֹן (*qiqayon*), "castor-bean plant."

symmetry above underscores the importance (especially for Gentiles) of appealing to/repenting before God. It also emphasizes the abundance of God's mercy, even relative to his commitment to justice. But these points only beg the question: Assuming that Jonah's original readers were not Gentiles, what sort practical lesson was this work trying to communicate?

To answer this question one must identify who those readers were. But scholars have yet to establish a definitive date for this work.[17] Broadly speaking, three possibilities exist: pre-exilic (eighth to early seventh centuries), exilic (sixth century), or post-exilic (fifth to third centuries). Space here forbids us from rehearsing the arguments and evidence for each of these options. Suffice it to say that the application of this narrative changes according to its original context. If it was written prior to Assyria's demise, then this work presents Nineveh as a sterling example for Israel and Judah to follow.[18] If it was written after the exile, it may serve to justify the authority that the Gentiles (specifically, the Persians) continued to wield over the Jews.[19]

However, one of the most intriguing possibilities is that Jonah was written during the Babylonian exile, specifically for the exiles themselves. The setting itself is quite suggestive. At twenty-five hundred acres, the magnitude of ancient Babylon surpassed even that of Nineveh. And surrounded as they were by their Gentile enemies, the Judahites would have had to learn to peaceably co-exist. Like Jonah among the Assyrians, this was the exiles' divinely appointed burden. Perhaps the ignominy of it could be eased with the knowledge that God cared about these foreigners, too?

Several other factors favor an exilic dating for the book of Jonah. (1) As previously discussed, the narrative presents Nineveh in a legendary way, suggesting chronological distance. (2) In some OT texts, Babylon and Assyria are closely interrelated and occasionally even

---

[17] We know that it could have been written no earlier than the eighth cent. B.C.E. (when the prophet lived), nor any later than the second cent. B.C.E. (when Sir 49:10 refers to the collection of Minor Prophets as "the book of the Twelve"). Virtually all of the periods within this time span have been proposed. Of course, the only one that doesn't have much support would be the period immediately following Nineveh's destruction.

[18] This seems highly unlikely, especially given the legendary characterization of Nineveh.

[19] This also seems unlikely, given the OT's generally positive portrayal of Persia, the nation responsible for releasing the exiles from their captivity.

confused.[20] (3) Jonah's theology resonates perhaps most strongly with that of the exilic prophets, especially Jeremiah and Ezekiel.[21] (4) Finally, as a parody of prophecy, the book of Jonah presumes that its readers are already familiar with the typical experiences and messages of the biblical prophets. Table 7.2 (next page) highlights some of these contrasts.

Beyond these reasons, the unique experience of the Babylonian exiles may serve to reveal Jonah's primary purpose. These exiles knew, of course, that Nineveh was but a distant memory. Ultimately, it failed to survive. Nevertheless, the narrative emphasizes God's concern for the Assyrians and his desire for their well-being. Given the generosity of God's mercy, a single act of genuine repentance was all that was needed to forestall their destruction. And if God was this invested in the Ninevites, how much more was he invested in Israel and Judah? This explains why God sent them even more prophets and gave them even more opportunities to repent. To some extent, then, the book of Jonah offers a rather scathing critique of the stubbornness of God's chosen people, a critique precisely along the lines of Ezek 3:5–7. It is a critique that both justifies their exile and vindicates the Almighty.

But the book of Jonah does more than account for this people's turbulent history. It also comments upon their then-current situation. Unlike the (historical) Assyrians, the exiled Judahites had not been obliterated. A remnant has survived. And this remnant is proof positive of God's deep-rooted and ongoing investment in his people. It is a remnant that, with just the right guidance, might learn to appreciate the power of repentance and come to experience the mercy of their Maker. Perhaps it is precisely this whale of a task that the little book of Jonah aims to accomplish.

---

[20] Assyria and Babylon are closely associated in passages like Jer 50:17–18 and Ezek 23:22–24. In the book of Judith (1:1) Nebuchadnezzar is referred to as "king of the Assyrians in the great city of Nineveh." This reference is historically inaccurate. Nebuchadnezzar was king of the Babylonians (605–562 B.C.E.). In fact, his father Nabopolassar had helped to destroy Nineveh prior to his son's reign.

[21] Cf. esp. Jer 18:1–10; 26:3, 12–13; Ezek 3:5–9; 18:21–32.

Comparison of Jonah's Experience with That of the Old Testament Prophets

Feature	Old Testament Prophets	Jonah
God's prophets sent to	God's people (Israelites and Judahites)	God's "enemies" (Assyrians)
Number of prophets sent	Many	One
Prophets' response	Obedient (some eager)	Disobedient (goes the other way)
When calamity befalls	Prophets endeavor to save the people	The people (sailors) endeavor to save the prophet
Lawlessness	The people are reluctant to abandon their crimes even after the prophets tell them to	The sailors are reluctant to commit a crime even after Jonah tells them to
Prophetic message	Lengthy, detailed	Only five Hebrew words
	Specific crimes cited	No crimes cited
	Pleas for repentance	No invitation to repent
	Vague timing	Specific timing
Prophets' audience	Ignores, counters, even persecutes the prophets	Repentance is swift (⅓ through city) and thorough (least to greatest, even animals)
Result	Israel and Judah devastated	Nineveh preserved
Prophetic outlook	Amid devastation, hope	Amid preservation, anger, disappointment, and despair
Gist of prophetic message	God's justification for the punishment of his people	God's justification for the preservation of the Ninevites

Table 7.2

8

The Book of Daniel —Prophecy of the End

FOCUS TEXT: DANIEL

A Modern Apocalypse: The Bible Code

One of the most recent, widespread, and sophisticated claims of prophecy in our time is *The Bible Code* (Simon & Schuster, 1997). This nonfiction work soared as high as number 3 during a remarkable eighteen-week debut on the *New York Times* best seller list.[1] While not quite as successful, its sequel, *The Bible Code II: The Countdown* (Penguin, 2002) also made the list.[2] Both books were written by Michael Drosnin, a well-respected investigative journalist with the *Washington Post* and the *Wall Street Journal,* and author of *Citizen Hughes,* an exposé of the private life of billionaire Howard Hughes.

The Bible Code begins quite dramatically, with Drosnin warning Israeli Prime Minister Yitzhak Rabin about an impending assassination: his own. The date was September 1, 1994, and Drosnin had found Rabin's full name encoded in the Bible with the words "assassin that will assassinate" crossing it. Although Drosnin's earnest admonition reached Rabin in plenty of time, the prime minister brushed it off. Just over a year later, on November 4, 1995, an assassin's bullet claimed Rabin's life. For Drosnin, this event solidified the authenticity of the Bible code.

[1] The eighteen weeks spanned from June 22 to October 19, 1997.
[2] Its stay lasted for four weeks between January 19 and February 2, 2003.

The Bible code is premised upon the principle of the Equidistant Letter Sequence (ELS). This is the process of detecting a meaningful word using letters spaced equally apart in a given text. In 1958, for instance, Rabbi Weissmandel discovered several relatively simple ELSs in the Torah. Most notably, he perceived that if one opens the book of Genesis and begins with the first Hebrew *t* (ת), and then counts exactly 50 letters to find *w* (ו), and then 50 more to find *r* (ר), and then 50 more to find *h* (ה), the resulting word (תורה, *torah*) is Torah. This could be the result of coincidence, except that the same pattern also emerges in the book of Exodus. Weissmandel found similarly compelling ELSs in the books of Leviticus, Numbers, and Deuteronomy.[3]

Using Weissmandel's observations as a starting point, a three-man Israeli team of mathematicians and computer scientists—Doron Witztum, Eliyahu Rips, and Yoav Rosenberg (henceforth, WRR)—created a computer program to perform more sophisticated searches for ELSs in Genesis. The algorithm they used provided an exhaustive, two-dimensional analysis of the text, permitting very high, and even negative, skip sequences. Essentially, the program turns the entire text into a series of word-search puzzles, whereby designated terms can be sought out in backward, forward, and even diagonal positions. (For a simplified yet portentous example, see Appendix G.) Statisticians universally agree that ELSs can be found in any text of sufficient length. But what this team sought to determine was whether the Bible contains associated word clusters (such as baseball/Yankees/Ruth, or Potter/Hogwarts/Rowling) in compact form more frequently than they would be expected to occur by chance.

For their experiment, WRR chose an encyclopedia list of thirty-two famous rabbis and searched Genesis to determine whether the names of these men could be found in proximity to the dates of their births and deaths. According to their results, they could. They then performed the same search on a control sample, a Hebrew version of Tolstoy's *War and Peace*. The latter experiment failed. Thus able to demonstrate the significance of their work, the trio published their findings in *Statistical Science*.[4] In a follow-up, independent test, Harold Gans, a senior code breaker at the National Security Agency, wrote his own

[3] H. M. D. Weissmandel, *Torath Hemed* (Mt. Kisco, N.Y.: Yeshivath Mt. Kisco, 1958).

[4] "Equidistant Letter Sequences in the Book of Genesis," *Statistical Science* 9 (1994): 429–38.

program to contest the Israelis' results. Using the text of Genesis, he tried cross-checking the names of the thirty-two rabbis with the names of the cities in which they were born or died. To Gans's surprise, the cities correlated as well.

Such findings so intrigued Drosnin that he taught himself Hebrew and obtained his own Bible code program, one that utilizes all 304,805 letters of the Torah. Drosnin claims that virtually every significant event or person from history can be found meaningfully encrypted within it. Some examples of the clusters that he cites can be found in table 8.1.

Bible Code Word Clusters		
Twin towers it knocked down twice airplane	The depression 1929 economic collapse stocks	Atomic holocaust 1945 Japan
Shakespeare Macbeth Hamlet presented on stage	Kennedy to die Dallas	Newton gravity
Hitler evil man Nazi and enemy slaughter	Edison electricity light bulb	Man on moon spaceship
Oswald marksman name of assassin who will assassinate	Watergate Who is he? President, but he was kicked out	Wright brothers airplane

Table 8.1

These clusters, of course, represent predictions after the event—what scholars call *ex eventu* prophecies. But Drosnin contends that the Bible code can effectively be applied to the future as well. In addition to the assassination of Rabin, the Bible code allegedly indicated the precise dates of the start of the Gulf War and of a significant Jupiter/comet collision prior to their occurrences. According to Drosnin, the Bible code also foretells a modern apocalypse: an atomic holocaust involving Israel that will usher in the end of the world. In this respect, Drosnin believes that the timing of the discovery of the Bible code—coinciding with the advent of the computer age—is fortuitous. Its embedded messages have emerged just in time to warn and perhaps even save civilization as we know it.

Of course, not everyone is convinced of the Bible code's legitimacy. Among its numerous critics, perhaps the most prominent is Brendan McKay, professor of computer science at Australian National University. McKay assembled his own team and refuted the findings of WRR and Gans in an article that was also published in *Statistical Science.*[5] Essentially, McKay's group found that the success of WRR and Gans was largely attributed to the wide variations of the rabbis' names, to the flexibility of Hebrew spelling (which allows a word to be constructed with vowels, without vowels, or some permutation thereof), and to the specific version of the Genesis text used.[6] The researchers discovered that once these factors were accounted for, similar results can indeed be obtained from comparable texts, including *War and Peace.*

Even in the face of such criticism, most Bible code proponents have continued to maintain their positions. Drosnin publicly responded to the skeptics by stating, "When my critics find a message about the assassination of a prime minister encrypted in *Moby Dick,* I'll believe them."[7] McKay promptly met Drosnin's challenge by finding numerous word clusters pertaining to the assassinations of Indira Gandhi, Rene Moawad, Leon Trotsky, Martin Luther King Jr., Robert Kennedy, John F. Kennedy, Abraham Lincoln, and Yitzhak Rabin, among others, all encoded within the English edition of *Moby Dick.*[8]

Some of Drosnin's harshest critics, however, have been those whose work he has relied upon so heavily. While Eliyahu Rips, Doron Witz-

---

[5] "Solving the Bible Code Puzzle," *Statistical Science* 14 (1999): 150–73.

[6] As McKay et al. point out, WRR used the widely accepted, standardized Koren version of the Hebrew text. This text is based on the Leningrad Codex, a complete OT manuscript from ca. 1009 C.E. However, the most recent and scholarly critical editions of the Hebrew text demonstrate a fair degree of alternative readings, scribal changes, and other such variants. Indeed, fragments from the Dead Sea Scrolls, which predate the Leningrad Codex by more than one thousand years, suggest the comparative rate of textual variation ranges anywhere from 1 out of 1,200 letters to 1 out of 20. Using the most conservative estimate in this range, these figures imply that of the 304,805 Hebrew letters of the Torah, at least 254 of them are in dispute. Because the Bible code's outcomes depend upon a fixed text, even a small number of letter changes (especially additions or omissions) completely alter the results.

[7] Sharon Begley, "Seek and Ye Shall Find," *Newsweek* (June 9, 1997), 66–67.

[8] These clusters and other information can be found on McKay's Web site, "Scientific Refutation of the Bible Codes," at http://cs.anu.edu.au/~bdm/dilugim/torah.html (accessed March 27, 2008). Other respondents have been less charitable, using the text of *The Bible Code* to reveal clusters such as hoax/fake/fraud/charlatan/snake oil.

tum, and Harold Gans continue to defend the statistical significance of their studies, they have publicly distanced themselves and their work from Drosnin and his conclusions. On this one point these three researchers agree: the Bible code cannot be used to predict future events.[9] In fact, the clusters that led Drosnin to envision an impending apocalypse specified the years in which it would occur—years that have since passed. Obviously, the world didn't end. But Drosnin hasn't conceded defeat. The unfulfilled prophecies have merely prompted rationales for the delay and revised timetables.

So what does Drosnin's *The Bible Code* have to do with our study of the OT prophets? As it turns out, this contemporary work provides an excellent basis for understanding the visions contained in the book of Daniel, though not through any type of ELS analysis. Rather, as we will demonstrate, these two works share a striking number of functional similarities.

An Old Testament Apocalypse: The Book of Daniel

In the Jewish Scriptures, the book of Daniel can be found among the Writings, alongside much of the Wisdom Literature. Christian tradition, by contrast, considers Daniel a major prophet, and so his book follows Ezekiel's. To be fair, this text contains elements of both wisdom and prophecy, yet it is distinctly neither.

Wisdom Elements (Dan 1–6)

Structurally speaking, the book of Daniel can be divided rather neatly in half. Daniel 1–6 contains heroic stories of its namesake, a clever Judahite courtier serving under foreign kings, and his associates during the period of their exile. Some of the most memorable and

---

[9]Rips: "For me, it was a catalyst to ask whether we can, from a scientific point of view, attempt to use the Codes to predict future events. After much thought, my categorical answer is no." Gans: "The book states that the codes in the Torah can be used to predict future events. This is absolutely unfounded." Witztum: "Mr. Drosnin's book is based on a false claim. It is impossible to use Torah codes to predict the future." The complete statements of these scholars can be found at http://leko2labs.free.fr/torah.htm (accessed March 27, 2008).

beloved tales of the OT are found here, including the three men in the fiery furnace (3:1–27) and Daniel in the lion's den (6:2–28). This first section presents models of Jewish wisdom, piety, and integrity. The stories maintain God's vindication of the upright and demonstrate how one can bear witness to a covenant-based faith and even prosper in the challenging and sometimes hostile conditions under Gentile rule. In this respect, the book bears the closest similarity to some of the writings of the Wisdom Literature. In subsequent chapters, we shall examine representatives of that literature more closely. For now, however, we will focus primarily on the second half of this book, which contains the bulk of the prophetic material.

Daniel's Visions (Dan 7–12)

Daniel 7–12 consists of a series of strange and fantastic visions whose meanings are subsequently revealed by angelic intermediaries. For Daniel, the experience is anything but pleasant. It causes him to feel "terrified" (7:1, 15, 28), "anguished" (7:15), "faint" (8:18, 9:9), "appalled" (8:27), "weak and ill" (8:27), and "powerless" (9:8, 16). He is "seized with pangs" (9:16), his "face blanched" (7:28) as he falls "prostrate in terror" (8:17) turning "the color of death" (9:8) with "no strength or even breath left" (9:17). What could possibly cause such tremendous physical and emotional distress? As it turns out, Daniel has been permitted a glimpse of the apocalypse, a period of unprecedented evil that will usher in the end of the world! Three consecutive visions convey the details.

The First Vision (Dan 7)

In his first vision (Dan 7), Daniel watches as four immense beasts come forth from the sea. The first is a lion with eagle's wings, the second a bear with three tusks, and the third a leopard with four heads and four wings. The last beast is exceedingly more powerful and horrifying than the rest. It devours everything in its path with its fearsome iron teeth and crushes what remains with its feet. This beast has ten horns, and another little horn that speaks arrogantly. The little horn provokes the Ancient One, who arises and convenes his divine court. In accordance with its judgment, the last beast and its little horn are destroyed. Their dominion is conferred upon "one like a son of man" and the holy people of the Most High.

The Second Vision (Dan 8)

In his second vision (Dan 8), Daniel sees a powerful ram with two great horns, one larger and newer than the other. The ram dominates the land until a goat with a prominent horn suddenly charges from the west and overthrows it. The prominent horn gives way to four others. From their midst emerges another little horn. This little horn persecutes the righteous ones and desecrates the holy sanctuary. After a time, this little horn is broken.

The Third Vision (Dan 10–12)

In his third vision (Dan 10–12), Daniel perceives four kings of Persia, who are supplanted by a powerful sovereign from Greece. The empire of the latter does not last long, however. Following his death, it is torn to pieces. A war breaks out between the rulers of the north and the south. The north prevails. Shortly thereafter, "a despicable person" rises to power in "the glorious land." He commits all sorts of atrocities against the righteous ones during a time of unsurpassed distress. His reign, however, is brought to an end when the forces of God arise against it. At that point, the dead are raised and the wise have their vindication.

Nebuchadnezzar's Dream (Dan 2)

To these three visions, we can also add the content of Nebuchadnezzar's dream, which Daniel describes and later interprets in Dan 2:

> "In your vision, O king, you saw a statue, very large and exceedingly bright, terrifying in appearance as it stood before you. The head of the statue was pure gold, its chest and arms were silver, its belly and thighs bronze, the legs iron, its feet partly iron and partly tile. While you looked at the statue, a stone which was hewn from a mountain without a hand being put to it, struck its iron and tile feet, breaking them in pieces. The iron, tile, bronze, silver, and gold all crumbled at once, fine as the chaff on the threshing floor in summer, and the wind blew them away without leaving a trace. But the stone that struck the statue became a great mountain that filled the whole earth." (Dan 2:31–35)

Collective Correspondence: The Meaning of the Visions

Although they vary in detail and symbolic representation, the three visions of Dan 7–12 and Nebuchadnezzar's dream in Dan 2 all

Daniel's Visions and Their Meanings

	Daniel 2	Daniel 7	Daniel 8	Daniel 10–12
	Second year of Nebuchadnezzar[10] *(586 B.C.E.?)*	*First year of Belshazzar (553 B.C.E.?)*	*Third year of Belshazzar (551 B.C.E.?)*	*Third year of Cyrus (537 B.C.E.?)*
	Large statue[11]	*Four beasts*	*Ram and goat*	*[None]*
Babylon (605–539)	Gold head	Lion with eagle's wings	[no mention]	[no mention]
Medes (605–539[12])	Silver chest, arms	Bear with three fangs	The smaller, older ram's horn	[no mention]
Persians (539–331)	Bronze torso, thighs	Leopard with four heads and four wings	The larger, newer ram's horn	Four kings
Greeks Alexander (336–323)	Iron legs	Strong, devouring beast with iron teeth	Goat (great horn)	Powerful king
Alexander's successors (323–164)	Iron and clay feet (Seleucids and Ptolemies)	Ten horns (Successive Greek/Seleucid kings[13])	Four other horns (Four divisions[14])	Four divisions (South = Ptolemies North = Seleucids)

[10] The narrative time frames given in the book of Daniel are notoriously ambiguous. Estimates are given here simply to establish a rough chronology for Daniel's supposed activities. Technically, Nebuchadnezzar's reign over the Babylonian Empire began ca. 605 B.C.E., making the second year of his reign ca. 604 B.C.E. This date makes no sense, however, given that Daniel and his cohort are exiled and living in Babylon (a situation that would not have happened until years later). The narrative context thus implies the second year in which the Jews were under Nebuchadnezzar (i.e., the second year of the exile). This would fix the date closer to ca. 586 B.C.E.

[11] The large statue, four beasts, etc., are the symbols used in each respective vision for the various reigns, kingdoms, and epochs addressed by the visions.

[12] Scholars today know that the Babylonian Empire fell to the Persians, not the Medes. In Greco-Roman historiography, however, it was widely held that the Assyrians fell to the Medes, the Medes fell to the Persians, and the Persians fell to the Greeks. For obvious reasons (namely, the Babylonian setting), it appears that the author of Daniel has simply replaced the Assyrians with the Babylonians. Technically, the kingdom of the Medes would have been roughly contemporaneous with that of the Babylonians.

[13] The ten Greek rulers as traced through the Seleucid Dynasty, up until the reign of Antiochus IV Epiphanes, include Alexander the Great (336–323 B.C.E.), Philip Aridaeus (323–316 B.C.E.), Alexander IV (316–309 B.C.E.), Seleucus I Nicator (312–280 B.C.E.), Antiochus I Soter (280–261 B.C.E.), Antiochus II Theos (261–246 B.C.E.), Seleucus II Callinicus (246–226 B.C.E.), Seleucus III Soter (226–223 B.C.E.), Antiochus III the Great (223–187 B.C.E.), and Seleucus IV Philopator (187–175 B.C.E.).

Daniel's Visions and Their Meanings, continued

	Daniel 2	Daniel 7	Daniel 8	Daniel 10–12
	Large statue	*Four beasts*	*Ram and goat*	*[None]*
Antiochus IV Epiphanes (177–164)	[no mention]	Little horn with human eyes, arrogant mouth	Little horn	Despicable person; king of the north
Antiochus's crimes	[no mention]	Blasphemes, persecutes the holy ones, changes observances and laws	Suspends cultic offerings, decimates the holy place, destroys the holy ones by catching them unaware	Breaks the covenant leader, plunders riches, abolishes cultic offerings, sets up the desolating abomination, blasphemes, persecutes the God-fearing, causes many to apostatize
Duration of Antiochus's persecution	[no mention]	A time, two times, and a half a time (=3½ years)	2,300 evening and morning sacrifices (=1,150 days)	A time, two times, and a half a time (=3½ years) 1,290 days 1,335 days
God's kingdom	Crushing stone; indestructible, eternal kingdom	Universal and everlasting dominion given to "son of man" and holy people of the Most High by the Ancient One	[no mention]	Michael arises; righteous delivered, dead raised, wise vindicated

Table 8.2

correspond to each other. Collectively, these passages foretell the rise and fall of four consecutive kingdoms in the ancient Near East: those of the Babylonians, the Medes, the Persians, and the Greeks. Their interest is primarily in this last one. They anticipate a strong leader, Alexander the Great, whose empire is divided after his death. Two of

[14] Following Alexander's death, four of his generals (Ptolemy Lagus, Philip Aridaeus, Antigonus, and Seleucus Nicator) divided up his empire. Ptolemy took Egypt and Palestine, and Seleucus eventually acquired Syria. The Ptolemies held Palestine until 198 B.C.E., when it was conquered and subsumed into the Seleucid kingdom by Antiochus III.

those divisions are especially pertinent: the kingdom to the north (the Seleucids) and that to the south (the Ptolemies). Once control over Palestine shifts from the latter to the former, a despicable Seleucid king, Antiochus IV Epiphanes, comes to power. He is responsible for a wide range of crimes against the holy ones. Fortunately, the duration of his persecution is relatively short—three and one-half years or so. At that point—the so-called end of time (2:28; 8:17; 10:14; 11:40)—the Ancient One dramatically breaks into human history. God condemns the Seleucid king, strips the empire of its power, raises the righteous ones to new life, and establishes a universal and everlasting kingdom for his people (see table 8.2 on pages 126–27).

Scholars have noticed that the details of Daniel's prophecies become conspicuously more accurate the closer they get to the reign of Antiochus IV Epiphanes. In fact, the prophet himself is relatively unknown until this period as well. These factors, coupled with the book's style, grammar, and language—portions of which are entirely in Aramaic—have led experts to conclude that Daniel was written at a relatively late date. In other words, this book is not the firsthand account of a Judahite exile who peers four hundred years into the future. Rather, it is the product of the very persecutions that it predicts. Because its author demonstrates full knowledge of Antiochus's "desolating abomination" in 167 B.C.E. but gets the details wrong about his death in 164 B.C.E, this work was almost certainly composed during that interval.

The vast majority of Daniel's visions, then, consist of prophecies *ex eventu*. With the 20/20 clarity of hindsight, the author could thus inspire full confidence in the legitimacy and certainty of Daniel's message. (He did, after all, correctly foresee nearly four centuries of political history.) In light of this track record, Daniel's original readers would be led to believe that those matters that yet remained (namely, the defeat of Antiochus and the establishment of God's kingdom) were sure to happen, and happen *soon*!

The text even accounts for the problematic historical gap—the reason why his readers had not heard of this particular prophet or his predictions before Antiochus's persecutions began. On two separate occasions, Daniel is specifically instructed to keep his visions a secret and to seal them away until that very time (8:26; 12:4). So despite being written (presumably) some four hundred years prior, their concealment explains the audience's ignorance. Moreover, because Daniel's visions were not to be revealed until the end, their sudden appearance, in the form of the book of Daniel, would be additional confirmation for the original audience that this event was indeed near.

The Bible Code and the Book of Daniel: Functional Similarities

At this point, the parallels between Drosnin's *The Bible Code* and the book of Daniel should begin to become evident. In each case, *ex eventu* prophecies serve to bolster the readers' trust in the accuracy and legitimacy of their source. Both rely upon information gleaned from hindsight but ascribe such knowledge to ancient origins. Both also purport to foresee the last days. Of course, neither source presents this information plainly. It remains artfully encoded for the wise to decipher and the faithful to believe.

In each case, the appearances of these books represent fortuitous and even deliberate timing. Drosnin has asserted that the messages within the Bible were specifically encrypted for computer-based technologies. As such, he contends that the encryption itself functions as a type of time capsule. It allows the secrets of the code to emerge at a very precise moment in human history, namely, just before its self-destruction. In much the same way, Daniel's visions are supposed to remain sealed and hidden right up until the end of time.

From the dates of their respective appearances, both books announce a relatively short interval until the world's demise. In fact, their timetables are nearly identical. Drosnin published *The Bible Code* in 1997 and therein predicted global annihilation as early as the year 2000. In *The Bible Code II,* published in 2002, Drosnin pushes for the year 2006. Drosnin's average turns out to be the same length of time that Daniel has given: three and one-half years. In both cases, the imminence of the end serves to heighten the urgency of the message. Impending apocalypses can be compelling rhetoric for decisive action!

Both works also get it wrong about the future, especially in their predictions of the apocalypse. Accordingly, efforts can be seen to extend their timetables. Drosnin has shifted from 2000, to 2006, to perhaps 2012 (that's when the planet-crushing comet arrives). Even Daniel's three-and-one-half-year forecast shows some signs of revision. The 1,150 days of Dan 8 (8:14) becomes 1,290 days in Dan 12 (12:11), and then 1,335 days at the conclusion of the book (12:12).[15]

These functional similarities beg the question of intention. Why were these books written? What were their authors hoping to achieve? We can presume a noble motive on the part of Drosnin, who seems genuinely convinced about the validity of the code. To avoid a nuclear showdown, he has sought to promote diplomacy and security in the Middle East, especially in Israel. To this end, he has personally become involved (or at least attempted to become involved) in attaining that goal. Although to his many critics Drosnin may be misguided—and perhaps even worse, misguiding others—his concern for the welfare of the planet is appropriate and perhaps even admirable.

But what about the author of Daniel? Why would someone pen such unconventional visions using such strange symbolism? Why would he go to such great lengths to fabricate such a convincing prediction of the approaching apocalypse? We cannot begin to answer these questions without some appreciation of the original context out of which this book emerged. To this end, we must consider the situation of the Jews in light of the specific policies and practices of the Seleucid King Antiochus IV Epiphanes.

The Purpose of the Book of Daniel in Light of Its Historical Context

In the Old Testament, our information about Antiochus IV Epiphanes comes from 1 and 2 Maccabees.[16] These texts paint a decidedly grim picture of his reign and attest to at least a dozen offenses that can be attributed either directly or indirectly to him (see list following).

- Selling off the high priesthood to the highest bidder. In fact, Antiochus purportedly did this not once but twice. He first replaced Onias III with his brother, Jason, when the latter promised to pay Antiochus 590 talents of silver. Three years later,

[15] Given their numerous similarities, I find the fact that the first words in both *The Bible Code* and *The Bible Code II* are taken from the book of Daniel (Dan 12:4 and 12:1, respectively) to be an altogether fitting irony.

[16] Roman Catholics and the Eastern Orthodox include these books in the regular canon of their Scriptures, whereas Protestants and Jews do not. Nevertheless, they are often found in the Apocryphal or Deuterocanonical appendixes of these Bibles.

Antiochus replaced Jason with Menelaus for a promise of 890 talents (2 Macc 4:7–10; 23–25).

- Establishing a Greek gymnasium in Jerusalem. The gymnasium was one of the chief means of spreading Greek culture. The young men who were enrolled in it were educated with a curriculum of Hellenistic philosophy and literature. It featured athletic contests that were held in the nude, giving circumcised Jews no place to hide (1 Macc 1:14–15; 2 Macc 4:12–15).
- Suppressing a "revolt" upon the rumor of his death. When a false report of Antiochus's demise reached Jason, he sought to forcibly reclaim the high priesthood from Menelaus via an attack on Jerusalem. When Antiochus heard of the incident, he assumed that all of Jerusalem was revolting. He sent in his troops, and within three days they had indiscriminately slaughtered an estimated 40,000 civilians and sold another 40,000 into slavery (1 Macc 1:20; 2 Macc 5:5–14).
- Raiding and looting the Jerusalem temple. Following his attack on Jerusalem, Antiochus entered the holy sanctuary and stripped it of everything valuable. This included the golden altar, lamp stands, utensils, tables, censers, cups, bowls, and even the plating that covered the walls. He also drained the temple treasury of some 1,800 talents of silver (1 Macc 1:21–23; 2 Macc 5:15–16; 21).
- Occupying Jerusalem and converting it into a Greek citadel. Two years after plundering the temple, Antiochus sent troops to Jerusalem under false pretenses. When the citizens let down their guard, the troops invaded. They plundered the city and burned it to the ground. They seized people and property and turned the city into their garrison (1 Macc 1:29–40; 2 Macc 5:24–26).
- Instituting a policy of Hellenization. By decree of Antiochus, the citizens of Jerusalem were compelled to abandon their laws, customs, sacrifices, and religious observances in favor of those of the Greeks. Jews could no longer keep kosher, observe the Sabbath, or celebrate their festivals. Rather, they were compelled to participate in pagan festivals such as that honoring Dionysus. They were forced to wear wreaths of ivy, walk in the tributary procession, and partake of the requisite sacrifices. Because refusal was punishable by death, these laws occasioned much apostasy (1 Macc 1:41–53; 2 Macc 6:6–9).

- Setting up the "desolating abomination." Antiochus rededicated Jerusalem's temple to the Olympian god Zeus. The sanctuary thus became the site of wild reveling and debauchery by the Gentiles, who engaged in prostitution within its sacred precincts. Antiochus also built a pagan altar upon the former one, and there he offered the preferred sacrifice of Zeus: pork (1 Macc 1:54–55; 2 Macc 6:1–5).
- Burning the Torah. As part of Antiochus's program of Hellenization, copies of the Torah were torn to shreds and burned. Anyone found possessing this book or adhering to its laws was sentenced to death (1 Macc 1:56–57).
- Executing women who had their children circumcised. In order to prevent the practice of circumcision, which the Greeks considered mutilation, all women who circumcised their infants were to be executed, with their infants hung from their necks. In addition, their families and those who performed the circumcisions were also to be put to death (1 Macc 1:60–61; 2 Macc 6:10).
- Attacking resisters on the Sabbath. In order to escape Antiochus's policies and practice their religion, some Jews fled to the wilderness regions outside of Jerusalem. Antiochus sent his troops to the hiding place of one such group. They waited until the Sabbath and then attacked. Because it was the Sabbath, the Jews refused to defend themselves. All one thousand of them were massacred (1 Macc 2:29–38; 2 Macc 6:11).
- Torturing and executing Eleazer. Antiochus's policy decreed that all Jews must partake of the Greek sacrifices, which included the consumption of pork. Eleazer, a noble and well-respected ninety-year-old scribe, refused. Antiochus showed him no pity. He was tortured and died upon the rack (2 Macc 6:18–31; see also 4 Macc 5–6).
- Torturing and executing seven brothers and their mother. Perhaps the most infamous story from Antiochus's reign involves the torture and execution of seven brothers and their mother for their refusal to eat the sacrificial pork. Because of their bold words against Antiochus, they suffered extraordinary cruelty. One by one, as their mother looked on, their tongues were cut out, their heads were scalped, their hands and feet were cut off, and they were fried alive in large, fire-heated pans (2 Macc 7:1–42; see also 4 Macc 8–12).

These incidents attest to the senseless cruelty that the Jews suffered simply because of their faith. As a rule, apocalyptic literature tends to proliferate under such conditions.[17] In light of them, the contents and purpose of the book of Daniel begins to make sense. For instance, the symbolic language in which Daniel's visions are encoded allows the author to escape the scrutiny of the authorities. Writing propaganda against Antiochus and the Greek establishment would have been extremely dangerous. It was far safer to write about multimetallic statutes, large rocks, beasts from the sea, rams, goats, and little horns.

As for the consummate end that Daniel's author envisioned, even this is rendered intelligible under his circumstances. Theologically speaking, the harsh discriminations and injustices that the Jewish people suffered all but demanded divine retribution. Daniel's author imagined just such a response. He sought to affirm that, despite appearances, God *was* still in control. In fact, the entire political history of the ancient Near East, from the Babylonians to the Greeks, was all part of God's design. It all had a purpose. It had been foreseen and preordained (or at least, permitted) by God for the good of God's people. Even Antiochus's persecutions achieved a greater good. In the long run, they served to "refine" the faith of the Jews (Dan 9:11–19; 2 Macc 6:12–16). But not even God would tolerate Antiochus for long.

By asserting that the Almighty would soon rise against this tyrant, the author of Daniel demonstrates hope in an otherwise hopeless situation. He thus encourages his contemporaries to remain loyal to God, to stand firm, and to take action—and then to admonish others to do the same (Dan 11:32–33). Fundamentally, he seeks to embolden his people in the midst of their unprecedented suffering to continue to honor God and stay true their covenant-based faith. No doubt it is for these reasons that the book was included in the OT, despite its evident shortcomings.

Postscript

By way of postscript, it should be noted that, to some extent, the Jews were vindicated, although not nearly as spectacularly as Daniel had predicted. According to the prophet, Antiochus would enjoy a decisive

[17] Aside from Daniel, the other biblical example is the book of Revelation, which was produced during the height of the Roman persecution of Christians.

victory against the kingdom of the south (the Ptolemies) and thus inherit Egypt, Libya, and Ethiopia. But reports from the east and north would alarm him, so he would swing his troops back up into Judea. There, between "the mountain" (Jerusalem) and "the sea" (the Mediterranean), he would meet his demise (Dan 11:40–45).

This account differs substantially from those of the ancient historians. They all indicate that Antiochus was in Persia attempting to raid a temple when he learned of the defeat of his forces in Judea.[18] According to 1 Macc 6:8–10, the report discouraged Antiochus so much that he grew violently ill and retired to his bed, where he lay confined for many days. He would not rise again. This varies somewhat from 2 Macc 9:4–12, where the news instead caused Antiochus to become enraged. The king immediately set out to "make Jerusalem a cemetery of Jews." En route, however, Antiochus was suddenly seized with intestinal pain. He suffered a hard fall from his chariot and physically deteriorated from there. Both books do agree, however, that Antiochus died in Persia. They also concur that before he died, Antiochus came to deeply regret his policies toward Jerusalem and the Jewish people.[19]

Following his death, Antiochus's nine-year-old son, Antiochus V Eupator, inherited the throne. He was placed in the care of Antiochus's general, Lysias. They did not retain power for long. Two years later, they were both put to death when Demetrius, the brother of Antiochus IV, claimed the kingship for himself. In the meantime, a small but determined band of Jews fought to regain possession of the Jerusalem temple. Against considerable odds, they succeeded. Its subsequent purification and rededication was such a momentous occasion that the Jews resolved to commemorate it forever (1 Macc 4:36–59; 2 Macc 10:1–8). It is celebrated nowadays as the festival of Hanukkah.

[18] The specific details of the accounts differ. In 1 Macc 6:1–16, Antiochus is in the city of Elymais (the biblical Elam) when he hears of Lysias's defeat. (This largely concurs with Polybius *History* 31.9 and Appian *The Syrian Wars* 11.66). However, in 2 Macc 9:2, Antiochus is in Persepolis when he learns of the losses of Nicanor and Timothy.

[19] So 1 Macc 6:10–13. In 2 Macc 9:13–17, Antiochus goes so far as to promise freedom for Jerusalem, equal citizenship for the Jews, restoration of the temple, and full restitution for its sacrifices. He even decides to convert!

Part III כתובים

The Writings (Kethuvim)

Having covered both the Law (Torah) and the Prophets (Nevi'im), we turn now in the third section of this book to the Writings (Kethuvim). In the Jewish canon, the Writings consist of thirteen books, including Psalms, Proverbs, Job, the Song of Songs, Ruth, Lamentations, Ecclesiastes, Esther, Daniel, Ezra, Nehemiah, and 1 and 2 Chronicles. As previously noted, Christian canons assign Lamentations and Daniel to the Prophets. They also group Ruth, Esther, Ezra, Nehemiah, and 1 and 2 Chronicles among the historical books. By genre, then, the closest and most distinctive category in the Christian canon to parallel the Jewish Writings is a subset within it called the Wisdom Literature. This classification includes Job, parts of Psalms, Proverbs, Ecclesiastes, and occasionally the Song of Songs. (To these, the Roman Catholics and Eastern Orthodox also add the Wisdom of Solomon and the book of Sirach.) Our remaining three chapters, therefore, are dedicated to the only three books that belong, indisputably and in their entirety, to this subset: Proverbs, Ecclesiastes, and Job.

In chapter 9, we will examine Proverbs as the OT's most conventional example of Wisdom Literature. As such, we will compare and contrast its message with some of the conventional wisdom of our own age. The next two chapters are devoted to instances of unconventional wisdom. In chapter 10, we'll see how the problems raised and the solution advanced by the book of Ecclesiastes somewhat defies the advice of Proverbs. In chapter 11, we will turn to consider the unfortunate lot of Job. There, we'll discover how his prolonged exchange with his three friends suggests a rather surprising purpose for this work. Following this, a short conclusion completes our study.

9

The Book of Proverbs —Conventional Wisdom

FOCUS TEXT: PROVERBS

When it comes to the subject of wisdom, it is not the abstract notion of learned experience that preoccupies contemporary discussions, but rather the conventional wisdom (CW) of our age.

Contemporary Conventional Wisdom (CW)

Originally, CW was a concept rather closely associated with "tradition" and "orthodoxy."[1] However, the definition and use of CW has evolved significantly. Its present usage accentuates the common, prevalent, or widespread sense of "conventional." Thus, CW has come to include any principle, belief, attitude, or prediction that is accepted as true or correct by the majority of a given population, regardless of its

[1] The phrase itself dates back to Harvard economist John Kenneth Galbraith, who first coined it in *The Affluent Society* (Boston: Houghton Mifflin, 1958). There, CW is understood as those long-held, familiar ideas with broad consensus that enable us to simplify complex social or natural phenomena. CW is not always accurate. It is, however, well-pedigreed, having been reinforced by academicians, political leaders, and reputable professionals. Consequently, the notions of CW tend to be resistant to change. A good example of this involves the current assertion that microorganisms such as bacteria and viruses are the primary culprits of disease and illnesses. CW, therefore, would dictate practices such as childhood vaccinations and frequent hand washing to combat a variety of maladies.

continuity with the past. Today, most dictionaries define CW as synonymous with public approval.[2] Indeed, this is the very nature of "CW Watch," a regular feature in *Newsweek* magazine. Thus, for instance, CW might approve of the president's performance one week and disapprove of it the next. It simply depends upon the latest events and the prevailing mood of the country.

In part, our fascination with CW stems from its potential influence over so many aspects of our society. Its effects can be seen in and upon our cultural norms, democratic government, advertising, fashion trends, entertainment offerings, and financial indicators (among others). Given its import, public relations experts, economists, marketing gurus, social scientists, and political analysts are constantly trying to measure it using randomly conducted, statistically significant, nationally representative surveys and public opinion polls. But determining our CW can be a bit like hitting a moving target, and the results aren't always as straightforward as they might seem. Take, for instance, our CW about God, religion, and spirituality.

CW and the Priority of Religion/Spirituality

According to the most recent Gallup polls, 86% of the population believes in God, 81% acknowledges the existence of heaven, and 84% rates religion as either "very" or "fairly" important in their own lives.[3] The United States was founded on the principle of religious freedom and our well-recognized mottos still proclaim "In God We Trust," "One Nation under God," and "God Bless America." Our CW, therefore, appears to support the contention that we are a God-fearing people.

But there is something of a paradox to these numbers. While 63% claim to be members of churches or synagogues, less than 31% attend

[2] So, for example, *Merriam-Webster's Dictionary:* "The generally accepted belief, opinion, judgment, or prediction about a particular matter." *Webster's New World College Dictionary:* "The generally accepted belief with regard to some matter, or the set of beliefs held by most people." *Encarta Dictionary:* "Popular notion: general or widespread belief."

[3] Data taken from surveys conducted between 2006 and 2007. Results obtained online at http://www.gallup.com/poll/1690/Religion.aspx (accessed March 27, 2008).

on a regular, weekly basis. Furthermore, a full 55% of the population believes that religion as a whole is losing its influence on our lives.[4]

If this last proposition is true, what might account for it? Given the alleged importance of faith, what could possibly be superseding it in priority? To answer these questions, one needs to identify the underlying wants, desires, values, and aspirations of our society. Fortunately, these are some of the very qualities that the Pew Research Center recently sought to examine in eighteen- to twenty-five-year-old Americans, members of the so-called Gen Next.[5] Their report, which utilizes a variety of data sources and nationally representative surveys, contains some rather surprising findings.[6]

For instance, members of Gen Next were asked which life goals (out of a list of five) they thought were the first and second most important to their peers. The results are summarized in table 9.1.

Gen Next's Life Goals

Life Goal	Most Important	Second Most Important	Top Two Aggregate
To get rich	64%	17%	81%
To be famous	10%	41%	51%
To help people who need help	12%	17%	30%
To be leaders in their community	7%	15%	22%
To become more spiritually aware	4%	6%	10%
None/don't know	3%	4%	7%
Totals	100%	100%	200%

Table 9.1

[4]Ibid.

[5]In the literature, "Gen X" refers to Americans born between 1965 and 1980. It is distinguished from Gen Next, which includes those born between 1980 and 2005.

[6]"How Young People View Their Lives, Futures and Politics: A Portrait of 'Generation Next,'" The Pew Research Center for the People and the Press (January 9, 2007). A full copy of this report can be found via the center's Web site at http://people-press.org/reports/pdf/300.pdf (accessed March 21, 2008).

The propensity "to get rich" was chosen as the first or second most important life goal among 81% of those polled. This was followed by the desire "to be famous," chosen as a top two among 51% of those asked. By contrast, the goal of becoming "more spiritually aware" came in dead last. It was highly prioritized by only 10% of the respondents. Now granted, these results may be somewhat skewed since those polled were asked not about themselves but about their peers. Nevertheless, their answers closely correspond to the results of two other personally based questions in the survey.

One of those examined the role models of Gen Next. It asked, "Other than friends or members of your own family, who would you say is the person you most admire these days?" Of those individuals specified, entertainers—actors, athletes, and performers—formed the largest subgroup, accounting for 14% of all responses. (It is difficult to imagine a segment of society that epitomizes the ideals of fame and fortune better than this one.) They were followed by teachers/professors (12%) and politicians (8%). Spiritual figures (from local congregational leaders all the way up to the Divine) were mentioned just 6% of the time.

Another pertinent question inquired about "the most important problem facing you in your life these days." This is how the Gen Next'ers answered (see table 9.2).

Gen Next's "Most Important Problems"

Issue	Percentages
Money/financial	30%
College/education	18%
Career/job	16%
Miscellaneous/other	12%
Family/relationships	7%
Health	2%
National/international conditions	2%
Spirituality/morality/general decline	*

Table 9.2

Here again, money topped the list. In fact, if we couple this designation with related career/job issues, we find that anxiety about one's employment and fiscal standing was judged "the most important problem" facing nearly half of all respondents (46%). At the other end of the spectrum, absolutely no one in this cohort mentioned spiritual or moral issues as their most significant concern.

Collectively, the Pew report findings depict Gen Next as placing a very high value on prosperity and prestige and a comparatively low value on spirituality. Is this profile accurate, or does it reflect certain biases and/or agendas of the reporting agency?

To answer this question, we can compare the Pew results with the much larger Cooperative Institutional Research Program (CIRP) Freshmen Survey conducted by the Higher Education Research Institute (HERI) at UCLA's Graduate School of Education and Information Studies (GSE&IS).[7] Among the most frequently analyzed sections of this survey is one in which students indicate which criteria (from a list of twenty or so) they consider to be "essential" or "very important" in life. Included in the list are goals such as "raising a family," "influencing social values," "becoming an authority in my field," and "keeping up to date with political affairs." Two criteria in particular are routinely highlighted for comparison. They are "developing a meaningful philosophy of life" and "becoming very well off financially." Here's how the college freshmen of 2005 compared to the incoming class of 1967 (see table 9.3).[8]

HERI Results: Class of 1967 vs. Class of 2005

Criterion judged as "essential" or "very important" in life	1967	2005
Developing a meaningful philosophy of life	74.5%	45.0%
Becoming very well off financially	41.9%	85.8%

Table 9.3

The 2005 freshmen results are just the latest manifestation of fairly consistent ascending/descending trends in these respective goals. Since

[7] Each year, the HERI oversees the administration of its national study to roughly 400,000 first-year students at seven hundred universities, four-year, and two-year colleges. Conducted since 1967, the HERI data sets allow for the longitudinal comparison of college freshmen over multiple decades. For more information, see UCLA's GSE&IS Web site at http://www.gseis.ucla.edu/heri (accessed March 27, 2008).

[8] Because students selected more than one criterion, the numbers do not add up to 100%.

1967, the gap between the two criteria gradually narrowed; it crossed around 1979 and has widened ever since. What these numbers suggest is this: today, nearly twice as many college freshmen judge the attainment of a comfortable life to be more crucial than establishing significance, spiritual or otherwise, for that life.[9]

It is tempting to consign the attitudes and inclinations noted above exclusively to the younger members of our society. To some extent, this is justifiable. Both the Pew report and the freshmen survey found that the emerging generation places a demonstrably greater emphasis on riches and renowned reputations than did those that preceded it. But several corresponding surveys imply that the propensities of the adult population in general may not be too far removed from Gen Next. For example, when a recent national Gallup poll of all adults were asked to name two men and two women they admired the most, the results were as follows (see table 9.4).[10]

Gallup Poll's Most Admired Men and Women

Category	Males	Females	Averages
Political leaders	35%	32%	33.5%
Businesspeople/entertainers	3%	13%	8.0%
Friends/relatives	7%	6%	6.5%
Religious leaders	7%	0%	3.5%
Other	21%	21%	21.0%
None	29%	30%	29.5%

Table 9.4

Of those individuals specified, politicians claimed the largest category (33.5%). Next came businesspeople/entertainers (8%) and

[9] Additional evidence from the HERI suggests that college education plays an effective role in tempering such attitudes. As a case in point, in the aftermath of college, only 57.1% of the senior class of 2005 rated "becoming very well off financially" as a "very important" goal—down from their previous CIRP response of 66.4% (a 9.3% drop). Moreover, 56.5% rated "developing a meaningful philosophy of life" as "very important"—up from their previous CIRP response of 47.4% (a 9.1% rise). Data taken from "Findings from the 2005 College Student Survey (CSS): National Aggregates," by Victor B. Saenz and Douglas S. Barreva, February 2007. See http://www.geis.ucla.edu/heri/PDFs/2005_CSS_REPORT_FINAL.pdf (accessed March 27, 2008).

[10] For the purpose of this table, the primary occupations of the individuals listed in the results of the Gallup poll were used. Totals do not add up to 100%.

friends/relatives (6.5%). On average, spiritual leaders accounted for only 3.5% of all responses.[11]

Another Gallup poll recently asked adults to identify the biggest problem facing our country. Topping the list was the war in Iraq, cited by 30% of respondents. It was followed by concerns about the economy (25%), health care (12%), government effectiveness (10%), and immigration (9%). By comparison, only 5% of those asked mentioned ethics, morality, or spiritual decline as a central concern of theirs.[12]

Finally, in a recent ABC News poll, more than one thousand adults in a random national sample were asked what they "would most like to have for Christmas." Cars and automotive accessories topped the list (16%), followed by computers (7%), clothes (6%), money (6%), jewelry (5%), travel (5%), home furnishings (4%), health products (4%), TVs (4%), houses (3%), appliances (3%), visits with family and friends (2%), and video games (2%). Only after all these things did intangible qualities such as love and peace join the ranks. They accounted for just 2% of all responses.[13]

Everyone knows that statistics can be made to support all sorts of propositions. Indeed, the contexts and wording of these questions should make us hesitant to draw any sort of definitive conclusions on the basis of them. But if the results of these surveys are at all telling, they intimate some possible trends about our society in general, and about our young adults in particular. With respect to what we want, what we desire, what we value, and what we most aspire to be, the findings seem to indicate that the pursuit of wealth, material acquisitions, and social power far surpasses in importance the development or expression of religious, spiritual, or moral attributes. From all appearances, this tendency looks to be "a widely held opinion accepted as true by the majority of our population." Practically speaking, then, it represents our CW. In principle, while we may seek heaven in the afterlife, we are much more preoccupied with Madison Avenue, Hollywood, Wall Street, and Washington, D.C., in this one.

---

[11] Results from a 2006 survey, obtained online at http://www.gallup.com/poll/1678/Most-Admired-Man-Woman.aspx (accessed March 27, 2008).

[12] Results from a September 2007 poll, obtained online at http://www.gallup.com/poll/1675/Most-Important-Problem.aspx (accessed March 27, 2008).

[13] The ABC News poll was conducted by telephone November 16–20, 2005, among a random national sample of 1,003 adults, with a three-point error margin. Sampling, data collection, and tabulation by TNS Telecoms, Inc., of Horsham, Pa.; analysis by Gary Langer; online at http://abcnews.go.com/images/Politics/999a2WishList.pdf (accessed March 27, 2008).

CW in the Old Testament: The Book of Proverbs

So how does our CW compare with that of the OT? Obviously, the popular opinions of the ancient Israelites are not as readily available to us today. No Gallup polls of an ancient Israelite "Gen א" ["Gen *alef*"] survive. But what we do have is their Wisdom Literature: a collection of writings that is primarily interested in the practical and sometimes confusing realities of everyday human experience. As mentioned in the sectional heading, titles typically associated with this genre include Job, Psalms, Proverbs, Ecclesiastes, the Song of Songs, Wisdom, and Sirach. Of these, scholars judge the most conventional work to be the book of Proverbs.[14] For this reason, it shall serve as an intriguing and appropriate basis of comparison for our own CW.

Technically speaking, the book of Proverbs is not a collection of sayings but rather an anthology of such collections. Following an introductory section that extols the virtues of Wisdom (1:1–9:18), six discrete headings serve to introduce "The Proverbs of Solomon" (10:1), "The Sayings of the Wise" (22:17), "Other Sayings of the Wise" (24:23), "Other Proverbs of Solomon" (25:1), "The Words of Agur, Son of Jakeh the Massite" (30:1), and "The Words of Lemeul, King of Massa" (31:1). Presumably, these subcollections circulated independently prior to their inclusion in the book of Proverbs. However, most scholars remain skeptical concerning their attributed origins, particularly in the case

[14] This assertion is based on a number of considerations. First, only parts of Psalms can rightly be classified as Wisdom Literature, and no scholarly consensus exists regarding the Song of Songs. Neither the book of Wisdom nor Sirach is contained in the Jewish or Protestant canons. So that leaves Job, Proverbs, and Ecclesiastes. The most conventional of this trio would have to meet the criteria of "orthodoxy" and "tradition." Relative to the mainstream theologies of the Hebrew Scriptures, Proverbs demonstrates considerably more overlap with the Torah and the Prophets—particularly in their emphasis on fidelity to God, ethical living, and cause/effect relationships—than either Job or Ecclesiastes. However, the most conventional work could also be defined by its "ordinary," "common," and "widespread" character. This standard suggests similarity and conformity to other wisdom writings, especially those throughout the ancient Near East. Here again, Proverbs not only exhibits more parallels, both in style and content, to such nonbiblical works, but at times it even borrows from them. (The clearest case of this involves Prov 22:17–23:11, which has been drawn from the "Instruction of Amenemope," an Egyptian text dating back to ca. 1200 B.C.E.) Therefore, even in light of varying definitions, the book of Proverbs easily emerges as the most conventional example of Wisdom Literature in the OT.

of Solomon.[15] As a whole, the dating of the book is notoriously difficult to determine. Aside from the headings, it contains remarkably few historical references, and virtually none from Israel's extensive and colorful narrative past.

The purpose of Proverbs is fairly clear. It sets forth principled advice on how to live a good and proper life via hundreds of maxims and adages. These sayings usually take the form of synonymous, antithetical, synthetic, or emblematic parallelism.[16] Though applicable to all, the work itself presupposes a younger, male audience (i.e., the emerging generation), as the dozens of references to "my son" imply. Couple these with the frequent mention of "father," "mother," and "parents," and it seems likely that Proverbs derived its origins and functions from the nexus of family life. Even so, the book was no doubt codified by the scribes of the royal court and probably also served instructional purposes for those associated with it. (In fact, references to the king slightly outnumber those to one's parents.)

Because they are presented without much literary or historical context, the contents of Proverbs enjoy something of a timeless quality. Consequently, more attention has been drawn to the ideology of this book than to its date or setting. The 915 verses of Proverbs somewhat defy comprehensive analysis. But for our purposes, a general overview shall suffice.

The Two Ways of Proverbs

The book of Proverbs presents two markedly different ways of life, each with its own corresponding set of characteristics, authorities, behaviors, and consequences. We can consider each of these aspects in turn.

---

[15] Solomon has been traditionally associated with all sorts of Wisdom Literature. According to rabbinic lore, Solomon wrote the Song of Songs when he was a youth, Proverbs when middle-aged, and Ecclesiastes when elderly. Even the book of Wisdom, written in Greek around the first cent. B.C.E., is attributed to him! Indeed, Solomon's wisdom was legendary. The narrative description of it can be found in 1 Kgs 3:4–28 and 5:9–14. There, it is claimed that Solomon composed some three thousand proverbs.

[16] Synonymous parallelism refers to the repetition of similar concepts: "He who confers benefits will be amply enriched, and he who refreshes others will himself be refreshed" (11:25). Antithetical parallelism refers to the contrasting of opposites: "Him who monopolizes grain, the people curse—but blessings be upon the head of him who distributes it" (11:26). In synthetic (or step) parallelism, the original thought is further amplified, explained, or developed: "Entrust your works to the LORD, and your plans will succeed" (16:3). In emblematic (or simile) parallelism, a figurative notion describes a literal one: "Like an open city with no defenses is the man with no check on his feelings" (25:28).

Characteristics

There is no concept that Proverbs emphasizes more than the virtue of wisdom (חכמה, *khokmah*). Be it in noun or adjective form, this term occurs more than one hundred times throughout the book's thirty-one chapters. In fact, more than a quarter of all OT references to it are found here. Proverbs portrays wisdom as having inestimable value. It surpasses the worth of any precious jewel and yields better returns than silver or gold (2:4; 3:14–15; 8:10–11, 19; 10:20; 16:16; 20:15). For this reason, wisdom is to be pursued relentlessly, obtained by any means, and safeguarded at all costs (4:5–7, 13; 7:1–4).

The introductory section of Proverbs (1:1–9:18) personifies wisdom as an honest, noble, powerful, and generous woman. It is she who is to be distinguished from folly, a tempting adulteress who entices the unwitting with her raw sensuality, sweet lies, and stolen goods. The (young, male) audience of Proverbs is thus encouraged to court wisdom like a lover. She must be appreciated and sought after, but special care must be taken to discern genuine wisdom from her many imposters and cheap imitators. Such discrimination separates those with "prudence," "intelligence," "understanding," "discernment," "discretion," and "knowledge" from the "foolish," the "simple-minded," and those "lacking judgment."

Following closely on the heels of wisdom is the notion of righteousness (צדקה, *tsedaqah*).[17] If wisdom is the primary virtue endorsed by Proverbs, then righteousness is its behavioral manifestation. It is marked by just, upright, and honorable living. The righteous are often contrasted with those who demonstrate the dark side of folly: the "wicked," "evil," "perverted," and "violent."

In addition to these primary characteristics, Proverbs presents a host of secondary attributes that one is admonished to either embrace or avoid. Thus, for example, it contrasts the industrious with the lazy, the humble with the proud, the honest with the dishonest, the peaceable with the troublemaker, the self-controlled with the quick-tempered, the generous with the stingy, the content with the greedy, the tight-lipped with the loquacious, the cautious with the reckless, and the restrained with the self-indulgent.

---

[17] The remarkable prevalence of these two terms can be demonstrated statistically. Forms of the word wisdom occur 114 times; forms of righteousness at least 90. Collectively, these words appear 204 times throughout 915 verses. That means that one or the other is mentioned, on average, every 4½ verses.

Authorities

In its emphasis on wisdom and virtuous living, the book of Proverbs is practically indistinguishable from much of the Wisdom Literature of the ancient Near East. What sets Proverbs and other representations of conventional wisdom in the OT apart is the attributed origin of such wisdom. Proverbs conceives of wisdom not merely as knowledge tempered by experience, and even less so as popular opinion. Rather, wisdom is the "firstborn" of God's creative work and the "craftsman" that contributed to the world's design (8:22–31).[18] So close is the relationship between God and wisdom that one cannot be known without the other. True wisdom leads one to God, just as God leads one to true wisdom (2:4–6). For this reason, the sages of the OT repeatedly insist that the fear of the LORD is the beginning of wisdom (Prov 1:7; 9:10; 15:33; Job 28:28; Ps 111:10; Sir 1:16).

Indeed, God is referenced some ninety times throughout the book of Proverbs. The Almighty is portrayed not only as the source of wisdom but also as its terminus. God sees and knows all (5:21; 15:3, 11; 16:2; 17:3; 21:2). Consequently, God is the arbitrator of wisdom's rewards and folly's punishments. Those who adhere to the paths of righteousness are blessed by God, whereas those who pursue wickedness experience his wrath (so, e.g., 3:33; 8:35; 10:3; 12:2; 15:25). In this respect, God can be said to control the fate and destiny of all individuals (16:1, 4, 9, 33; 19:21; 20:24; 21:30).

Two other authority figures are closely patterned upon God's role. The first is the king. Proverbs affirms that all monarchs are accountable to the precepts of wisdom if they desire long and successful reigns (16:12; 20:8, 28; 25:5; 29:4, 14; 31:4). But it also recognizes them as a source of God's wisdom (8:15; 16:10; 21:1) and as a means by which wisdom's benefits and folly's penalties are bestowed (14:35; 16:13–15; 19:12; 20:2, 26; 22:11, 29). The prudent are thus advised to fear both God and king (24:21).

One's parents are also prominent authority figures acknowledged by Proverbs. They, too, are a source of wisdom and discipline (1:8; 4:1; 6:20; 13:1; 15:5; 23:22). As with the king, obedience or disobedience to them results in positive or negative consequences (19:26; 20:20; 28:24; 30:17). But Proverbs tends not to portray the parents as the issuers of

---

[18] Because of its purported role in creation, the principles of wisdom can be gleaned through the careful observation of nature (so, e.g., 6:6; 30:24–28, 29–31, 33).

such consequences. Rather, they themselves reap the effects of their children's wisdom or folly (10:1; 15:20; 17:6, 21, 25; 19:13; 23:24–25; 28:7; 29:3, 15).

The above authorities constitute the sources of the numerous "teachings," "corrections," "instructions," "disciplines," "commands," "laws," and "counsels" that the reader is advised to follow. These references apply principally to the lessons contained within Proverbs itself (so 4:4–5, 20; 5:7; 7:1, 24; 22:17). There is no mention, for example, of the Abrahamic covenant or of obedience to the precepts of the Torah. Conspicuously absent as well is any acknowledgment of Israel's cult or religious establishment. In fact, Proverbs never even touches upon the dangers of idolatry—the premier transgression in the Law and the Prophets. Such is the cosmopolitan nature of this literature.

So if it is not the worship of false gods that leads a person to folly, then what does? According to Proverbs, it is one's trust in oneself (1:32; 3:7; 12:15; 21:2; 26:12, 16; 28:11, 26; 30:12). Misplaced self-confidence is the enemy of wisdom, since it inevitably prevents an individual from perceiving, much less correcting, the error of his or her ways.

Behaviors

It is personal conduct that defines one as virtuous or not. To paraphrase a modern-day sage: "Folly is as folly does." But what exactly constitutes wise or foolish activity? Proverbs both recommends and condemns a multitude of specific behaviors. Broadly construed, most of these can be grouped into one of six subcategories.[19] (1) The wise heed correction and submit to the proper authorities. The foolish spurn admonition and hold authority in contempt. (2) The wise use their speech prudently, speaking sparingly and honestly. The foolish talk excessively. Their words are boisterous and deceptive. (3) The lives of the wise are marked by diligence and integrity. These qualities manifest themselves in work and business settings, judicial contexts, and virtuous lifestyles. The foolish tend to be lazy and dishonest. They are professionally unreliable and lack self-control over their vices. (4) The wise seek peace. They are slow to anger and quick to forgive. They often have the best interests of all at heart. The foolish are often the instigators of trouble. They are

[19] For the sake of time and space, we will only briefly touch on these behaviors here. For those wishing a more comprehensive analysis, including the accompanying citations, please see Appendix H.

quick-tempered and hot-headed. They meddle in other people's affairs and set traps for the unsuspecting. (5) The wise behave generously. They share their material resources liberally and are socially unpretentious. The foolish behave greedily. Their appetites are never satisfied. They are stingy, haughty, and ostentatious. (6) Finally, the wise surround themselves with wise companions. This includes selecting a spouse who embodies the appropriate virtues. The foolish, however, surround themselves with evildoers. They also end up regretting the spouses whom they have chosen.

Consequences

Accompanying these opposing sets of characteristics, authorities, and behaviors are a related set of consequences. One of the central principles underlying the book of Proverbs is that "the scoundrel suffers the consequences of his ways, and the good man reaps the fruit of his paths" (14:14). In other words, there is a direct correlation between one's behavior and its aftereffects. For Proverbs, rewards and punishments are not consigned to the hereafter—at no point do heaven or hell factor into the equation. Rather, one reaps what one sows in the here and now. Such is one's incentive to pursue virtue and avoid vice.

The consequences recorded throughout the sayings are at least as varied as their associated behaviors. However, they can be generally classed into one of six subcategories.[20] (1) The righteous enjoy the good favor of God, the king, and their parents. Accordingly, they reap their associated blessings. The wicked are condemned by God, punished by the king, and a source of grief to their parents. (2) The wise enjoy good health and a long life. The foolish are plagued by suffering, and they often die before their time. (3) The virtuous are materially blessed. They acquire tremendous wealth and abundant possessions. Evildoers squander whatever wealth they have, and are quickly reduced to poverty and debt. (4) The righteous receive the praise and honor of those around them. The wicked face shame and disgrace. People rejoice at their downfall. (5) The wise enjoy lives of peace and security. Even when times are tough, no harm befalls them. The foolish are pursued by misfortune. They are frequently visited by disaster and destruction. (6) Finally, the

[20] Again, for the sake of time and space, we will only briefly touch on these consequences here. For those wishing a more comprehensive analysis, including the accompanying citations, please see Appendix I.

upright are happy and satisfied. They take pleasure in life and gain their hearts' desires. The wicked are constantly frustrated. Their plans usually fail and their souls crave in vain.

Summary/Conclusion

Having concluded our overview of Proverbs' contents, we can illustrate its two ways accordingly (see table 9.5).

Proverbs' Two Ways

Characteristics	Wisdom Righteousness Seek virtues	Folly Wickedness Indulge vices
Authorities	God King Parents	Self
Behaviors	Heed correction Right use of speech Demonstrate diligence/ integrity Seek peace Act generously Good choice of companions	Despise correction Wrong use of speech Demonstrate laziness/ dishonesty Cause trouble Act greedily Poor choice of companions
Consequences	Favor Life Wealth Honor Security Satisfaction	Abomination Death Poverty Shame Ruin Frustration

Table 9.5

Several points can be made on the basis of our survey. First, the message of Proverbs obviously challenges some of the CW of our day. If the latest popular opinion polls are to be believed, then we as a society and especially the emerging generation tend to pursue material acquisitions and social status as ends unto themselves. Indeed, our fascination with these things appears to have contributed to the diminished importance of spiritual attributes. Proverbs advocates the complete reversal of these priorities, especially for the emerging generation. It maintains that the cultivation of wisdom, righteousness, and virtue should be one's paramount goal. Furthermore, it insists that it is only through this pursuit that life's genuine, abundant, and permanent blessings can be attained and enjoyed. In this regard, there are no shortcuts to success. Any other approach, according to Proverbs, is invariably bound to fail.

Second, relative to some of the trends that we have already seen in the OT, we find both continuity and contrast in the message of Proverbs. Like the Law and the Prophets, Proverbs attests to the preeminence of God. However, on the question of how best to honor the Divine, we encounter a plurality of approaches. For the Torah, faith is most clearly demonstrated by obedience to the covenantal law, including support for and participation in the religious establishment. For the Prophets, fidelity to God is marked primarily by the rejection of idolatry and the practice of social justice. For Proverbs, the ultimate expression of one's fear of the Lord is to be found in the pursuit of wisdom, righteousness, and virtuous living. There are, to be sure, varying degrees of overlap among these three paradigms. Nevertheless, each possesses its own unique emphasis and exhibits its own distinctive way of approaching, respecting, and interacting with the Almighty.

Collectively, the Law, the Prophets, and Proverbs affirm the existence of a divinely appointed system of causes and effects, and they all forecast certain consequences depending on one's conformity to the ideal. Thus, those who follow the law, care for the socially vulnerable, and cultivate virtue enjoy God's blessings. Those who break the law, trample on the lowly, and indulge their vices suffer his wrath. As we have seen, Proverbs promotes this cause/effect relationship *ad nauseam.* It maintains, consistently and repeatedly, that one reaps what one sows. As far as Proverbs is concerned, then, life is essentially fair. But not all of the Wisdom Literature agrees. Our final chapters are devoted to two texts that take issue with precisely this point—and they do so in remarkably clever and creative ways.

10

The Book of Ecclesiastes —Unconventional Wisdom I

Focus Text: Ecclesiastes

"Chaff" and the Meaning of Life

He is widely considered to be one of the brightest lights of the High Middle Ages (1000–1299 C.E.): an intellectual giant whose *opera omnia* consists of more than one hundred works, including his voluminous *Summa theologiae,* one of the most comprehensive philosophical and theological treaties ever produced. (The complete American edition totals more than two million words!) Even to this day, the *Summa* or portions of it is required reading for undergraduate and graduate students at many Roman Catholic universities, colleges, and seminaries throughout the world. The fact that Thomas Aquinas died just prior to his fiftieth birthday (1225–1274 C.E.) only makes his literary output all the more remarkable. Indeed, the Roman Catholic Church officially bestowed upon this scholar its highest possible honor when it canonized him to sainthood in 1323 C.E.

It was during the process of canonization that a puzzling anecdote about Aquinas first surfaced. Its source was Reginald of Piperno, Aquinas's confessor and friend. According to Reginald, three months before Aquinas died he abruptly stopped writing, abandoning his *Summa* and a commentary on the Psalms midstream. Thomas became withdrawn, forlorn, and despondent. Concerned for his physical and mental health, Reginald implored him to return to his work. But the great doctor of the church refused. Only when Reginald repeatedly pressed him for a reason did Thomas finally divulge:

> I adjure you by the living almighty God, and by the faith you have in our order, and by charity that you strictly promise me you will never reveal in my lifetime what I tell you. Everything that I have written seems to be chaffy in respect to those things that I have seen and have been revealed to me.[1]

Reportedly, Aquinas never wrote another word. Of course, his odd behavior begs the question, What exactly was it that Thomas saw? What was it that caused him to dismiss his entire life's work as "chaff," a meaningless by-product of grain threshing; the wispy shell borne away by the wind and burned for lack of use? To this day, theories abound. Some think he had a mystical experience; others a nervous breakdown. Given the events that followed, perhaps he glimpsed his imminent demise and despaired over the limits of his own mortality. Nobody knows for sure. But seven centuries later, Aquinas's sentiment strikes a familiar chord with, of all people, a mother of four from Ohio.

"Sunshine" (her moniker in cyberspace) recently posted the following question on the Philosophy section of Yahoo! Answers, an online messaging board:

> Did something ever happen to you that makes EVERYTHING else seem trivial?

Sunshine reveals that she has had this feeling ever since her dad has started "slipping away" due to the sudden onset of dementia. Judging from the responses, most readers identify with her experience. They share their own profound events, including the birth of a child, a sudden death, a tragic accident, and the diagnosis of a terminal disease.[2]

On the same site, "Dan" asks a similar question but from a decidedly different angle:

---

[1] Processus canonizationis s. Thomae, Neapoli 79, ed. M.-H. Laurent, fascicule 4 of *Fontes vitae s. Thomae Aquinatis,* ed. Dominic M. Prümmer (Toulouse, n.d.), 376–77, quoted in Marjorie O'Rourke Boyle, "Chaff: Thomas Aquinas's Repudiation of His *Opera omnia,*" *New Literary History* 28 (1997): 383–99.

[2] See http://malaysia.answers.yahoo.com/question/index;_ylt=At_fH61HN9a_XWrMkUZKt7aGQgx.;_ylv=3?qid=20071209173338AA0IFl (accessed March 27, 2008).

> Why does life seem utterly meaningless and pointless when you draw back and look at it? From outer space as it were, lots of tiny humans running around, living and then dying, what's the point?

How would *you* answer him? The twenty posted replies fall generally into one of three categories. Nearly one third agree with Dan: life *is* meaningless; deal with it. Another third advises him to simply establish his own purpose—to pursue his passions and share his unique gifts and talents with those around him while he can. A final third professes the existence of a spiritual realm beyond this material world—a realm that ultimately informs the true meaning of life.[3]

Even within the relatively modest confines of this online domain, Sunshine and Dan represent only a tiny fraction of the interest in this subject. A phrase-specific search for the "meaning of life" reveals more than two thousand matches among its Q&A postings. In fact, the question is so ubiquitous that at least one inquirer wonders if and when people will ever stop raising it!

Indeed, since the dawn of consciousness, humanity has pondered the purpose of life. And throughout human history, significant events have triggered existential crises that resulted in the radical reevaluation of priorities. Indeed, if the crisis is great enough, virtually everything else can pale in comparison. Suddenly, it all seems . . . well . . . *chaffy*. Evidently, this is a situation that the author of Ecclesiastes was quite familiar with. And his experience with it poses some serious challenges for the conventional wisdom of his time.

Qoheleth

From its outset, the book of Ecclesiastes claims to consist of "the words of David's son, Qoheleth, king in Jerusalem" (Eccl 1:1). This attribution logically suggests King Solomon, the traditional source of much Wisdom Literature, even though he is never mentioned by name. However, the semantic and literary evidence strongly favors a much later compositional date, most likely during the fourth or third century B.C.E.[4] The scholarly consensus, therefore, is that Solomon could not have been its author.

[3] See http://ph.answers.yahoo.com/question/index?qid=20061119142855AAAMYo2 (accessed March 27, 2008).

[4] This assessment is based on several observations, including the presence of numerous Persian loan words and possible engagement with Greek philosophy.

As for the designation "Qoheleth" (קהלת), this title is derived from the Hebrew word קהל, *qahal* or "assemble." A *qohelet* is the agent of assembly—the "assembler," so to speak. Thus, Qoheleth could denote the leader of an assembly. This is how the LXX translates it. The Greek ἐκκλησιαστής, *ekklēsiastēs*(brought into English as Ecclesiastes) is one who heads a church or a congregation (ἐκκλησία, *ekklēsia*). But "qoheleth" could also refer to an assembler of sayings—a collector of proverbs (see Eccl 12:9–11). So while the former definition gave rise to the English title for this book, the latter is decidedly more consistent with the actual role of our author.

Affiliation with the Wisdom Literature

As previously noted, the book of Ecclesiastes is classed among the Wisdom Literature of the HB. Its placement there is due to more than just its Solomonic attribution. Some of the contents of Ecclesiastes also reflect the same ideologies of conventional wisdom. For example, Ecclesiastes recognizes the two paths of wisdom and folly (2:13–14; 10:2). It extols the virtues of peace (4:6), humility (5:1–5), integrity (5:1–5), patience (7:8b–9), self-restraint (7:21–22; 10:4), industriousness (11:6), verbal discretion (5:1–5; 9:17; 10:12–14), fear of God (5:6), and obedience to the king (8:2–6a; 10:20). It even acknowledges the benefits of righteous behavior and the disadvantages of foolishness. According to Ecclesiastes, the wise curry God's favor (2:26; 8:12–13) and preserve their own lives (7:11–12). They obtain happiness (2:26; 8:1), honor (7:1a), wealth (2:26), and power (7:19). The foolish, by contrast, forfeit their wealth (2:26). They are lazy (10:18; 11:4), self-destructive (4:5), and condemned by God (3:17; 8:12–13).

As familiar as these assertions may be, they are relatively minor notes in the overall composition of Ecclesiastes. They are set within, and at times seem discordant with, a grander and more sophisticated arrangement that resonates throughout this work—one that pronounces all things as הבל, *hebel* (lit. "vapor," "mist," or "breath").

All Things "Vapor"

Ecclesiastes begins by proclaiming: "Vapor of vapors," says Qoheleth, "vapor of vapors. All is vapor" (הבל הבלים אמר קהלת הבל הבלים הכל הבל,

habel habalim 'amar qohelet habel habalim hakkol habel). This declaration is also repeated at the book's conclusion (12:8). Together, these bookends create an *inclusio* around the entire work, thus drawing attention to its central theme: "Vapor!" (הבל, *habel*).[5]

So what exactly does it mean to profess everything as "vapor"? As it turns out, this term has a well-established use throughout the Wisdom Literature. There, it is frequently employed to denote the fragility of human life (Job 7:16; Ps 39:5–6, 12; 62:10; 78:39; 144:3–4). It is often paired with other ephemeral entities, such as a "breeze" (Job 7:7), "vanishing cloud" (Job 7:9), "phantom" (Ps 39:7), "cobweb" (Ps 39:12), "illusion" (Ps 62:10), and "shadow" (Ps 144:3). (Among these, Aquinas's "chaff" would be right at home.)

The beginning and ending of Ecclesiastes present *hebel* in its superlative form: "vapor of vapors." The superlative emphasizes a term's most extreme quality. (The "King of kings," for instance, is the supreme regent above all other rulers.) "Vapor of vapors," therefore, refers to the most transitory of the transitory; the most fleeting of the fleeting; the faintest of the faint. It is the vestige of a dream; the echo of a whisper; the tail of a zephyr. *This* is what the author of Ecclesiastes has determined *everything* to be.

Qoheleth bases his assessment on his experience, specifically, on his quest "to search and investigate in wisdom all things that are done under the sun" (Eccl 1:13). In essence, our sage had set out to ascertain the meaning of life.

Qoheleth's Experiment and the Problem with Death

Qoheleth began his experiment by pursuing "pleasure and the enjoyment of good things" (2:1). He surrounded himself with laughter and mirth, wine and frivolity. These things, however, disappointed him (2:2–3). So instead, he turned his hand to "great works" (2:4):

---

[5] As it turns out, these phrases may also hold the key to unlocking Ecclesiastes' literary structure as well. For more, see A. G. Wright's series of articles in the *Catholic Biblical Quarterly:* "The Riddle of the Sphinx: The Structure of the Book of Qoheleth," *CBQ* 30 (1968): 313–34; "The Riddle of the Sphinx Revisited: Numerical Patterns in the Book of Qoheleth," *CBQ* 42 (1980): 38–51; "Additional Numerical Patterns in Qoheleth," *CBQ* 45 (1983): 32–43.

> I built myself houses and planted vineyards; I made garden and parks, and set out in them fruit trees of all sorts. And I constructed for myself reservoirs to water a flourishing woodland. (Eccl 2:4–6)

As a result of his industriousness and ambition, Qoheleth obtained unprecedented prosperity:

> I acquired male and female slaves, and slaves were born in my house. I also had growing herds of cattle and flocks of sheep, more than all who had been before me in Jerusalem. I amassed for myself silver and gold, and the wealth of kings and provinces. I got for myself male and female singers and all human luxuries. I became great, and I stored up more than all others before me in Jerusalem. . . . Nothing that my eyes desired did I deny them, nor did I deprive myself of any joy, but my heart rejoiced in the fruit of my toil. This was my share for all my toil. (Eccl 2:7–10)

But when he considered all of his acquisitions and material possessions, Qoheleth found them, too, to be "vapor" and "a chase after the wind" (2:11). Why? Because he understood that, sooner or later, he would be replaced by his successor. Once that happened, all that he had labored for would be of no profit to him (2:11–12). Qoheleth came to realize that, no matter how prosperous one might be, ultimately, you can't take it with you (2:17–21; 5:15–16; 6:1–2).

So finally, Qoheleth examined the value of wisdom. He perceived that "wisdom has the advantage over folly as much as light has the advantage over darkness" (2:13). Nevertheless, neither the wise nor the foolish can escape the inescapable. Inevitably, the same fate befalls them both. Death proves to be the great equalizer. As such, it levels the playing field and in the long run renders all human enterprise futile. This recognition led Qoheleth to the following conclusion:

> So I said to myself, if the fool's lot is to befall me also, why then should I be wise? Where is the profit for me? And I concluded in my heart that this too is vanity ["vapor"]. Neither of the wise man nor of the fool will there be an abiding remembrance, for in days to come both will have been forgotten. How is it that the wise man dies as well as the fool! Therefore I loathed life, since for me the work that is done under the sun is evil; for all is vanity ["vapor"] and a chase after the wind. . . . So my feelings turned to despair. . . . (Eccl 2:15–17, 20)

It is in this, Qoheleth's deduction, that the conventional wisdom of the Old Testament is directly confronted by the book of Ecclesiastes. Whereas the former champions the virtuous life and touts its associated blessings, the latter regards these things as null and void—or transient, at best—against the backdrop of death. In other words, regardless of whether one is wise or foolish, rich or poor, righteous or sinful, or even human or animal, a common destiny awaits all (2:14b–16; 3:18–21; 6:3–6, 8; 7:2b; 9:2–3; 12:3–7). According to Qoheleth, there is no immortality, no retribution, or any meaningful existence after death (9:5–6).[6] Not even the memory of the departed lasts for long (1:11; 12:13–16).[7] As a result, death renders life unfair, and, as Sunshine put it, "makes EVERYTHING else seem trivial."

Qoheleth's Problems with Life

As the remainder of the book unfolds, we find that Qoheleth's complaints are not only limited to death. Our author also takes issue with the problems of life—problems that, again, defy the conventional wisdom of his time. Chief among these is the supposed cause/effect relationship between one's behavior and its consequences. This system doesn't jibe with Qoheleth's experience. He cites numerous injustices: the righteous perish while the wicked thrive (7:15; 10:14); the sinner commits a hundred crimes and receives no punishment (8:10–12); slaves ride on horseback while princes walk the ground (10:5–7). In fact, he finds very little correspondence between merit and success:

> The race is not won by the swift, nor the battle by the valiant, nor a livelihood by the wise, nor riches by the shrewd, nor favor by the experts. . . . (Eccl 9:11)

In short, Qoheleth discovers no consistent application of justice. Wickedness, oppression, and corruption prevail, and they frequently outweigh the good accomplished by virtue (4:1–3; 5:7; 9:18; 10:1). Even mere chance contributes to the randomness of life (9:8–9), further jeopardizing the notion of divine retribution.

---

[6] At Qoheleth's time, one's afterlife consisted only of a shadowy, underground existence in Sheol.

[7] According to Jewish tradition, one attained "immortality" primarily through remembrance, via the legacy of one's name. In the Torah, this legacy is associated with children. For this reason, offspring, especially sons, were crucial for establishing a lasting memory. (This is also why the most heinous crimes in the HB resulted not only in the death of the perpetrator but of his family as well [e.g., Num 16:20–34; Josh 7:6–26]. In this way, his name would be "blotted out" forever.) The Wisdom tradition maintains that a "good name" will also be long remembered. It is this assertion that Qoheleth denies. The book of Sirach (second cent. B.C.E.) would eventually mediate by acknowledging that while the names of the virtuous may be forgotten (Sir 44:9–10), the fruits of their virtues would nevertheless endure (44:11–15).

This is not to say that Qoheleth doesn't believe in God. He concedes God's sovereignty over all (3:14–15; 7:13–14) and even acknowledges a cyclical balance to the created order—a patterned, "appointed time" for everything (1:4–10; 3:1–8). In accordance with God's wisdom, the sun rises and the sun sets; seasons pass from one to the next; generations come and generations go. (Here our author's perspective resembles Dan's: "from outer space, as it were.") But despite such coherence in the grand scheme of things, Qoheleth contends that wisdom's particulars lie far beyond our abilities to grasp. Specifically, nobody can know for certain what the future holds for them (3:11; 6:12; 7:13–14; 8:6–8; 9:1, 12; 10:14; 11:5). Such wisdom is unattainable (1:16–17; 7:23–24; 8:16–17), though glimpses of it can be found in life's somber occasions (7:1b–6; 11:8). Thus, while death, mourning, and sorrow may be more instructive than happiness and frivolity, too much of this sort of wisdom can become depressing (1:18). For this reason, Qoheleth cautions against becoming "too wise" (7:16)!

Qoheleth's final complaint has to do with the pitfalls of ambition and wealth. As he has seen, excessive toil leads to excessive acquisitions. Such prosperity is not only useless at death; it also proves problematic during life. According to Qoheleth, riches trigger an increase in greed and demand (4:8; 5:9–10; 6:7). In turn, rivalry lies at the heart of ambition (4:4). Therefore, the rich are in a constant state of anxiety, preoccupied with their affairs during the day and restless at night (2:23; 5:11). They obsess over their wealth and suffer regardless of whether it is retained or lost (5:12–13). Clearly this is no advantage, even within a fleeting life.

Qoheleth's Solution

So what is the solution, the consummate answer to the "meaning of life" question? The book of Ecclesiastes presents one. If death constitutes the most inevitable and insurmountable of problems, then Qoheleth upholds life as its principal solution. After all, "a live dog is better off than a dead lion" (9:4). To make the most of their lives, Qoheleth advises his readers to

> Go, eat your bread with joy and drink your wine with a merry heart, because it is now that God favors your works. At all times let your garments be white, and spare not the perfume for your head. Enjoy life with the wife whom you love, all

> the days of the fleeting life that is granted you under the sun. This is your lot in life, for the toil of your labors under the sun. Anything you can turn your hand to, do with what power you have; for there will be no work, nor reason, nor knowledge, nor wisdom in the nether world where you are going. (Eccl 9:7–10; similarly 2:24; 3:12–13, 22; 5:18–20; 8:15; 11:9–10)[8]

To recap, then, Qoheleth has deemed the conventional pursuits of wisdom, virtue, and ambition and all that they promise as "a meaningless chase after the wind." This position places him squarely at odds with the Wisdom Literature. At the same time, however, he doesn't completely reject the truth claims of that tradition, as we noted at the start. Rather, our author seems intent upon striking a precarious balance. If anything, he favors moderation. For Qoheleth, all excesses, good or bad, are to be avoided. One should become neither too industrious nor too lazy, neither too wise nor too foolish, neither too righteous nor too sinful, neither too somber nor too frivolous, neither too wealthy nor too poor, neither too bold nor too cautious. Rather, one ought to be content with one's lot in life and find satisfaction in the simple pleasures of food, wine, work, and family. According to this ideology, one can do no better than to "eat, drink, and be merry" in appreciation of each day, always mindful that life passes quickly.

Ecclesiastes' Conclusion (Eccl 12:1–8)

The book of Ecclesiastes closes on this last note, with a wonderfully poetic description of the physical decline that accompanies old age. Its text, and proposed interpretation, is as shown in table 10.1.

---

[8] In this respect, Qoheleth's counsel bears striking resemblance to a passage from the Gilgamesh Epic. When Gilgamesh wrestles with his own mortality following the death of his friend, Enkidu, he solicits the help of Siduri, an alewife, to point him in the direction of Utnaphishtim (a mortal who has successfully achieved immortality). Siduri tries to dissuade Gilgamesh from his quest by explaining:

> "You will not find the eternal life you seek. When the gods created humanity they appointed death for it, and kept eternal life for themselves. So Gilgamesh, let your stomach be full; make merry day and night, every day feast and rejoice. Day and night, dance and play; adorn yourself in fresh clothes. Keep your head washed, bathe in water, and appreciate the child who holds your hand. Let your wife delight herself in your embrace. This is the task [of humanity]." (Translation revised on the basis of Stephanie Dalley, *Myths from Mesopotamia: Creation, the Flood, Gilgamesh, and Others* (rev. ed.; Oxford's World Classics; New York: Oxford University Press, 2000), 150, and *ANET,* 90.)

Remember your Creator in the days of your youth,
  before the evil days come
And the years approach of which you will say,
  I have no pleasure in them; . . .

Ecclesiastes 12:1–8 Interpreted

Biblical Text	**Text Describes**
Before the sun is darkened, and the light, and the moon, and the stars, while the clouds return after the rain	A description of the Palestinian winter, a natural metaphor for old age
When the guardians of the house tremble,	Shakiness in the arms
And the strong men are bent	Crooked legs
And the grinders are idle because they are few,	Loss of teeth
And they who look through the windows grow blind	Dimming of the eyes
When the doors to the street are shut And the sound of the mill is low	Loss of hearing
When one waits for the chirp of a bird, but all the daughters of song are suppressed	Decline of the voice
And one fears heights, and perils in the street	Growing trepidation or mental confusion
When the almond tree blooms,	White hair
And the locust grows sluggish	Arthritic stiffness or sexual decline
And the caper berry is without effect	An appetite stimulant; signals the loss of appetite

Table 10.1

Because man goes to his lasting home,
  and mourners go about the streets;
Before the silver cord is snapped
  and the golden bowl is broken,
And the pitcher is shattered at the spring,
  and the broken pulley falls into the well,
And the dust returns to the earth as it once was,
  and the life breath returns to God who gave it.
Vanity of vanities, says Qoheleth,
  all things are vanity! (Eccl 12:1, 5–8)

The Epilogue (Eccl 12:9–14)

To this, the proper conclusion of the work, a brief epilogue has been appended (12:9–14). Because the epilogue refers to Qoheleth in the third person, it was obviously penned by a later author or authors. Unfortunately, at least for the integrity of this book, the subsequent writer didn't subscribe to Qoheleth's philosophical outlook. Rather, with a sweeping generalization, he endeavors to dovetail the entire work into the tongue and groove foundation of Torah orthodoxy:

> The last word, when all is heard: Fear God and keep his commandments, for this is man's all; because God will bring to judgment every work, with all its hidden qualities, whether good or bad. (Eccl 12:13–14)

The fact that Qoheleth never even mentions God's commandments seems to be of no concern for our redactor.[9] Rather, his gloss suggests that soon after Ecclesiastes was composed, its message proved to be far too controversial for some of its readers. Evidently, they preferred a more substantial, if not conventional, meaning to life. But a more innovative solution was about to emerge—a solution that found its way into Judaism during the Greco-Roman period.

The Aftermath: Immortality and the Legacy of Ecclesiastes

In its clash with Hellenization, Judaism confronted and subsequently adopted belief in the immortality of the soul and in retributive justice in the afterlife. In the OT, these concepts first appear in the book of Daniel (Dan 12:2–3). Among the sapiential works, they find their clearest representation and staunchest ally in the book of Wisdom (ca. first century B.C.E./C.E.). In fact, it is on the basis of these tenets that the book of Wisdom advances what some scholars take to be an explicit refutation of the book of Ecclesiastes.[10]

---

[9]In Eccl 8:5–6, Qoheleth affirms that the wise man "keeps the command," avoids evil, and recognizes that there is "a time and a judgment for everything." However, given the subject of its preceding context —obedience to the king (8:2–4)—these references most likely refer to civil laws and courts. As for God's judgment, this notion is maintained in 3:17 and 11:9, but scholars remain divided over the meaning of these passages. Given the thrust of the epilogue, some question their originality as well.

[10]Wis 2 contains the argument in question. Its parallels are indeed compelling. The full text can be found in Appendix J.

Beyond Daniel and Wisdom, the notion of eternal rewards and punishments is woven into a considerable number of intertestamental writings (works that were composed in the period between the OT and NT, e.g., *1 Enoch,* the *Book of Jubilees,* the *Testaments of the Twelve Patriarchs,* the *Testament of Moses*). Collectively, this literature indicates that by the time Christianity appeared on the scene, it inherited and in turn contributed to a fairly prevalent and well-developed theology of the afterlife. Such theology has all but alleviated the fundamental crisis faced by Qoheleth. Consequently, Ecclesiastes' solution is considered by many to be somewhat obsolete—the remnant of a less enlightened era.

However, as long as the "meaning of life" question is raised—and judging by the Internet, there's no sign of a letup—this work will continue to have relevance. Because it grounds the lofty idealisms of conventional wisdom (and even our own CW, for that matter) in the harsh realities of the human experience, Ecclesiastes' message is as applicable today as it was back then. It recognizes that life is *not* always fair. Injustices abound on many different levels. Most problematically, death appears to have the final say, ultimately threatening to obscure whatever it is that one hopes to be, to acquire, or to accomplish. Irrespective of one's views on the afterlife, virtually all human beings can recognize the validity of these assertions. Qoheleth simply refuses to sugar-coat them.

But it is not our author's intent to depress his readers. Just the opposite. He submits that the brevity of our mortal existence, properly understood, should lend true clarity to our perspective. It should motivate us to balance our lives, to readjust our priorities, and to appreciate the simple pleasures we might otherwise take for granted. It should further enable us to place our ambitions in their proper contexts, to cultivate a healthy detachment from our possessions, to acknowledge our achievements with humility, and to face our failures with a due sense of proportion. Regardless of whatever awaits us in the great hereafter, such advice can certainly lead to a better quality of life in the great here and now.

Having thus concluded our consideration of Ecclesiastes, we turn finally to the book of Job. Like Ecclesiastes, Job contends with some of the fundamental principles of the Wisdom tradition. But it does so in an entirely different, not to mention unexpected, sort of way.

11

The Book of Job —Unconventional Wisdom II

Focus Text: Job

The "Iron Horse"

By the time he retired from baseball in 1939, Lou Gehrig had amassed some extraordinary accomplishments. During his seventeen-season career (1923–1939), Gehrig led his team, the New York Yankees, to six World Series victories. He was elected to seven consecutive All-Star teams (1933–1939) and was twice honored with the American League's Most Valuable Player Award (1927, 1936). In 1934, Gehrig captured baseball's elusive Triple Crown when he led the league in batting average (.363), home runs (49), and runs batted in (165). He holds the record for most grand slams in a career (23) and became the only player in history to drive in more than 500 runs during a three-year period (with 509 from 1930 to 1932). Gehrig's most storied achievement, however, was his consecutive playing streak of 2,130 games—a record that shattered Everett Scott's former one of 1,307.[1] The streak came not without cost, however. Late in his career, X-rays revealed that

[1] Gehrig's record stood for fifty-six years, until Cal Ripken Jr. broke it in 1995. Ripken's record, set in 1998, now stands at 2,632 consecutive games.

Gehrig had suffered seventeen fractures in his hands. He had simply played through the pain. It was this feat that earned him the nickname the "Iron Horse."

Without question, Gehrig's playing streak would have continued had sudden tragedy not struck. The Iron Horse contracted amyotrophic lateral sclerosis (ALS), forcing him into retirement just eight games into the 1939 season. On July 4, 1939, sixty-two thousand fans gathered at Yankee Stadium to pay tribute to the legendary first baseman. As Gehrig stood at home plate and addressed the crowd, he dwelled not on his misfortune but on his overwhelming feelings of gratitude. "Today," he said, "I consider myself the luckiest man on the face of this earth." The ballplayer thanked his fans, his teammates, his coaches, and his family for all of the support he had received from them. "I may have had a tough break," he concluded, "but I have an awful lot to live for."[2]

Unfortunately, Gehrig would not live much longer. Even iron, it would seem, can be broken. He succumbed to ALS on June 2, 1941. Before he died, however, Gehrig was inducted into the Baseball Hall of Fame. The Yankees also retired his number 4 jersey, making Gehrig the first professional athlete ever to have received this honor.

ALS: The Disease and Its Victims

The malady that stole Gehrig's life would eventually bear his name: Lou Gehrig's disease. It is a nefarious and, to date, incurable neuromuscular ailment characterized by progressive muscular weakness. It attacks nerve cells in the brain and in the spinal cord, causing motor neurons, which control the movement of voluntary muscles, to break down and die. As a result, the brain becomes incapable of signaling voluntary muscles to initiate and control their movements. Lacking the necessary signals, these muscles gradually weaken and deteriorate. The disease is inevitably fatal. Most people diagnosed with it survive less than five years. It eventually affects speech, swallowing, and breathing. However, because ALS affects only the body's voluntary muscles, patients' minds, senses, and internal organs are generally not impaired.[3]

---

[2] This scene was immortalized in the 1942 motion picture, *Pride of the Yankees,* starring Gary Cooper.

[3] Information taken from the Lou Gehrig Web site: http://www.lougehrig.com/about/als.htm (accessed March 27, 2008).

This creates a fearsome condition: helpless victims watch their bodies decline even while their cognitive abilities remain fully sound.[4]

Aside from Gehrig, ALS has plagued the lives of other notable individuals (see list following).

- Professor Morrie Schwartz (the subject of Mitch Albom's bestseller, *Tuesdays with Morrie*)
- Nobel physicist Stephen Hawking
- Hall of Fame pitcher Jim "Catfish" Hunter
- Senator Jacob Javits
- Actors Michael Zaslow and David Niven
- Creator of *Sesame Street* Jon Stone
- Television producer Scott Brazil
- Boxing champion Ezzard Charles
- NBA Hall of Fame basketball player George Yardley
- Pro football player Glenn Montgomery
- Golfer Jeff Julian
- Golf caddie Bruce Edwards
- British soccer player Jimmy Johnstone
- Musician Leadbelly (Huddie Ledbetter)
- Photographer Eddie Adams
- Entertainer Dennis Day
- Jazz musician Charles Mingus
- Composer Dimitri Shostakovich
- Former Vice President of the United States Henry A. Wallace
- U.S. Army General Maxwell Taylor[5]

To this list, we can also add at least one more name: Leonard L. Bridge, my father.

I was eleven years old when my dad's diagnosis was confirmed by the Mayo Clinic. Prior to that, he had been the picture of good health.

---

[4]So intimidating is this disease that victims of it comprised a significant percentage of Dr. Jack Kevorkian's infamous physician-assisted suicide clientele. According to records, 12 of Kevorkian's 69 clients had ALS ("Dr. Jack Kevorkian and Cases of Euthanasia in Oakland County, Michigan, 1990–1998," L.A. Roscoe et al., *New England Journal of Medicine* 434:23 [December 7, 2000]: 1735–36). Given the relatively low incidence of this disease, this percentage of representation (17.4%) is very high indeed.

[5]Information gathered from the ALS Association's Web site at http://www/alsa.org (accessed March 27, 2008).

In his younger days, he had attended college on a golf scholarship. (To my knowledge, his state record for the lowest score on seventy-two holes played in a single day still stands.) There, at an athletic banquet, he had met my mother, a cheerleader. The two soon married and had three children. He was a good-natured, diligent, and caring man. He taught economics at the local community college, coached our sports teams, served as the school board president, and was active in our church. He avoided caffeine, alcohol, and cigarettes. He never even swore. Even though he received his diagnosis at the prime of his life (he was then thiry-nine), he handled it with Gehrig-like courage and optimism.

The physicians had given my dad one year to live. He lasted six. During that time, I witnessed his physical decay. He went from walking, to using a cane, to using a wheelchair, to finally using a motorized wheelchair. Yet the weaker his body became, the stronger his spirit grew. He tried to remain as active as possible and continued to teach up until the last two weeks of his life. His faith never seemed to waver. Despite the circumstances, it remained a rock-solid source of comfort for him and for our family. Nevertheless, we all struggled to make some sort of sense of the cruel fate he had been dealt.

Throughout those six years, I read the book of Job with some degree of regularity. I remember reading it cover to cover the morning after my father had died. I was hoping that it contained some sort of answer, some sort of explanation as to why bad things happen to good people. After all, this is the book's widespread reputation. Ultimately, however, I found it confusing and disappointing. While the book is about the terrible suffering endured by a righteous man, it provides no satisfactory answer as to why his suffering occurs. In fact, even within God's master plan, Job's affliction seems to contribute very little to the greater good. In my opinion, the book failed to deliver what it had purportedly promised.[6]

Over a decade later, I returned to this book again. This time, it was for a very different reason. I had been assigned to teach a college-level

---

[6] Surely others have reached this same conclusion. As a case in point, this assessment was alluded to in the television series *Providence* (NBC, 1999–2002). In one episode, an anxious mother has to decide whether or not to consent to some fairly invasive and risky medical procedures for her sickly newborn. Following a restless night in the chapel, she hands Dr. Sydney Hansen (Melina Kanakaredes) a Bible and confesses, "I've been reading this all night long, but the book of Job doesn't say anything about exploratory surgery."

course on "The Sacred Writings of Israel." Job was part of the curriculum. In preparation for the course, I was forced to re-examine this text from a more academic point of view—to read it in light of its original, historical context. Only then did I begin to appreciate Job's theological contributions to the wisdom tradition. But even more importantly, I finally began to grasp the true rhetorical aim of this work.

The Literary Structure of the Book of Job

The book of Job can be neatly divided into two parts, according to its differing literary styles. The beginning (1:1–2:13) and ending (42:7–17) of the book are written in narrative prose. This is what contains the plot and the story line of the work. Between these sections lies the substantial core (3:1–42:6). This core consists of a series of extended, poetic dialogues between the characters of the book. For clarity's sake, we shall examine these two parts separately.

The Narrative Prose

The book begins by describing the righteousness of a man named Job:

> In the land of Uz there was a blameless and upright man named Job, who feared God and avoided evil. Seven sons and three daughters were born to him; and he had seven thousand sheep, three thousand camels, five hundred yoke of oxen, five hundred she-asses, and a great number of work animals, so that he was greater than any of the men of the East. His sons used to take turns giving feasts, sending invitations to their three sisters to eat and drink with them. And when each feast had run its course, Job would send for them and sanctify them, rising early and offering holocausts for every one of them. For Job said, "It may be that my sons have sinned and blasphemed God in their hearts." This Job did habitually. (Job 1:1–5)

All goes well for Job until a certain day, when the heavenly court is assembled before God. Among them is "the satan" (הַשָּׂטָן, *hassatan*), or literally, "the accuser."[7] When God boasts of Job's blamelessness, the accuser challenges the grounds of Job's loyalty. Surely if Job were

---

[7] With the definite article, this word is clearly *not* a proper name, despite the tendency of modern translations to render it as such. These tendencies stem from the later Jewish and Christian practice of ascribing this name, Satan, to the devil.

to lose what he had, his disposition toward God would change. Confident of his man, God thus sanctions the collapse of Job's life. He places Job in the accuser's power on the condition that Job himself remain unharmed.

> And so one day, while his sons and his daughters were eating and drinking wine in the house of their eldest brother, a messenger came to Job and said, "The oxen were plowing and the asses grazing beside them, and the Sabeans carried them off in a raid. They put the herdsmen to the sword, and I alone have escaped to tell you." While he was yet speaking, another came and said, "Lightning has fallen from heaven and struck the sheep and their shepherds and consumed them; and I alone have escaped to tell you." While he was yet speaking, another came and said, "The Chaldeans formed three columns, seized the camels, carried them off, and put those tending them to the sword, and I alone have escaped to tell you." While he was yet speaking, another came and said, "Your sons and daughters were eating and drinking wine in the house of their eldest brother, when suddenly a great wind came across the desert and smote the four corners of the house. It fell upon the young people and they are dead; and I alone have escaped to tell you." Then Job began to tear his cloak and cut off his hair. He cast himself prostrate upon the ground, and said, "Naked I came forth from my mother's womb, and naked shall I go back again. The LORD gave and the LORD has taken away; blessed be the name of the LORD!" In all this Job did not sin, nor did he say anything disrespectful of God. (Job 1:13–22)

As tragic as the fallout is, it is apparently not enough. When God lauds Job's response, the accuser provokes the Almighty even further: "Skin for skin! All that a man has will he give for his life. But now put forth your hand and touch his bone and his flesh and surely he will blaspheme you to your face" (2:4–5). So once again, God relinquishes Job, permitting everything short of his death. Accordingly, the accuser

> went forth from the presence of the LORD and smote Job with severe boils from the soles of his feet to the crown of his head. And he took a potsherd to scrape himself, as he sat among the ashes. Then his wife said to him, "Are you still holding to your innocence? Curse God and die." But he said to her, "Are even you going to speak as senseless women do? We accept good things from God; and should we not accept evil?" Through all this, Job said nothing sinful. (Job 2:7–10)

It is at this point in the story that Job's three friends arrive. Their arrival sets the stage for the poetic discourses that follow. The discourses—the bulk of this book—consist of three cycles of speeches that alternate between Job and his three friends, Eliphaz, Bildad, and Zophar. We can illustrate this section as shown in table 11.1.

The Three Cycles of Speeches in Job 4–31			
	First Cycle (4–14)	**Second Cycle (15–21)**	**Third Cycle (22–31)**
Eliphaz's speech	4–5	15	22
Job's reply	6–7	16–17	23–24
Bildad's speech	8	18	25
Job's reply	9–10	19	26–27:12
Zophar's speech	11	20	[27:13–21?]
Job's reply	12–14	21	29–31

Table 11.1

It should be noted that the structure of Job follows this fairly consistent outline up until Bildad's third speech (Job 25). At that point, some textual corruption affects Job's reply and Zophar's final speech. In Job 28, an independent treatise on the inaccessibility of wisdom has been inserted, and in Job 32–37, the speeches of a fourth character, Elihu, have been awkwardly interjected. (Most scholars agree that these are subsequent emendations to the original text.[8]) Finally, beginning in Job 38, God booms forth from a storm. He delivers two speeches (38:1–40:2 and 40:6–41:26), each of which is followed by a short recant by Job (40:3–5 and 42:1–6).

At 42:7 the narrative prose resumes. Job's friends are criticized for their words and Job intercedes on their behalf. As the book draws to its conclusion, God restores Job's former prosperity:

> The Lord even gave to Job twice as much as he had before. Then all his brethren and his sisters came to him, and all his former acquaintances, and they dined with him in his house. They condoled with him and comforted him for all the evil which the Lord had brought upon him; and each one gave him a piece of money and a gold ring. Thus the Lord blessed the latter days of Job more than his earlier ones. For he had fourteen thousand sheep, six thousand camels, a thousand yoke of oxen, and a thousand she-asses. And he had seven sons and three daughters.

[8] It is not clear to whom the wisdom poem in Job 28 is to be attributed. Its themes, the inestimable value of wisdom and its attainment through fear of the Lord, resonate most closely with the theologies of Job's friends. As for Elihu, he is missing from both the prologue and the epilogue of this work. In fact, Job doesn't even respond to him. These factors strongly suggest that this character is the product of a much later editor. Curiously, Elihu's dialogues add remarkably little to the positions already espoused by Eliphaz, Bildad, and Zophar.

> ... In all the land no other women were as beautiful as the daughters of Job; and their father gave them an inheritance among their brethren. After this, Job lived a hundred and forty years; and he saw his children, his grandchildren, and even his great-grandchildren. Then Job died, old and full of years. (Job 42:10–16)

So what is the point of this book? Perhaps it seeks to present Job as a model of patience—as an example of the ideal way to respond to calamity. Certainly this is Job's reputation among the earliest Christians (see, e.g., Jas 5:11). Or perhaps it intends to assert that God ultimately rewards those who suffer unjustly—those who endure their difficulties with humility and grace. Judging from the narrative, either of these options are legitimate possibilities. Just one problem remains. The book is more—substantially more—than just the narrative. The vast majority of it consists of the poetic disputations. If an author simply wanted to convey the ideas above, he surely could have accomplished this in three chapters. Why add another forty chapters of dialogue—dialogue that, in fact, contradicts both the characterization of Job's patience and the notion of divine retribution? Why, indeed? Obviously, the core is there for a reason: it contains the central message of this book. Of course, getting at it requires that we first go through it.

The Poetic Dialogues

In the wake of Job's afflictions, his three friends have rallied around him. Together, they sit on the ground for a whole week. No one speaks a word. Finally, it is Job who first breaks the silence. He curses the day he was born (3:3–10) and bemoans his very existence (3:11–19). Job finds himself in such discomfort that death would be a welcome relief (3:20–26).[9]

Following his lamentation, each one of Job's friends takes a turn speaking to him. They always speak in order—Eliphaz, Bildad, and Zophar—and allow Job an immediate response. Over the course of three cycles, then, the friends account for nine dialogues and Job contributes nine replies.

---

[9] We can thus contrast Job's view of death with that of Qoheleth's. While both concede the brevity of life, they hold decidedly different attitudes toward death. For Qoheleth, death constitutes humanity's principal and insurmountable problem. For Job, death represents rest and peace—a preferable alternative to his acute pain and agony.

There are certain themes that the friends consistently touch upon. The most prominent (it appears in eight of the nine dialogues[10]) is the assertion that God punishes the wicked. Even though they may seem to prosper for a while, those who practice evil will always suffer the consequences of their ways. This is a position resolutely maintained by Eliphaz (4:7–11; 4:18–5:7; 5:12–14; 15:17–35; 22:15–18), Bildad (8:8–19; 18:5–21), and Zophar (11:11–12; 20:4–29; 27:13–21). As a corollary to this, the friends also contend that God delivers the righteous (5:11, 15–27; 8:6, 20–22). It may be observed that this motif is not emphasized nearly as much as the former. Nevertheless, on both of these points, Job's friends embody the fundamental tenets of conventional wisdom theology.

In light of their theological premises, the friends urge Job to appeal his case to God. They reason that if Job is truly innocent, God will alleviate his suffering and vindicate his cause (5:8; 8:5–7; 11:13–20; 22:21–30). Of course, they fail to appreciate the crux of Job's dilemma. Job recognizes that God is the source of his terrible anguish (6:4; 7:12–15; 10:13–17; 12:7–10; 16:11–14; 19:7–12; 23:13–16; 30:20–22). At the same time, he also realizes his own innocence (6:8–10; 27:2–12). But what compounds his frustration is that Job knows that God knows that he's innocent (10:5–7; 23:10–12; 31:4–6)!

Job implores God to leave him alone (10:20–22; 13:20–27). Delusional with pain, he speaks without restraint (6:2–3; 23:2). Job's patience has reached its limits (6:11–12; 21:4). Life is short and fragile (7:1–10, 16–19; 9:25–28), and Job reasons that any offenses that he might have committed are, in the grand scheme of things, relatively harmless to God (7:20–21). Accordingly, Job begs God for compassion (30:23–24). The Almighty, however, remains reclusive and silent—deaf to Job's questions, prayers, and appeals (16:15–17; 19:6–12; 23:8–9; 30:20–22). This leaves Job at the mercy of God's whims. The sufferer has no third-party arbitrator to secure him justice (9:32–35; 16:18–19; 31:35–37).

Here we must recognize that Job's situation puts his friends in an awkward position. Either Job is right (he is innocent) and God is wrong (for unjustly afflicting him) or God is right (for afflicting him) and Job is wrong (he's guilty).

---

[10] It is missing only from Bildad's third reply (25:1–6), a portion of which appears to have been lost to textual corruption.

Job's friends opt for the latter scenario. They take issue with Job's supposed righteousness. After all, who can be righteous before God (4:12–17; 15:14–16; 25:2–6), the all-knowing, all-seeing, all-powerful Creator (22:12–14)? Evidently, the mistake must lie with Job. He has accounted himself as upright, whereas God's "punishment" speaks for itself (22:2–4). This conclusion leads the trio to turn on their friend. They take offense at his words (8:2), calling them "garrulous babblings" which demand rebuke (11:2–3). They label Job as "impatient" (4:5) "arrogant," "impious," and "wicked" (15:2–5). They invent specific crimes which they level against him:

> You have unjustly kept your kinsmen's goods in pawn,
> left them stripped naked of their clothing.
> To the thirsty you have given no water to drink,
> and from the hungry you have withheld bread;
> As if the land belonged to the man of might,
> and only the privileged were to dwell in it.
> You have sent widows away empty-handed,
> and the resources of orphans you have destroyed. (Job 22:6–9)

They even go so far as to raise suspicions about Job's ill-fated children (8:4)!

Job feels the attacks of his friends—not to mention those of his wife, relatives, servants, and acquaintances (19:13–19; 30:1–19)—almost as deeply as God's (19:22). They have proven themselves to be wholly undependable (6:13–21). Job accuses them of glossing over falsehoods and offering vain remedies (13:4). With their trite maxims and worthless advice (13:12), Job's companions lack true wisdom and understanding (17:10). Their words vex Job's soul (19:2–3), and their barrage of insults and mockery (16:6–11, 20; 17:2–12) proves nearly unbearable.

In his own defense, Job never claims to be perfect (14:4). After all, who can be (9:2–14)? But he knows himself well enough to recognize his innocence. He has lived a good life (29:12–17) and realizes that the pain and torment he has been forced to endure is disproportionate to whatever minor faults he may possess (19:4–6). In this respect, God is not just (31:2–3). And here is where God's justice seems to fail yet again: while Job suffers, the wicked flourish! While Job has become an object of scorn and ridicule (12:4–5), the godless thrive and prosper (12:6; 21:7–15; 24:2–17)! Where, Job wonders, is their punishment (21:16–34)?

Near the conclusion of the dialogues, Job fondly reminisces about his former life (29:2–11). He longs to return to the time when he enjoyed God's favor. He makes a final, heartfelt appeal to God's sense of justice (31:2–34) and implores the Almighty to answer him (31:37). Shortly thereafter, God does.

For some three dozen chapters, the reader has anticipated God's response. However, when he finally appears, God offers no insight into Job's predicament or into suffering in general, for that matter. Rather, in his first treatise (38:1–40:2), God asserts his omnipotence, his creative activities, and his knowledge of the ways of the natural order: the earth, sea, sky, firmament, stars, land, animals, and birds. He emphasizes that his knowledge and abilities lie far beyond human capacities. God's second speech (40:6–41:26) picks up where the first left off, describing God's command over two mighty sea creatures, the behemoth and the leviathan.[11]

In many respects, God's dramatic appearance is disappointingly anti-climactic. Not only does he fail to address Job's condition, but also he merely reiterates divine qualities that both Job and his friends have previously and repeatedly acknowledged (e.g., 9:3–19; 11:5–12; 12:13–25; 22:12–14; 26:5–14). Though its finale leaves much to be desired, the poetic dialogues nevertheless provide some important clues as to the fundamental purpose of this book.

The Rhetorical Aim of Job

The key to understanding Job lies in the proper orientation of the reader. The prevailing assumption about this work—a mistake that I and many others have made—is that the reader who approaches the text is one who is intimately acquainted with suffering. In other words, they identify, either directly or indirectly, with Job. But from that vantage point, this book proves paradoxical and disorienting. In the poetic core, Job wrestles with utter tragedy, unmerited suffering, and absolute abandonment. Yet in the prose narrative, he receives restorative justice—his "happily ever after" ending. A reader in Job's position, therefore, might be led to expect the same. But this notion runs entirely contrary to Job's message throughout the dialogue section. Sometimes horrible calamities befall even the best of people. Life is not fair, and the reasons are not always forthcoming. Furthermore, readers seeking an explanation

[11] Elsewhere in the HB, these creatures are somewhat mythical and legendary. Here in Job, however, they refer to the hippopotamus and crocodile, respectively.

for their own adversities will inevitably be disappointed by the solutions found here. If Job's experience is at all indicative, then such misfortunes are either the result of some cosmic contest between God and his celestial cohort or part and parcel of the unfathomable ways of the Almighty and therefore utterly beyond human comprehension. Who can take comfort in that?

In short, reading this book from Job's perspective locks the reader into a conceptual stalemate that becomes impossible to resolve. But there is a solution to this enigma. One simply needs to approach this book from a different point of view.

In its time, it is likely that the author expected his readers not to identify with Job but with Job's friends. Their theological outlook embodies the cause/effect relationship of rewards and punishments endorsed throughout the Law, the Prophets, and the Writings. In other words, any faithful Israelite, Judahite, or Jew would have subscribed to it! Despite its title, then, this book is not so much about Job (the sufferers themselves) as it is about Job's friends (those who witness the suffering of others). To these readers, the book of Job becomes an object lesson in how not to respond to the victims of tragedy.

Job conveys some keen insights into the emotional, psychological, and even theological responses of those who behold catastrophe, yet remain unscathed by it. Initially, the trio is shocked by their friend's appearance. Job has deteriorated to the point of becoming unrecognizable (2:12). His wretched state provokes their fear (6:21). After all, if this happened to Job, it could also happen to them. Instinctively, they set about creating some cognitive distance by differentiating their behavior from his: "If I were in your place, I would . . ." (5:8). They distance themselves from Job even further by attributing Job's sufferings to his moral deficiencies—deficiencies that they themselves evidently don't possess. This leads them to attack Job's character and to imagine all sorts of sins that would justify such a punishment. Job's dogged insistence of his innocence simply proves (to their minds, anyway) the depths of his delusion and depravity.

In all of this, their positions are supported by their theology. Job levels some serious accusations against God, whom the trio is quick to defend. But by deigning to speak for the Almighty, the three friends fail spectacularly. They wind up misrepresenting the Divine and condemning an innocent victim. Because of this, they court their own judgment and dishonor (19:28–29; 42:7–9).

So what advice does this book offer to those in the positions of Job's friends? How should one treat the victims of tragedy? We find that the friends are at their best at the beginning of this story (2:11–13). Initially, they come from afar and meet to offer Job their sympathy and comfort. They weep for him, tear their clothes, and cover their heads with dust. Then, for seven days and seven nights, they sit on the ground and suffer in silence and in solidarity at their companion's side. Their mistake comes when they venture to reply to Job's lamentation. The sufferer asks precious little of them (6:22–23). Job desires only that they show him compassion (19:21), listen to his words (21:2), allow him to vent his feelings (13:13), and judge aright (6:28–30). As Job observes, the trio's wisest course of action would have been to simply refrain from speaking (13:5).

Job's Original Setting?

Surely this timeless lesson is as applicable for us today as it was back then. But what were the circumstances that originally gave rise to it? This text, like its wisdom counterparts, Proverbs and Ecclesiastes, is notoriously difficult to date. There is no scholarly consensus regarding its original setting, with proposals ranging from the tenth to the third century B.C.E. But if our rendering of it is correct, the book presupposes a tragedy, perhaps one familiar to the vast majority of its readers. At least two possibilities present themselves. The first is the Assyrian destruction of Israel in 722 B.C.E. In conjunction with this event, thousands of Israelite refugees sought safety in the southern kingdom of Judah. Scripture from that period attributed Israel's downfall to its own moral deficiencies, beginning with its initial break from the Davidic dynasty in the south. Among its other sins, Israel's mistreatment of the poor is specifically cited by the book of Amos as one of the chief causes of its downfall. (Recall that this is the same indictment that Job's friends leveled against him.) It is possible, therefore, that this work stems from a northern refugee seeking to solicit compassion from the self-righteous Judahites in the aftermath of Israel's destruction. If this is the case, then references to the friends' own judgment and condemnation may represent veiled allusions to Judah's own future. But whether or not the book of Job can be dated so early remains a matter of debate.[12]

---

[12] Among others, Marvin H. Pope, *Job* (AB 15; 3d ed.; Garden City, N.Y.: Doubleday, 1979) believes it can. He settles for a seventh-century dating. This assessment may

Another possibility is that the tragedy in question is the destruction of Jerusalem and the Babylonian exile (587–538 B.C.E.). Of course, the majority of Judahites living at that time underwent the exile, putting them in the position of Job, not his friends. If this book does presuppose that event, then it seems likely that it was written to those who may have beheld it from a distance. One such group might have been the Judahite community that took refuge in Egypt. From the book of Jeremiah, we know that there was both contact and animosity between the Judahites exiled in Babylon and those residing in Egypt (see Jer 41:11–44:30). Furthermore, it has been observed that a variety of elements in the book of Job appear to have been drawn from an Egyptian environment.[13] In this case, the work may have been composed in order to soften the attitudes of the Egyptian Judahites toward their counterparts in Babylon. The hopes of restoration that permeates the writings of the exilic prophets might then also account for Job's own eventual restoration at the narrative's conclusion.

Summary and Conclusion

It should be emphasized that both of these scenarios remain speculative. What is decidedly more certain is that, regardless of whether Job was written in the tenth century or the third, its original readers surely would have identified with the theological convictions of Job's friends. They would have tended to ascribe life's blessings to God's favor and life's afflictions to God's disapproval. The book of Job takes issue with these positions by asserting that terrible disasters sometimes befall upstanding individuals. It is beyond the purview of this book to explain why. Even to this day, such calamities—ALS, for example—remain mysterious and uncontrollable. But when they strike, the one

---

also be corroborated by the details contained within the prose narrative. For example, Édouard Dhorme has observed at least nine parallels between Job and the patriarchal stories of Genesis, including the terms used to describe wealth, sacrifices offered without priestly intervention, the longevity of the main characters, and the specific phrasing of their deaths (*A Commentary on the Book of Job* [trans. H. Knight; London: Thomas Nelson & Sons, 1967], xx–xxi). What is unclear is whether such elements are indeed archaic or the result of a later writer archaizing the story.

13. Dhorme has found the author's knowledge of Egypt to be "indisputable." His conclusion is based on specific terms that appear throughout the book, including references to Egyptian canals (lit., "Niles"), sailing vessels, indigenous flora and fauna, and precious native stones and metals (*Commentary on the Book of Job,* clxxi–clxxii).

thing that we *can* control is our response to their victims. In this respect, Job offers us some valuable guidelines. By imposing our own theologies upon their situations or rushing to the Almighty's defense, we run the very real risk of alienating the sufferers and misconstruing reality. Ultimately, we're much better off remaining silent and demonstrating our solidarity with attentive compassion. We ought to allow the afflicted to give vent to their feelings, without judgment or blame, and let God take responsibility for the rest.[14]

[14]Happily, this is how my father's three closest friends—Bob Hunt, Dick Shilts, and Ray Anderson—treated him during his illness. My family and I owe these exemplary men a tremendous debt of gratitude. In that spirit, I dedicate this chapter to them.

Conclusion

Prior to this book, readers may well have held certain assumptions about various biblical notions—notions like "creation," "Noah's ark," "the covenant," "the commandments," "prophecy," "Jonah's whale," "the apocalypse," "wisdom," and "Job's suffering." In most cases, their assumptions were probably based on some sort of encounter with the Bible—an inadvertent eavesdropping on ancient conversations. In our preceding study, we've sought to re-examine these conversations in their original contexts. By adopting the perspectives of our ancient authors and their audiences, we've endeavored to approach this material from their points of view. As we have seen, the results derived from this exercise frequently challenge and occasionally even contradict our own popular notions about the purposes and meanings of these conversations. This process, therefore, has proven to be a valuable one, one that conveys a more authentic sense of our authors' originally intended messages. In short, it enables us present-day readers to really "get" the Old Testament.

As mentioned in the introduction, this book is by no means exhaustive. We have left literally thousands of passages unexplored, awaiting their discovery by patient, well-prepared, and attentive readers. In this respect, perhaps we can liken the OT to an archaeological dig site. To the unassuming, it may appear to be just a weathered old mound—an insignificant contour easily overlooked amidst a well-developed literary landscape. But now we know otherwise. Although our survey has barely scratched the surface, our findings offer an encouraging hint of what else might lie beneath. The artifacts we've recovered may be ancient and foreign, but there is an unmistakable timelessness and relevance about them.

Throughout their narrative history, from the very beginning to the apocalyptic end, the Hebrew Scriptures have ventured to express the dynamic relationship between God and his creation. But the story doesn't end there. Those who take their lessons to heart—those who conscientiously apply them to their own life circumstances—infuse them with new life, fresh meaning, and unique purpose. Such transactions suggest that yet-unwritten chapters are destined to be added to the grand and epic saga that, even now, continues to unfold between God and his people.

Appendix A

Narrative Timeline 1 (Creation to the United Monarchy)

The timeline on the following page portrays the biblical narratives' timeline from creation to the end of the United Monarchy at the death of Solomon in approximately 920 B.C.E.

Below the major characters, the biblical books covering each period are provided.

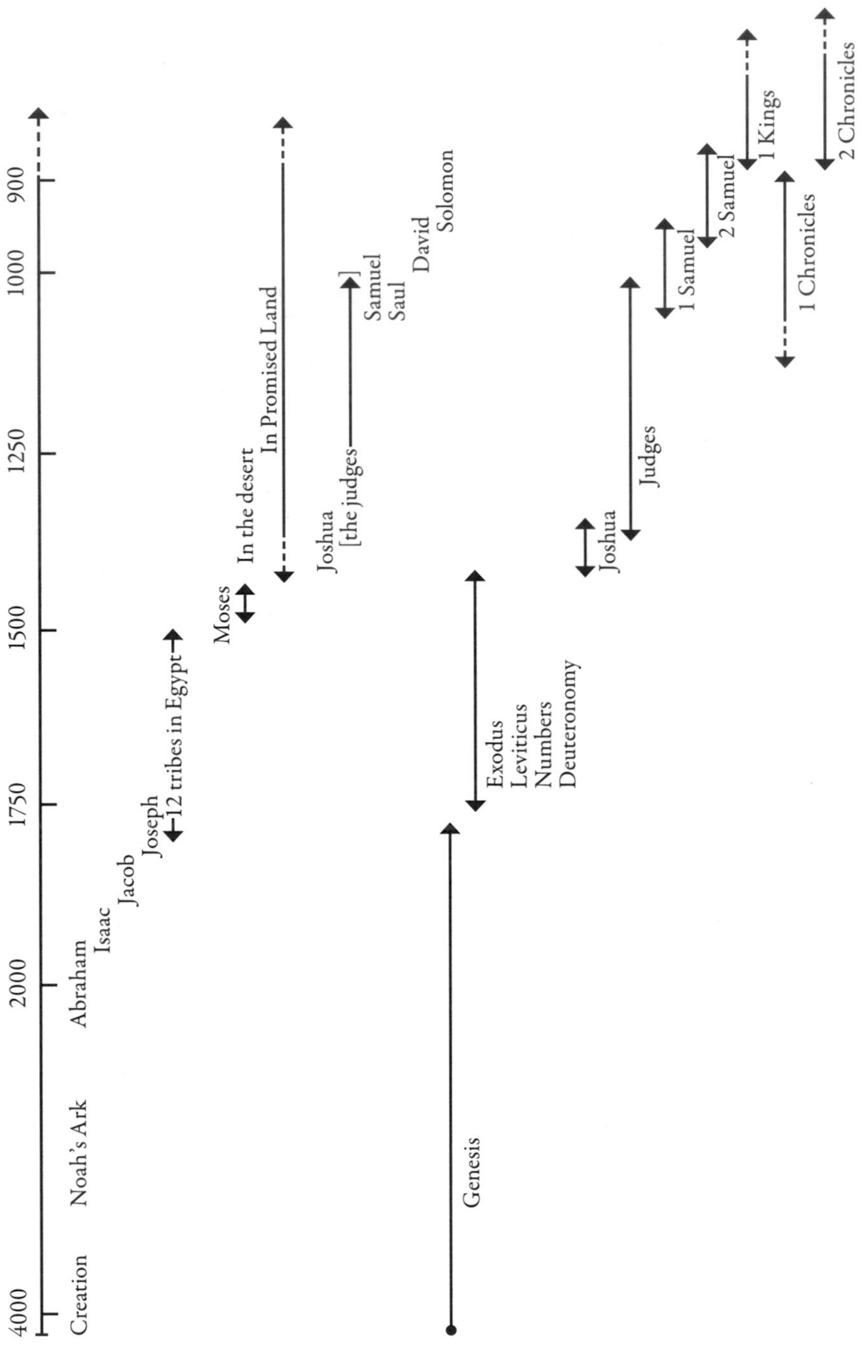
4000
2000
1750
1500
1250
1000
900
Creation
Noah's Ark
Abraham
Isaac
Jacob
Joseph
12 tribes in Egypt
Moses
In the desert
In Promised Land
Joshua
[the judges
]
Samuel
Saul
David
Solomon
Genesis
Exodus
Leviticus
Numbers
Deuteronomy
Joshua
Judges
1 Samuel
2 Samuel
1 Kings
1 Chronicles
2 Chronicles

Appendix B

Ancient Near Eastern Laws and the Torah

For comparative purposes, the Mesopotamian law codes of Lipit-Ishtar (nineteenth century B.C.E.) and Hammurabi (1728–1686 B.C.E.) are frequently utilized by biblical scholars.[1] Like the Torah, they claim to have been divinely commissioned. They are all promulgated by "shepherds." They each conclude with a series of "blessings" and "curses" relative to the injunctions contained within them. Even their specific contents exhibit some striking similarities:

Early Mesopotamian Laws	Torah
If, when a seignior gave a field to a gardener to set out an orchard, the gardener set out the orchard, he shall develop the orchard for four years; in the fifth year the owner of the orchard and the gardener shall divide equally, with the owner of the orchard receiving his preferential share.[2]	"When you come into the land and plant any fruit tree there, first look upon its fruit as if it were uncircumcised. For three years, while its fruit remains uncircumcised, it may not be eaten. In the fourth year, however, all of its fruit shall be sacred to the LORD as a thanksgiving feast to him. Not until the fifth year may you eat its fruit." (Lev 19:23–25)
If an obligation came due against a seignior and he . . . has been bound over to service, [he] shall work (in) the house of [his] purchaser or obligee for three years, with [his] freedom reestablished in the fourth year.[3]	"If your kinsman, a Hebrew man or woman, sells himself to you, he is to serve you for six years, but in the seventh year you shall dismiss him from your service, a free man. When you do so, you shall not send him away empty-handed, but shall weight him

[1] The complete text of the Lipit-Ishtar and Hammurabi law codes can be found in *ANET,* 159–61 and 163–80, respectively.

[2] *ANET,* 169, §60.

[3] *ANET,* 170–71, §117.

	down with gifts from your flock and threshing floor and wine press, in proportion to the blessing LORD, your God, has bestowed on you." (Deut 15:12–14)
If a seignior's ox was a gorer and his city council made it known to him that it was a gorer, but he did not pad its horns or tie up his ox, and that ox gored to death a member of the aristocracy, he shall give one-half mina of silver.[4]	"If an ox was previously in the habit of goring people and its owner, though warned, would not keep it in; should it then kill a man or a woman, not only must the ox be stoned, but its owner also must be put to death." (Exod 21:29)

But despite the close resemblance, there is at least one fundamental difference between these Mesopotamian law codes and the Torah. The former were generated by the kings (namely, Lipit-Ishtar and Hammurabi) in response to the gods' calls for just and equitable societies. Ultimately, their law codes are designed to define an individual's rights and responsibilities within the commonwealth, for the protection and peace of its citizenry. Such objectives are virtually identical (in theory, anyway) to ours today.

In the Torah, however, most of the laws emanate directly from God. This leads to a paradigmatic shift in emphasis. It places prominence not on one's duty to one's fellow man, but on one's responsibility to the Divine. In other words, the statutes of the Torah are designed not merely for the sake of justice and equality but for the purpose of forging a nation uniquely consecrated to the Almighty—a people who would become, in all aspects of their existence, the living embodiment of the covenantal promise between Yahweh and Abraham.

[4] *ANET,* 176, §251.

Appendix C

Comparative Canons of Scripture

Jewish (39 Books)	**Roman Catholic (46 Books)**	**Protestant (39 Books)**	**Eastern Orthodox (51 Books)**
Torah	***Pentateuch***	***Pentateuch***	***Pentateuch***
Genesis	Genesis	Genesis	Genesis
Exodus	Exodus	Exodus	Exodus
Leviticus	Leviticus	Leviticus	Leviticus
Numbers	Numbers	Numbers	Numbers
Deuteronomy	Deuteronomy	Deuteronomy	Deuteronomy
Prophets	***Historical Books***	***Historical Books***	***Historical Books***
(Former Prophets)	Joshua	Joshua	Joshua
Joshua	Judges	Judges	Judges
Judges	Ruth	Ruth	Ruth
1 Samuel	1 Samuel	1 Samuel	1 Samuel
2 Samuel	2 Samuel	2 Samuel	2 Samuel
1 Kings	1 Kings	1 Kings	1 Kings
2 Kings	2 Kings	2 Kings	2 Kings
	1 Chronicles	1 Chronicles	1 Chronicles
	2 Chronicles	2 Chronicles	2 Chronicles
	Ezra	Ezra	Ezra
			1 Esdras
			2 Esdras
	Nehemiah	Nehemiah	Nehemiah
	Tobit		Tobit
	Judith		Judith
	Esther	Esther	Esther
	1 Maccabees		1 Maccabees
	2 Maccabees		2 Maccabees
			3 Maccabees

Prophets	***Prophets***	***Prophets***	***Prophets***
(Latter Prophets)	*(Major Prophets)*	*(Major Prophets)*	*(Major Prophets)*
Isaiah	Isaiah	Isaiah	Isaiah
Jeremiah	Jeremiah	Jeremiah	Jeremiah
Ezekiel	Ezekiel	Ezekiel	Ezekiel
	Daniel	Daniel	Daniel
	+	+	+
	Lamentations	Lamentations	Lamentations
	Baruch		Baruch
			Letter of Jeremiah
(The Twelve)	*(Minor Prophets)*	*(Minor Prophets)*	*(Minor Prophets)*
Hosea	Hosea	Hosea	Hosea
Joel	Joel	Joel	Joel
Amos	Amos	Amos	Amos
Obadiah	Obadiah	Obadiah	Obadiah
Jonah	Jonah	Jonah	Jonah
Micah	Micah	Micah	Micah
Nahum	Nahum	Nahum	Nahum
Habakkuk	Habakkuk	Habakkuk	Habakkuk
Zephaniah	Zephaniah	Zephaniah	Zephaniah
Haggai	Haggai	Haggai	Haggai
Zechariah	Zechariah	Zechariah	Zechariah
Malachi	Malachi	Malachi	Malachi
Writings	***Wisdom Books***	***Wisdom/Poetic Books***	***Wisdom/Poetic Books***
Job	Job	Job	Job
Psalms	Psalms	Psalms	Psalms
Proverbs	Proverbs	Proverbs	Proverbs
Ecclesiastes	Ecclesiastes	Ecclesiastes	Ecclesiastes
Song of Songs	Song of Songs	Song of Songs	Song of Songs
	Book of Wisdom		Book of Wisdom
	Sirach		Sirach
Ruth			
Lamentations			Prayer of Manasseh
Esther			
Daniel			
Ezra			
Nehemiah			
1 Chronicles			
2 Chronicles			

Appendix D

Narrative Timeline 2 (United Monarchy to Greek Rule)

The timeline on the following pages portrays the biblical narratives' timeline from the United Monarchy (1000–920 B.C.E.) until the beginning of the Greek (Hellenistic) period beginning with Alexander's defeat of the Persian Empire in 331 B.C.E.

Below the major characters/nations, the biblical prophetic books covering each period are provided. Note that Elijah and Elisha's narratives are found in 1 Kgs 17–2 Kgs 9.

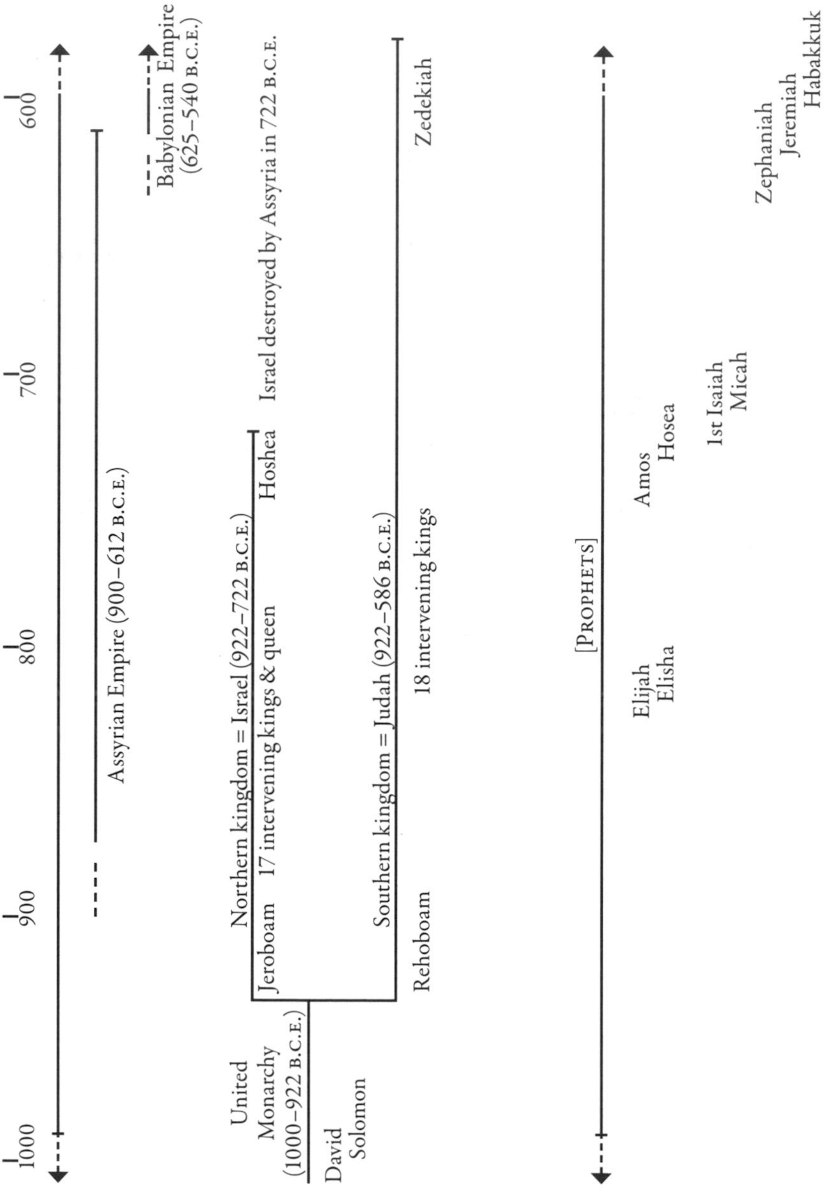
1000
900
800
700
600
Assyrian Empire (900–612 B.C.E.)
Babylonian Empire
(625–540 B.C.E.)
United
Monarchy
(1000–922 B.C.E.)
David
Solomon
Northern kingdom = Israel (922–722 B.C.E.)
Jeroboam
17 intervening kings & queen
Hoshea
Israel destroyed by Assyria in 722 B.C.E.
Southern kingdom = Judah (922–586 B.C.E.)
Rehoboam
18 intervening kings
Zedekiah
[PROPHETS]
Elijah
Elisha
Amos
Hosea
1st Isaiah
Micah
Zephaniah
Jeremiah
Habakkuk

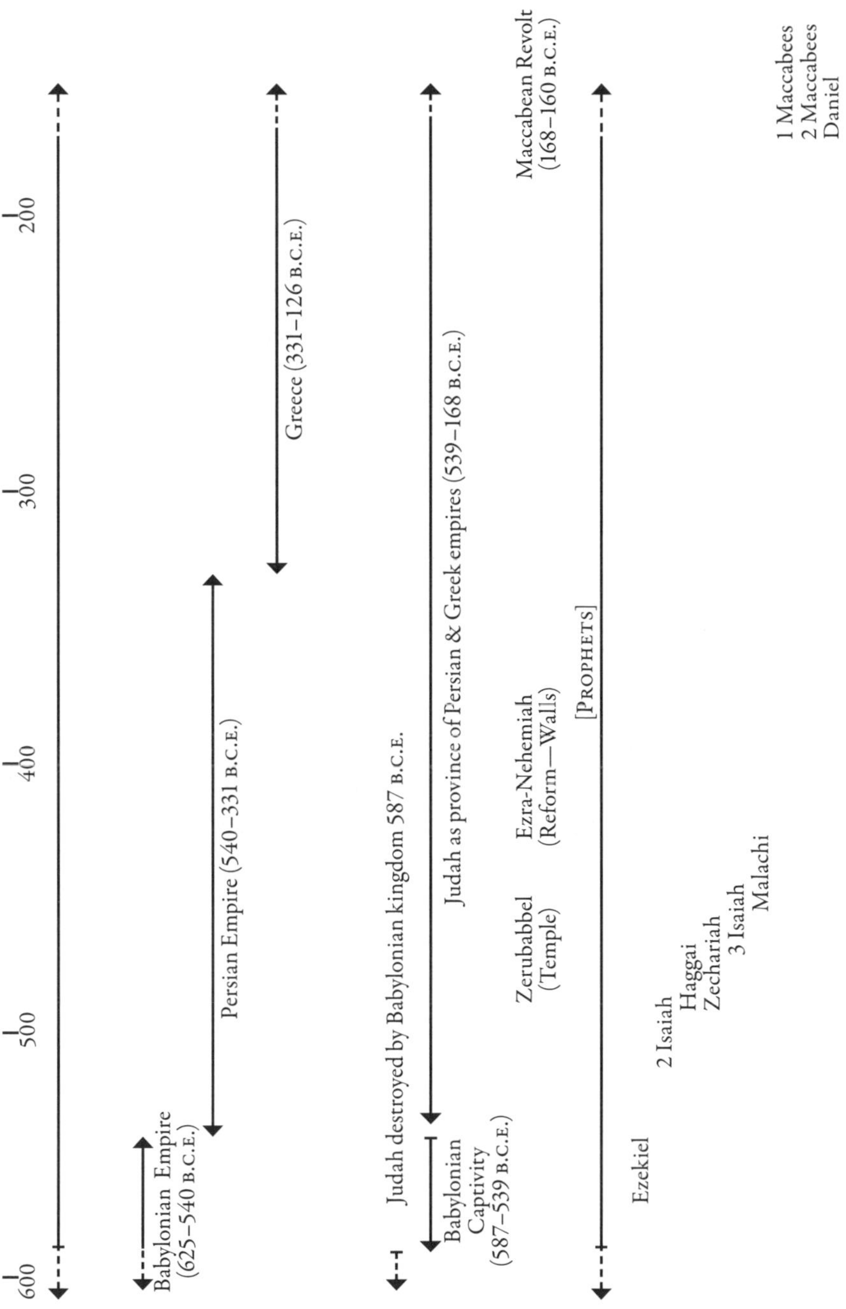
600
500
400
300
200
Babylonian Empire (625–540 B.C.E.)
Persian Empire (540–331 B.C.E.)
Greece (331–126 B.C.E.)
Judah destroyed by Babylonian kingdom 587 B.C.E.
Babylonian Captivity (587–539 B.C.E.)
Judah as province of Persian & Greek empires (539–168 B.C.E.)
Zerubabbel (Temple)
Ezra-Nehemiah (Reform—Walls)
Maccabean Revolt (168–160 B.C.E.)
[Prophets]
Ezekiel
2 Isaiah
Haggai
Zechariah
3 Isaiah
Malachi
1 Maccabees
2 Maccabees
Daniel

Appendix E

The Writing Prophets

Dates (B.C.E.)	Prophet	Kingdom	World Power
786–746	*[Jonah]*	Israel (Northern)	Assyria
760–740	*Amos*	Israel (Northern)	Assyria
750–725	*Hosea*	Israel (Northern)	Assyria
742–700	ISAIAH 1–39	Judah (Southern)	Babylonia
722–701	*Micah*	Judah (Southern)	Babylonia
640–622	*Zephaniah*	Judah (Southern)	Babylonia
590–540	[DANIEL]	Judah (Southern)	Babylonia
627–562	JEREMIAH	Judah (Southern)	Babylonia
ca. 612	*Nahum*	Judah (Southern)	Babylonia
608–598	*Habakkuk*	Judah (Southern)	Babylonia
593–571	EZEKIEL	Judah (Southern)	Babylonia
587–539?	*Jonah*	Judah (Southern)	Babylonia
ca. 586/5	*Obadiah*	Judah (Southern)	Babylonia
546–538	ISAIAH 40–55	Judah (Southern)	Babylonia
520–515	*Haggai*	Judah (Southern)	Persia
520–515	*Zechariah*	Judah (Southern)	Persia
515–500	ISAIAH 56–66	Judah (Southern)	Persia
500–350	*Joel*	Judah (Southern)	Persia
500–450	*Malachi*	Judah (Southern)	Persia
167–164	DANIEL	Judah (Southern)	Greece

Key
[Brackets] = Narrative settings
Italics = Minor Prophets
SMALL CAPS = MAJOR PROPHETS

Appendix F
The Prophetic Notion of Justice

When it comes to the prioritization of social justice above religious observance, the following passages echo the sentiments of Isa 1:10–16:

> Cry out full-throated and unsparingly,
>   lift up your voice like a trumpet blast;
> Tell my people their wickedness,
>   and the house of Jacob their sins.
> They seek me day after day,
>   and desire to know my ways,
> Like a nation that has done what is just
>   and not abandoned the law of their God;
> They ask me to declare what is due them,
>   pleased to gain access to God.
> "Why do we fast, and you do not see it?
>   afflict ourselves, and you take no note of it?"
> Lo, on your fast day you carry out your own pursuits,
>   and drive all your laborers.
> Yes, your fast ends in quarreling and fighting,
>   striking with wicked claw.
> Would that today you might fast
>   so as to make your voice heard on high!
> Is this the manner of fasting I wish,
>   of keeping a day of penance:
> That a man bow his head like a reed,
>   and lie in sackcloth and ashes?
> Do you call this a fast,
>   a day acceptable to the LORD?
> This, rather, is the fasting that I wish:
>   releasing those bound unjustly,
>   untying the thongs of the yoke;
> Setting free the oppressed,

breaking every yoke;
Sharing your bread with the hungry,
sheltering the oppressed and the homeless;
Clothing the naked when you see them,
and not turning your back on your own.
Then your light shall break forth like the dawn,
and your wound shall quickly be healed;
Your vindication shall go before you,
and the glory of the LORD shall be your rear guard.
Then you shall call, and the LORD will answer,
you shall cry for help, and he will say: Here I am!
If you remove from your midst oppression,
false accusation and malicious speech;
If you bestow your bread on the hungry
and satisfy the afflicted,
Then light shall rise for you in the darkness,
and the gloom shall become for you like midday. (Isa 58:1–10)

Thus says the LORD of hosts, the God of Israel: Reform your ways and your deeds, so that I may remain with you in this place. Put not your trust in the deceitful words: "This is the temple of the LORD! The temple of the LORD! The temple of the LORD!" Only if you thoroughly reform your ways and your deeds; if each of you deals justly with his neighbor; if you no longer oppress the resident alien, the orphan, and the widow . . . will I remain with you in this place, in the land which I give your fathers long ago and forever. (Jer 7:3–7)

For it is love that I desire, not sacrifice,
and knowledge of God rather than holocausts. (Hos 6:6)

Woe to those who turn judgment to wormwood
and cast justice to the ground!
They hate him who reproves at the gate
and abhor him who speaks the truth.
Therefore, because you have trampled upon the weak
and exacted of them levies of grain,
Though you have built houses of hewn stone,
you shall not live in them!
Though you have planted choice vineyards,
you shall not drink their wine!
Yes, I know how many are your crimes;
how grievous your sins:
Oppressing the just, accepting bribes,
repelling the needy at the gate!
I hate, I spurn your feasts,
I take no pleasure in your solemnities;
Your cereal offerings I will not accept,
nor consider your stall-fed peace offerings.

Away with your noisy songs!
  I will not listen to the melodies of your harps.
But if you would offer me holocausts,
  then let justice surge like water,
  and goodness like an unfailing stream. (Amos 5:7, 10–12, 21–24)

> Say to all the people of the land and to the priests: When you fasted and mourned in the fifth and in the seventh month these seventy years, was it really for me that you fasted? And when you were eating and drinking, was it not for yourselves that you ate, and for yourselves that you drank? [Thus says the Lord of hosts:] Render true judgment, and show kindness and compassion toward each other. Do not oppress the widow or the orphan or the poor; do not plot evil against one another in your hearts. (Zech 7:5–6, 9–10)

With what shall I come before the Lord,
  and bow before God most high?
Shall I come before him with holocausts,
  with calves a year old?
Will the Lord be pleased with thousands of rams,
  with myriad streams of oil?
Shall I give my first-born for my crime,
  the fruit of my body for the sin of my soul?
You have been told, O man, what is good,
  and what the Lord requires of you:
Only to do the right and to love goodness,
  and to walk humbly with your God. (Mic 6:6–8)

The reader may note that in most of these examples, the recurring emphasis is upon justice, especially as it pertains to the poor. As far as God is concerned, this duty is to occupy an even higher priority than prayer, sacrifice, or liturgical celebration. But what exactly do the prophets mean by justice for the poor?

Today, "justice" is usually defined as "fairness" and "impartiality," especially concerning rewards and punishments. The OT prophets speak to this legal aspect of justice in their repeated references to "the gate." The city gates were where the elders of the town often assembled to hear and settle disputes among their kinsmen. The prophets decry the discrimination that was occurring at these gates—discrimination that inevitably benefited the rich and influential at the expense of the poor. They advocated a spirit of blind justice by maintaining that objective merit, not self-serving biases, should inform such decisions.

The OT also recognizes an economic aspect to justice, one that differs quite significantly from our contemporary understanding of it. The ideals of modern capitalism suggest that those who diligently choose to take advantage of available educational resources and employment opportunities reap the financial rewards of their labors, whereas those who squander them receive what little they deserve. In other words, there is an inherent justice to the free-market system. Accordingly, charity, as it involves the redistribution of wealth, could be considered a type of injustice, since it reallocates to the undeserved what rightfully belongs to another.

As we have seen, the HB speaks of rewards and punishments, particularly as they pertain to the fidelity or infidelity of God's people. It also contrasts the material consequences of virtuous and non-virtuous living, especially in the Wisdom Literature. But it takes a decidedly different view of personal ownership. In the ancient Near East, material wealth was measured primarily in terms of land, agriculture and livestock. Because these things, along with the elements necessary to sustain them, are created by and depend upon God, they rightfully "belong" to him (so Ps 24:1; 50:12). Humans thus occupy the role of stewards, or caretakers, of God's creation. And good stewardship, according to the Law and the Prophets, means ensuring that God's abundant gifts reach even the most vulnerable members of society, especially the widows, orphans, and resident aliens. In this respect, charity to the disenfranchised is one of the most concrete expressions of justice in the Bible. Indeed, as if to reinforce this point, the Hebrew word for "charity" (צדקה, *tsedaqah*) is a derivation of the word "justice" (צדק, *tsadaq*). Both linguistically and theologically, then, charity is one of the principal forms of justice.

Appendix G
Equidistant Letter Sequencing Explained

The Bible Code uses Equidistant Letter Sequencing (ELS) to find keywords and their associated terms. The process begins by removing all spacing and punctuation from a given text. So, for example,

> In the beginning, when God created the heavens and the earth. . . .

becomes

> inthebeginningwhengodcreatedtheheavensandtheearth. . . .

Next, starting with the first letter, the computer runs a series of skip counts—reading every second letter, every third letter, every fourth letter, and so on. Our example above contains 49 letters, so the "skip" can go as high as 47 (begin with the first letter, skip 47, and read the last letter). At that point, the computer can run reverse skip counts. In this case one would begin with the forty-ninth letter and work backwards, with skips of -1, -2, -3, and so on, all the way back to -47. Obviously, this process produces a lot of different readings. But that's just the beginning. The computer then runs through this entire process again, using the second letter as a starting point. Eventually, it uses the third, then the fourth, and so on. The idea is to account for every possible skip sequence within a given text. So here would be the initial outcomes from our sample:

Equidistant Letter Sequencing (ELS)			
	Skip 1	**Skip 2**	**Skip 3**
Letter 1	iteeinnwegdraeteevnadherh	ihennhgcadeannhah	ieinedatendeh
Letter 2	nhbgnighnocetdhhaesnteat	negngeortthvsder	nbngncthasta
Letter 3		tbiiwndeeheeatet	tenwgreevahr
Letter 4			hgihoedhenet
Etc.			

Table G.1

You can imagine how many letter strings might result even from our relatively small sample of 49 letters. Imagine how many more would be produced by a continuous strand containing 304,805 letters!

Once all the letter strings are produced, they can be searched for specific keywords. Suppose I wanted to know the date of the end of the world. Does this passage contain the answer? (Wouldn't it be ironic—the date of the end encoded in the beginning of the Bible!) I could run a search for the word "END." As it just so happens, it appears in the table above, beginning with the first letter and skip counting three. A skip count of three divides this text into twelve four-letter rows, with one letter left over:

ELS: Skip 3 Results			
I	N	T	H
E	B	E	G
I	N	N	I
N	G	W	H
E	N	G	O
D	C	R	E
A	T	E	D
T	H	E	H
E	A	V	E
N	S	A	N
D	T	H	E
E	A	R	T
H			

Table G.2

This configuration can now be searched for other, associated terms. These terms may appear backwards or forwards, in vertical, horizontal, or diagonal positions. As it just so happens in our example, the words "THE" "DATE" of "THE" "END" all converge above the word "EARTH":

ELS: Skip 3 Further Results

I	N	T	H
E	B	E	G
I	N	N	I
N	G	W	H
E	N	G	O
D	C	R	E
A	T	E	D
T	H	E	H
E	A	V	E
N	S	A	N
D	T	H	E
E	A	R	T
H			

Table G.3

But when is the date? Some more creative searching reveals the number TEN that appears not once, not twice, but three times. In fact, it is encoded right between DATE and END:

ELS: Skip 3 Resulting Data

I	N	T	H
E	B	E	G
I	N	N	I
N	G	W	H
E	N	G	O
D	C	R	E
A	T	E	D
T	H	E	H
E	A	V	E
N	S	A	N
D	T	H	E
E	A	R	T
H			

Table G.4

So there we have it! Gen 1:1 has given us the precise date of the end of the world: 10/10/10! Convinced? Well, don't cash in your 401(k) just yet.

Appendix H

Proverbs' Two Ways (Behaviors)

The book of Proverbs contains at least six sets of behaviors that are characteristic of the wise or the foolish. Here we consider them in a little more detail.

Heed/Despise Correction

According to Proverbs, the hallmark of the wise is their attitude concerning instructional discipline. Ultimately, such attitudes reflect one's stance toward the aforementioned authorities. The virtuous, therefore, revere the commands (10:8; 13:8, 13), accept admonition (10:17), love correction (12:1; 13:1), listen to advice (12:15), take counsel (13:10; 19:20), heed reproof (13:18; 15:5, 32), keep the law (28:4; 29:18), accumulate knowledge (10:14; 15:14; 18:15), and are concerned with wisdom (17:24; 23:12).

Such attitudes are contrasted with those of the foolish, who remain stiff-necked (29:1), spurn admonition (15:5, 32), disregard correction (10:17; 13:18), despise counsel (1:30; 13:13), disobey the word (19:16), hate reproof (1:30; 12:1; 13:1, 8; 15:10, 12), and abandon the law (28:4).

Right/Wrong Use of Speech

The flip side of hearing and listening, of course, is speech. And there is no corporeal aspect of humanity—neither the mind nor the heart, neither the hands nor the eyes—that receives as much attention in Proverbs as the organs of speech.[1] So potent are their effects that "death and life" are said to be within their power (18:21). Readers are thus admonished to voice their opinions sparingly (13:3; 17:27) and measure their words carefully (10:19; 15:28; 21:23). The maxims portray the virtuous as inclined toward silence (11:12; 17:28; 24:7). They keep another's confidence (11:13; 25:9) and are reluctant to reveal their own knowledge (12:23). When they do speak, they do so quietly. Their words are mild (15:1) and soothing (15:4). They state only what they are sure of (12:27). With truthful lips they seek to please others (10:32). However, when the occasion calls for it, they are not afraid to frankly reprove (10:10) or rebuke (28:23). When they themselves fail, they are quick to confess and forsake their sins (28:13).

The foolish, of course, demonstrate the opposite behaviors. They are boisterous (13:3; 27:14) and boastful (20:14). They are hasty in their words (29:20) and often speak before listening (18:13). Their responses are harsh (15:1) and angry (12:16). They gossip (16:28; 20:19), betray secrets (11:13; 20:19), and promise what they don't deliver (17:20; 25:14). They use their lies to pervert the truth (10:32), to condone the wicked (17:15; 24:24), to deceive others (12:17), and to conceal their own shortcomings (28:13).

Diligence and Integrity/ Laziness and Dishonesty

Acts of diligence and integrity also occupy many of the aphorisms. Most of these pertain to one's laboring or business practices. According to Proverbs, those who are virtuous work industriously to complete their tasks. They till their own fields (12:11), care for their own flocks and herds (12:10), and establish their own households (24:27). They utilize strong oxen (14:4) and fill their granaries in the summer (10:5). They become skilled in their trade. They plan carefully and build their wealth gradually (13:11). They are attentive to their superiors (27:18), employ honest weights and measures (11:1), and avoid contracts that they cannot fulfill (11:15; 22:26–27).

[1] The frequencies of bodily references include the heart (69), eyes (37), hands (26), ears (13), the mind (10), and feet (9). Collectively, the mouth (46), lips (35), and tongue (18) exceed them all (99).

The wicked, by contrast, fail to plow their seeds (20:4). They are slack in their work (21:25) and prefer sleep (10:5) and idle pursuits (12:11) to honest jobs. They enter into imprudent contracts (11:15; 20:25) and tend to employ sluggards (10:26), drunkards (26:10), and fools (13:17; 26:6). They use false scales (11:1) and weights (20:10, 23), interest, and overcharge (28:8) to gain money and possessions quickly (13:11; 20:21). However, their dishonest wealth dissipates rapidly (23:4–5).

Beyond the business realm, integrity distinguishes the wise from the foolish in juridical matters as well. The righteous, for instance, hate bribes (15:27). In court, they stand up for the vulnerable (31:8–9) and innocent (24:11–12), and they convict evildoers (24:25). The wicked, however, both offer and accept bribes (17:23). Accordingly, they condemn the just (17:15), fine the innocent (17:26), reject rightful claims (18:5), and show undue partiality toward the guilty (18:5; 24:23–24).

In their personal lives, the virtuous demonstrate integrity by avoiding temptations. Cautious (14:16) and patient (16:32), they are not afraid to discipline their children (13:24; 22:6, 15; 23:13–14; 29:17). Those without virtue yield to the whims of their desires. They cavort with harlots and prostitutes (29:3), drink wine and strong liquor excessively (20:1; 23:29–35), gorge themselves upon succulent foods (23:20–21), and chase the trappings of wealth (1:13–14; 23:4–5; 28:22). They are self-indulgent and reckless (14:16), and their children are, too (29:15).

Seek Peace/Cause Trouble

A propensity toward peace and tranquility is another characteristic that defines the wise. To achieve it, they will pass over an insult (12:16), check a quarrel (17:14), overlook an offense (19:11), and cover a misdeed (17:9). The virtuous are slow to anger (14:29; 15:18; 16:32; 19:11). They counsel peace (12:20), confer blessings (11:25; 20:7), refresh others (11:25; 25:13), and seek the greater good (11:27). They even refuse to rejoice at the downfall of their enemies (24:17–18).

Those who demonstrate folly behave contentiously. They pick quarrels (18:1; 20:3), spread accusations (10:18), sow discord (13:10), and enkindle strife (15:18; 26:21). They upset their own households (11:29; 15:27) and revile their neighbors' (11:12). They meddle in other people's affairs (26:17), plot evil (14:22), and set traps for the unsuspecting (1:11–12; 26:27). Quick-tempered (14:17) and merciless (12:10), they crave violence (13:2) and delight in another's downfall (17:5).

Act Generously/Greedily

The behaviors of the wise and those of the foolish can also be differentiated according to their material generosity. The upright are kind and compassionate to the poor and the needy (14:21, 31; 19:17; 22:9; 29:7). They distribute their grain unsparingly (11:26; 21:26). They are also socially generous. Wholly unpretentious (13:7), they frequently bestow gifts upon others (11:25; 18:16; 21:14) and occupy lower places of honor (25:6–7). The wicked, however, are consumed with greed (21:26). They mock the poor (14:31; 17:5), despise the hungry (14:21), and monopolize grain (11:26). They are stingy (11:24), haughty (14:16), and ostentatious (13:7).

Choose Good/Bad Companions

Finally, it is not only one's behavior but also that of one's friends and associates that can lead one toward wisdom or folly. In other words, "Walk with wise men and you will become wise, but the companion of fools will fare badly" (13:20). The reader is thus advised to avoid evildoers (1:10–19), drunkards and gluttons (23:20; 28:7), harlots (29:3), thieves (29:24), gossips (20:19), rebels (24:21), the violent (28:24), and the volatile (22:24). Instead, they are encouraged to make genuine friends—those whose loyalty transcends all circumstances (17:17; 18:19, 24; 27:10) and whose correction and counsel proves beneficial (27:6, 9). Surrounded by such advisors, their plans are sure to succeed (11:14; 15:22; 24:6).

Proverbs further cautions its audience about selecting a spouse—in this case, a wife. Her ideal attributes are described in detail at the conclusion of the book (31:10–31). Not surprisingly, she embodies the characteristics of wisdom, righteousness, and the other virtues mentioned in Proverbs. Such a woman is considered a valuable gift from God (12:4; 18:22; 19:14). She is contrasted with domestic partners who are "disgraceful," "quarrelsome," "cantankerous," and "nagging." Proverbs likens them to "rot in [the] bones" and "a persistent leak" (12:4; 19:13; 21:9, 19; 25:24; 27:15).

Appendix I

Proverbs' Two Ways (Consequences)

The book of Proverbs contains at least six sets of consequences that correspond to wise/righteous or foolish/wicked behavior. Here we consider them in a little more detail.

Favor/Abomination

The wise are pleasing to God, the king, and their parents. And with such favor comes reward. Proverbs affirms that the virtuous are loved by God (15:9). Both they (11:20; 12:22) and their prayers (15:8, 29) are his delight. In turn, the Almighty is their stronghold (10:29; 18:10) and their defense (14:26). God blesses their dwellings (3:33) and serves as a refuge for their children (14:26). Likewise, the righteous enjoy the king's favor (14:35). He befriends them (22:11), loves them (16:13), and employs them in his service (22:29).

The foolish, however, are condemned as an abomination to God (3:32; 11:20; 12:2, 22; 15:9, 26; 16:5). He curses their houses (3:33) and ignores their cries (21:13; 28:9) and sacrifices (15:8; 21:27). God is said to defeat their projects (22:12), plunder their lives (22:23), and cause their downfalls (10:29). In much the same way, the wicked are also the object of the king's wrath (14:35; 16:14; 20:2). Accordingly, they are severely punished (15:10) and chastened (16:22) with rods (10:6; 14:3; 26:3) and blows (19:29), beatings (18:6; 20:26), lashings (20:30), and scourgings (20:30).

Life/Death

One of the benefits of wisdom, according to Proverbs, is a prolonged life (3:16; 4:10; 8:35; 10:16, 17, 27; 12:28; 19:16; 21:21; 22:4). The wise bask in good health (4:22), vigor (3:8), and the glory of old age (16:31). Virtue enables one to avoid the snares of the nether world (13:14; 14:27; 15:24) and remain in the land (2:21). The righteous ones not only save themselves from death (11:4), but they also act as a source of life for others (10:11; 11:19, 30; 13:14; 14:27; 16:22).

The foolish fail to thrive (21:28) and face premature demise (10:21; 11:19; 12:28; 19:16). They endure only momentarily (12:19) and then forfeit their lives (20:2). They have no future (24:20). Their years are brief (10:27), and their lamp goes out (13:9; 20:20; 24:20). Cut off from the land (2:22; 10:30), they abide in the assembly of the shades (21:16). What little hope they had while living is extinguished upon their death (11:7).

Wealth/Poverty

During their lives, the virtuous are blessed materially. They accumulate great wealth (8:21; 10:22; 12:27) and riches (3:16; 8:18; 11:24; 21:5; 22:4; 24:25). Their crops are large and abundant (3:10; 20:13; 28:19), and their flocks supply ample resources (15:6; 27:26–27). They receive numerous possessions (24:3–4) and precious treasures (21:2), and they establish lasting inheritances for their grandchildren (13:22).

Evildoers are reduced to poverty (6:11; 13:18; 21:5; 23:21; 24:34; 28:19). They have no harvest (20:4). Their fields are overgrown with thorns and snares (22:5), thistles and nettles (24:31). Their bordering walls are broken down (24:31). Whatever wealth they may have had goes to the righteous (13:22; 22:16). Their profits are empty (11:18), and their earnings are constantly in turmoil (15:6). Eventually, they grow poor (11:24) and become enslaved on account of their debts (11:29; 12:24; 22:7). They have nothing to pass along as a heritage for their children except empty air (11:29).[1]

[1]It should be noted that although Proverbs associates wealth and poverty with virtue and folly, it doesn't maintain a strict, two-way correspondence. In other words, Proverbs recognizes that some of the foolish are wealthy, just as some of the virtuous are poor. Given Proverbs' tendency toward recompense, these may simply be temporary conditions. At any rate, the dictums are quick to promote a virtuous life over a comfortable one (so, e.g., 15:16, 17; 16:8, 16, 19, 32; 17:1; 19:22; 22:1; 28:6).

Honor/Shame

On account of their virtue, the righteous nourish many. The cities and nations in which they live are exalted on their behalf (11:11; 14:34). Accordingly, the region rejoices at their prosperity (11:10; 28:12; 29:2). They garner the esteem (3:4), favor (3:4; 13:15), thanks (28:23), praise (12:8), and honor (3:35; 13:18; 21:21; 22:4; 29:23) of those around them.

The wicked set their cities ablaze with turmoil and strife (29:8). They stir up disputes (29:22), sow discord (6:14; 16:28), and separate neighbors and friends (16:28; 17:9). Their towns are overthrown by trouble (11:11; 12:7). For this reason, they are cursed (24:24), denounced (24:24), despised (12:8), and disgraced (13:5). They are the objects of contempt and scorn (18:3). Covered with shame (3:35; 13:5), their names are left to rot (10:7) while people rejoice at their perishing (11:10).

Security/Ruin

Because the wise promote peace by allaying discord (15:18) and calming wrath (15:1), they are able to avoid misfortune (16:17; 19:23) and escape trouble (11:8, 9, 21; 12:12). Thus, they are never disturbed (10:30; 12:3). No harm befalls them (12:21) because even their enemies are on good terms with them (16:7). Therefore, the house of the righteous stands firm (12:7) and endures (12:12). It is established forever (10:25; 12:19) in safety and security (1:33; 10:9).

The foolish are pursued and overwhelmed by misfortune (12:21; 13:21). Terror comes upon them like a storm (1:27), bringing disaster and doom (1:26), distress and anguish (1:27). They cannot escape the evil that befalls them (10:24; 11:27). Their houses are overturned (15:25), destroyed (14:11), ruined and torn down (14:1). Their strongholds are demolished (12:12). They are overthrown (10:8; 14:32), swept away (21:7), and erased by the tempest of calamity (10:25).

Satisfaction/Frustration

Finally, the upright do well and benefit themselves (11:17; 19:8). They are happy and refreshed (3:18; 8:33–34), and their hearts are full of joy (10:28; 12:20). They find pleasure in their work and in its sure rewards (11:18; 12:14). Their desires are granted (10:24) and their hungers appeased (13:2, 25). They flourish (14:11) and are amply satisfied (12:14; 13:4).

The wicked are caught in their own intrigue (11:6) and ruined by their own duplicity (11:3). They bring about their own downfall (5:22; 13:3). Their plans fail miserably (15:22), and they fare poorly (10:9). Their prey escapes (12:27), and they suffer from hunger (19:15) and want (13:25; 21:17). Their desires are thwarted (10:3), their expectations come to nothing (10:28), and their souls are left to crave in vain (13:4).

Appendix J
Wisdom 2:1–3:11

They said among themselves, thinking not aright:
"Brief and troublous is our lifetime;
  neither is there any remedy for man's dying,
  nor is anyone known to have come back from the nether world.
For haphazard were we born,
  and hereafter we shall be as though we had not been;
Because the breath in our nostrils is a smoke
  and reason is a spark at the beating of our hearts,
And when this is quenched, our body will be ashes
  and our spirit will be poured abroad like unresisting air.
Even our name will be forgotten in time,
  and no one will recall our deeds.
So our life will pass away like the traces of a cloud,
  and will be dispersed like a mist
  pursued by the sun's rays
  and overpowered by its heat.
For our lifetime is the passing of a shadow;
  and our dying cannot be deferred
  because it is fixed with a seal; and no one returns.
Come, therefore, let us enjoy the good things that are real,
  and use the freshness of creation avidly.
Let us have our fill of costly wine and perfumes,
  and let no springtime blossom pass us by;
  let us crown ourselves with rosebuds ere they wither.
Let no meadow be free from our wantonness;
  everywhere let us leave tokens of our rejoicing,
  for this our portion is, and this our lot.
Let us oppress the needy just man;
  let us neither spare the widow
  nor revere the old man for his hair grown white with time.
But let our strength be our norm of justice;
  for weakness proves itself useless.
Let us beset the just one, because he is obnoxious to us;
  he sets himself against our doings,

Reproaches us for transgressions of the law
  and charges us with violations of our training.
He professes to have knowledge of God
  and styles himself a child of the LORD.
To us he is the censure of our thoughts;
  merely to see him is a hardship for us,
Because his life is not like other men's,
  and different are his ways.
He judges us debased;
  he holds aloof from our paths as from things impure.
He calls blest the destiny of the just
  and boasts that God is his Father.
Let us see whether his words be true;
  let us find out what will happen to him.
For if the just one be the son of God, he will defend him
  and deliver him from the hand of his foes.
With revilement and torture let us put him to the test
  that we may have proof of his gentleness
  and try his patience.
Let us condemn him to a shameful death;
  for according to his own words, God will take care of him."
These were their thoughts, but they erred;
  for their wickedness blinded them,
And they knew not the hidden counsels of God;
  neither did they count on a recompense of holiness
  nor discern the innocent souls' reward.
For God formed man to be imperishable;
  the image of his own nature he made him.
But by the envy of the devil, death entered the world,
  and they who are in his possession experience it.
But the souls of the just are in the hand of God,
and no torment shall touch them.
They seemed, in the view of the foolish, to be dead;
  and their passing away was thought an affliction
  and their going forth from us, utter destruction.
But they are in peace.
For if before men, indeed, they be punished,
  yet is their hope full of immortality;
Chastised a little, they shall be greatly blessed,
  because God tried them
  and found them worthy of himself.
As gold in the furnace, he proved them,
  and as sacrificial offerings he took them to himself.
In the time of their visitation they shall shine,
  and shall dart about as sparks through stubble;

They shall judge nations and rule over peoples,
and the LORD shall be their King forever.
Those who trust in him shall understand truth,
and the faithful shall abide with him in love:
Because grace and mercy are with his holy ones,
and his care is with his elect.
But the wicked shall receive a punishment to match their thoughts,
since they neglected justice and forsook the LORD.
For he who despises wisdom and instruction is doomed.
Vain is their hope, fruitless are their labors,
and worthless are their works. (Wis 2:1–3:11)

Whether or not this passage from Wisdom is an explicit refutation of Ecclesiastes remains a matter of scholarly debate. The complaints of the "wicked" about their lack of legacy and the transitory nature of life (specifically comparing it to a "mist"), coupled with their resolve to "enjoy the good things," including "costly wine" and "perfume," are decidedly familiar elements. But extending these notions so as to lead to the oppression of the just is hardly something Qoheleth endorsed.

Theoretically speaking, the scenario presented by Wisdom—wicked men condemning the righteous "son of God" to see what would happen to him, and then the latter being raised to immortality—finds a close parallel to the NT's take on Jesus.[1] To some extent, then, the Gospel portrayals of Jesus' death and resurrection can be understood as sort of a case study or practical application of Wisdom's theology. And as such, they somewhat defy Ecclesiastes' assertion that a righteous life ultimately amounts to nothing more than "vapor."

[1] Additional parallels can be found in Wisdom's treatment of premature death in Wis 4:10–5:23.

Suggested Reading

Study Bibles

The Catholic Study Bible. Donald Senior and John J. Collins, eds. 2d ed. New York: Oxford University Press, 2006.

The New Interpreter's Study Bible. New Revised Standard Version with the Apocrypha. Walter J. Harrelson, ed. Nashville: Abingdon, 2003.

The Jewish Study Bible: Featuring the Jewish Publication Society TANAKH Translation. Adele Berlin, Marc Zvi Brettler, and Michael Fishbane, eds. New York: Oxford University Press, 2003.

Old Testament Introductions

Bandstra, Barry. *Reading the Old Testament: An Introduction to the Hebrew Bible.* 3d ed. Belmont, Calif.: Wadsworth, 2004. Written by my former professor at Hope College, this work is one of the first to feature an accompanying CD, filled with helpful supplementary material such as charts, maps, timelines, and ancient texts. Furthermore, the online site associated with this work (http://www.hope.edu/bandstra/RTOT/RTOT.HTM) is, in my opinion, the best OT Web resource available.

Boadt, Lawrence. *Reading the Old Testament: An Introduction.* Mahwah, N.J.: Paulist Press, 1984. A classic textbook. Very popular and widely used for good reason. Informed, yet accessible.

Collins, John J. *Introduction to the Hebrew Bible.* Minneapolis: Augsburg, 2004. Written by a top-notch biblical scholar. This book lacks some of flashier visual elements many students desire, but they can be found on the accompanying CD. I found the treatment of Daniel and the Wisdom Literature especially well done.

Coogan, Michael D. *The Old Testament: A Historical and Literary Introduction to the Hebrew Scriptures.* New York: Oxford University Press, 2006. An excellent work. Coogan's scholarship is as good as it gets, and the layout of this book, with lots of pertinent pictures and textboxes, makes it very user-friendly.

Ancient Near Eastern Background

Dalley, Stephanie. *Myths from Mesopotamia: Creation, the Flood, Gilgamesh, and Others.* Rev. ed. Oxford's World Classics. New York: Oxford University Press, 2000. Less comprehensive than Prichard's work, but the translations are more recent.

Prichard, J. B., ed. *Ancient Near Eastern Texts Relating to the Old Testament.* 3d ed. Princeton, N.J.: Princeton University Press, 1969. Although dated, it remains one of the most comprehensive collections of such documents available to the general public.

Sparks, Kenton L. *Ancient Texts for the Study of the Hebrew Bible: A Guide to the Background Literature.* Peabody, Mass.: Hendrickson, 2005.

Chapter-Specific Booklist

Chapters 1–4: Genesis

Brueggemann, Walter. *Genesis.* Interpretation: A Bible Commentary for Teaching and Preaching. Louisville, Ky.: Westminster John Knox, 1982. A popular commentary, lucid and informed. Designed primarily for church-based audiences.

Gunkel, Hermann. *Genesis.* Translated by Mark E. Biddle. Mercer Library of Biblical Studies. Macon, Ga.: Mercer University Press, 1997. Although somewhat dated (the original was first published in Germany in 1901), this commentary offers a wealth of insight and remains a classic among scholars.

Westermann, Claus. *Genesis: A Continental Commentary.* Translated by John J. Scullion, S.J. 3 vols. Minneapolis: Fortress, 1994. Very thorough and more recent than Gunkel's work. The degree of detail is a boon for scholars but can be somewhat overwhelming for novices.

Chapter 5: Torah

Alter, Robert. *The Five Books of Moses: A Translation with Commentary.* New York: W. W. Norton, 2004. A terrific blend of scholarship and accessibility. Considered one of the best one-volume commentaries on the Torah ever published in English.

Chapter 6: The Prophets

Blenkinsopp, Joseph. *A History of Prophecy in Israel.* Rev. and enl. ed. Louisville, Ky.: Westminster John Knox, 1996. A classic text from one of the leading scholars in this field.

Brueggemann, Walter. *The Prophetic Imagination.* Rev. ed. Minneapolis: Augsburg Fortress, 2001. Another classic text from another leading scholar.

Miller, John W. *Meet the Prophets: A Beginner's Guide to the Books of the Biblical Prophets, Their Meaning Then and Now.* New York: Paulist Press, 1987. A very accessible introductory survey of the Writing Prophets.

Chapter 7: Jonah

Limburg, James. *Jonah: A Commentary.* Old Testament Library. Louisville, Ky.: Westminster John Knox, 1993. Scholarly, yet succinct.

Sasson, Jack M. *Jonah.* AB 24B. Garden City, N.Y.: Doubleday, 1990. One of the most comprehensive Jonah commentaries available. Considerable references to the Hebrew text, which can be intimidating to non-Hebrew readers.

Trible, Phyllis. "The Book of Jonah: Introduction, Commentary, and Reflections." Pages 461–529 in *The New Interpreter's Bible.* Volume 7: *Introduction to Apocalyptic Literature, Daniel, The Twelve Prophets.* Leander E. Keck et al. eds. Nashville: Abingdon, 1996. Takes more of a literary approach to Jonah. Trible's writing approaches a poetic quality and is filled with interesting insights.

Chapter 8: Daniel

Collins, John J. *Daniel: A Commentary on the Book of Daniel.* Hermeneia. Minneapolis: Augsburg Fortress, 1993. The definitive commentary on Daniel to date. Top-notch scholarship, yet accessible to most readers. Extensive bibliography and secondary references are an academician's dream.

Chapter 9: Proverbs

Von Rad, Gerhard. *Wisdom in Israel.* Nashville: Abingdon, 1972. A classic work, dubbed the most profound theological treatment of Proverbs available.

Whybray, R. N. *Proverbs.* New Century Bible Commentary. Grand Rapids, Mich.: Eerdmans, 1994. A careful analysis of Proverbs from a well-recognized scholar.

Chapter 10: Ecclesiastes

Murphy, Roland E. *Ecclesiastes.* WBC 23A. Waco, Tex.: Word, 1992. Generally recognized as one of the strongest commentaries on Ecclesiastes.

Chapter 11: Job

Clines, David J. A. *Job 1–20.* WBC 17. Dallas: Word, 1989. Perhaps the most exhaustive of recent commentaries on Job. In particular, its fifty-two-page bibliography is perhaps the most comprehensive ever compiled.

Dhorme, Édouard. *A Commentary on the Book of Job.* Translated by Harold Knight. Nashville: Thomas Nelson, 1984. Although a little dated (the original was first published in 1926), this work has been called one of the best commentaries on any biblical book, ever. Indeed, Dhorme's command over all facets of biblical exegesis is impressive. His contributions continue to remain relevant.

Pope, Marvin H. *Job.* 3d ed. AB 15. Garden City, N.Y.: Doubleday, 1979. A solid, user-friendly commentary that's a little less intimidating, and considerably shorter, than those of Clines and Dhorme.

Index of Subjects

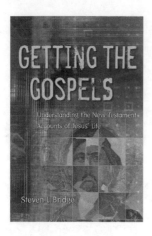